EXECUTIVE PRIVILEGE

STUDIES IN GOVERNMENT
AND PUBLIC POLICY

EXECUTIVE PRIVILEGE

Presidential Power, Secrecy, and Accountability

THIRD EDITION, REVISED AND UPDATED

Mark J. Rozell

UNIVERSITY PRESS OF KANSAS

Published by the University Press of Kansas (Lawrence, Kansas 66045), which was organized by the Kansas Board of Regents and is operated and funded by Emporia State University, Fort Hays State University, Kansas State University, Pittsburg State University, the University of Kansas, and Wichita State University

Originally published with the title *Executive Privilege: The Dilemma of Secrecy and Democratic Accountability* by Johns Hopkins University Press in 1994.

Library of Congress Cataloging-in-Publication Data

Rozell, Mark J.
Executive privilege : presidential power, secrecy, and accountability / Mark J. Rozell. — 3rd ed., rev. and updated.
    p. cm.
Includes bibliographical references and index.
ISBN 978-0-7006-1712-8 (cloth : alk. paper)
ISBN 978-0-7006-1713-5 (pbk. : alk. paper)
1. Executive privilege (Government information)—United States. 2. Executive privilege (Government information)—United States--History. I. Title.
JK468.S4R67 2010
342.73'06--dc22

2009052161

British Library Cataloguing in Publication Data is available.

Printed in the United States of America

10 9 8 7 6 5 4 3 2 1

The paper used in this publication is recycled and contains 30 percent postconsumer waste. It is acid free and meets the minimum requirements of the American National Standard for Permanence of Paper for Printed Library Materials Z39.48-1992.

For Nadine and Renée

CONTENTS

PREFACE

The first edition of this book (1994) examined executive privilege controversies from the presidencies of George Washington through George H. W. Bush. At that time, executive privilege appeared to be dormant, and President Bill Clinton expressed an interest in reviving that presidential power. Because of the Watergate taint, President Richard M. Nixon's successors had made little effective use of executive privilege. Presidents Gerald R. Ford, Jimmy Carter, and George H. W. Bush generally avoided mentioning executive privilege and looked to other constitutional and statutory sources of authority for withholding information. President Ronald Reagan made some efforts to revive executive privilege, but he ultimately backed down in each of his battles with Congress and thus further weakened that presidential power. By the mid-1990s, it appeared that executive privilege was either dead or weakened beyond repair.

Presidents Bill Clinton and George W. Bush changed all of that. Neither of these presidents was reluctant to use executive privilege. Each of them tried to reestablish the viability of executive privilege as a legitimate presidential power. In so doing, each precipitated substantial controversy over attempts to withhold testimony, documents, and other sources of information about the operations of the executive branch.

Executive privilege was a controversial issue during the scandal that led to Clinton's impeachment. The Clinton White House was also involved in an extraordinary number of other executive privilege disputes over its two terms. Some of the Clinton-era controversies resulted in important legal decisions regarding executive privilege. The George W. Bush White House also became embroiled in a number of controversies over the president's expansive and highly dubious exercises of executive privilege.

The executive privilege controversies of the Bill Clinton and George W. Bush years were the impetus for the new editions of this book. The second edition appeared in 2002, and thus covered executive privilege battles through the very early stages of George W. Bush's first term in office. Since publication of that edition, there have been a number of significant executive privilege conflicts that will have a lasting impact on the future exercises of this presidential power. This latest edition provides substantial new material on the Bush years and also covers the very early period of the Barack

Obama presidency. Importantly, one of Obama's first acts as president was to reverse a Bush executive order on executive privilege, and he thus gave a meaningful victory to advocates of government transparency who had fought many Bush-era secrecy practices. Yet, there already is evidence that in the area of government secrecy, Obama is not poised to make a fundamental break from the policy approaches of his latest predecessors.

I wrote the first edition in the early 1990s largely in response to the controversial much earlier work on executive privilege by Raoul Berger (1974). At the time, my purpose was to offer what I perceived to be a much-needed corrective to an enormously influential and flawed work of scholarship. Berger had written an entirely single-sided analysis of a complex constitutional issue and declared executive privilege a "myth." Leading presidential observers and many constitutional scholars referred to Berger's work as the authoritative and even the last word on the subject. I believed then that a different voice was needed on this subject. The first edition of this book therefore stands largely as a rebuttal to Berger's analysis. This edition provides a needed updating of executive privilege controversies in light of what has happened since 1994.

The events of the Clinton, Bush, and now Obama years have also provided an opportunity for additional reflection on this topic. At the end of the first edition I had expressed the hope that some future administration would take up the charge to reestablish the presidential use of executive privilege. I argued that executive privilege is a legitimate, and sometimes necessary, presidential power and that with the benefit of enough time and distance from Watergate, it would become possible once again some day for a president to use this authority without embarrassment.

Bill Clinton and George W. Bush gave me a lot more than I had hoped for, as both of these presidents used executive privilege in a number of interbranch disputes and therefore revived the national debate over this presidential power. Yet in so doing, they did far more damage to this constitutional principle than if they had just followed the lead of their predecessors and avoided executive privilege as much as possible. This latest edition reflects the development of my thinking on this topic in light of the many executive privilege controversies over the past fifteen years. Furthermore, in that period there have been important court decisions that have provided legal guidance on the meaning of executive privilege, the components of that principle, and its limitations. Although I believe today, as I did then, that executive privilege disputes are best handled outside of the courts through an accommodation process, any current analysis of this constitutional principle must consider the newer legal standards in this area.

Another noteworthy change is that since the second edition of this book, most of my work on Bush, Obama, and executive privilege has been in collaboration with my former PhD student and now colleague Mitchel A. Sollenberger (a professor at University of Michigan–Dearborn). The new chapter seven of this book is also a coauthorship between us. My work has grown and benefited a great deal from this collaboration that I look forward to continuing into the future.

I am grateful for the support and encouragement of a number of persons and organizations. I thank Fred Woodward and the University Press of Kansas for the opportunity to update and revise this book. I appreciate the cooperation and support of Henry Y. K. Tom and the Johns Hopkins University Press as I made the transition to a new publisher. The Lynde and Harry Bradley Foundation fellowship provided me with the financial support necessary to spend a semester to work on the first edition. The National Endowment for the Humanities summer research grant program provided additional financial support for writing the first edition.

Henry J. Abraham and James W. Ceaser were important sources of ideas for this project when I began thinking about writing on executive privilege back in the 1980s. Joseph Bessette and Michael Nelson read early drafts of the first edition and offered many helpful suggestions. Lou Fisher of the Law Library of the Library of Congress has become my best critic and source of ideas on this topic since *Executive Privilege* first appeared. He read and made exceptionally detailed and helpful comments on drafts of the second edition as well as on a number of my more recent cowritten papers on the topic. Morton Rosenberg has also been a most valuable source of ideas and information on executive privilege.

I have also benefited more recently from a number of opportunities to discuss my work on executive privilege with constitutional law professors, particularly John Yoo and Michael Stokes Paulson. I thank Michael for the invitation to present some of my research at the Minnesota Law School conference on presidential powers held in 1998. I benefited from the wonderfully detailed comments on my paper by Professor Saikrishna Prakash and Judge Kenneth Starr. The *Minnesota Law Review* published my essay in its May 1999 issue. I thank the *William and Mary Bill of Rights Law Journal* for the opportunity to contribute to its April 2000 special issue on executive privilege, where I elaborated on my earlier critique of Berger's analysis. I also benefited from the invitation to present my analysis of executive privilege in the Clinton and Bush years at a Duke Law School conference in March 2002 and from the opportunity to contribute an essay on that topic to the *Duke Law Journal*. More recently, I cowrote a lengthy analysis of former president George W. Bush's use of executive privilege in the *Journal of Law and Politics*. That article is one of several new works on executive privilege—some appearing as journal articles and others as book chapters—I have written with Mitch Sollenberger.

Research for this book derives substantially on presidential papers and other government documents. I thank the staffs at the Gerald Ford, Jimmy Carter, and George H. W. Bush presidential libraries for all of their good help during my research visits. The Gerald Ford Fellowship Program supported my visit to the Ford Library in Ann Arbor, Michigan. The Center for Presidential Studies at Texas A&M University supported my visit to the Bush Library in College Station, Texas, and the attendant opportunity to participate in the presidency conference organized by center director George C. Edwards III.

Numerous congressional staff members, past and present, have assisted my searches for various executive privilege materials. I thank David Kass, Jim Wilson, Henry Wray, Sandy Harris, Kevin Sabo, Monica Wrobelewski, James Lewin, Kathryn Seddon, Charles Tiefer, Eric Thorsen, and especially Morton Rosenberg.

I am truly grateful to work in a most supportive academic environment in the School of Public Policy at George Mason University. Dean Kingsley Haynes and Associate Dean Jim Finkelstein are exemplary leaders who make it possible for faculty to keep focused on scholarship and teaching. I have many wonderful colleagues, too many to name here, who make it a pleasure to be a part of this intellectually vibrant interdisciplinary program.

This new edition, as the previous one, is dedicated to my daughters Nadine and Renée, with love.

INTRODUCTION: THE DILEMMA OF SECRECY
AND DEMOCRATIC ACCOUNTABILITY

Executive privilege poses a complex dilemma: a presidential administration sometimes needs to conduct the duties of government in secret, yet the coordinate branches and the public need information about the executive branch so that they can fulfill their democratic responsibilities. This study proposes that the resolution to the dilemma of executive branch secrecy and democratic accountability is in the founders' theory of the separation of powers. That theory allows for a carefully exercised and properly constrained presidential power of executive privilege.

Not all will agree. In a political system predicated on democratic accountability, many analysts believe that there can be no legitimate basis at all for executive privilege. Raoul Berger certainly is not alone in the view that executive branch secrecy is indefensible. In his 1885 book *Congressional Government,* political scientist and future president of the United States Woodrow Wilson argued that representative government must be predicated on openness. He explained that Congress had the high responsibility of investigating administration activities. "It is the proper duty of a representative body to look diligently into every affair of government and to talk much about what it sees."[1] The Wilsonian view is echoed by David Wise, who maintains that executive privilege is a "dubious doctrine." Wise believes that executive privilege cannot be legitimate under a separation of powers system in which the legislative branch has extensive investigating powers.[2] Among the justifications given for withholding information, none is more prominent than national security concerns. Although most would agree that some limits on access to national security information are reasonable, Wise argues that because "*all* information is of possible value to an adversary," adopting a standard is not possible. "Moreover, 'national security' is a term of political art, which can be defined by a given administration to coincide with its political interests. The men in power tend, sometimes unconsciously, to equate their own personal and partisan interests with the national interest, no matter how noble their motives."[3]

Wise is particularly concerned about freedom of the press issues. Democratic accountability cannot exist, he believes, in a society in which the press is limited in what it can investigate and report. Consequently, executive

1

privilege cannot coexist with the Bill of Rights and accountable government. "Freedom to publish about government is either absolute, or it does not exist," Wise says. "Once qualified, it may be described as something else, but not as freedom of the press."[4]

Morton H. Halperin and Daniel N. Hoffman also argue that executive branch leaders use national security as a reason to withhold vital information from Congress, the bureaucracy, and the public and thus destroy democratic accountability. In their view, secrecy often originates from "a domestic political need."[5] Furthermore, they maintain that secrecy threatens the basic liberties guaranteed by the Bill of Rights. "The Framers sought to design a structure for effective leadership that would not threaten liberty."[6] Halperin and Hoffman argue that the Framers—concerned with individual liberties—purposefully did not grant a presidential power of privilege in Article II of the Constitution. According to them, secrecy fosters official "lying," and consequently, public policy must be based on complete openness in governmental deliberations.[7] They believe that openness is "constitutionally necessary" and that it protects citizens against those leaders who scheme to "prevent the American public from learning the truth."[8]

Halperin and Hoffman also admit that they are concerned with more than just protecting liberty and democratic accountability. They believe that open government will also ensure a number of policy changes that they desire, such as decreased defense budgets and less U.S. intervention in international affairs.[9]

For our purposes, the major concerns about executive privilege are the rights of citizens and governmental accountability. Nearly five decades ago, James Wiggins wrote that "each added measure of secrecy measurably diminishes our freedom."[10] During the Watergate period, investigative reporter Clark Mollenhoff testified before Congress that executive privilege "would eventually destroy all of our freedom. . . . It is unfortunate that shortsighted editorial writers and superficial politically motivated legal scholars have occasionally given a degree of support to this so-called time honored doctrine and this phony well-established precedent of executive privilege."[11]

A classic slippery-slope argument characterizes many of the critiques of executive privilege: allow any measure of withholding of information, and ultimately all our liberties will be undermined and democratic accountability destroyed. This argument is countered by the views of other analysts who believe that current limitations on secrecy policies are not in the public interest.

Michael A. Ledeen, former consultant to the Reagan administration National Security Council, has criticized the argument of former representative

Lee Hamilton (D-Ind.) that secretly arrived at policies are inferior to ones arrived at in full public view. Ledeen countered that "it is all wonderfully high-minded and unexceptionable; it is also unworkable. These abstract principles are in conflict with a world where secrecy makes its own demands. If secrets—of various sorts—cannot be kept, good policy and good relations are impossible."[12] Contrary to the arguments of the critics of executive privilege, Ledeen maintains that our political culture is overly suspicious of secrecy. He believes that Americans are unimpressed with "reason of state" as a justification for government secrecy; this is in stark contrast to Great Britain, where the Official Secrets Act and libel laws render "the British government—and media—far more close-mouthed than ours."[13]

Former editor of the *Sunday Times* of London, Harold Evans, also finds the differences between the U.S. and British secrecy policies telling. For example, under U.S. law, it is a felony to lie to Congress, whereas in Great Britain, there is no penalty for deceiving Parliament. Instead, "punishment is meted out to those who dare expose the deception."[14] In Great Britain, unauthorized disclosure of official information is a crime, whereas in the United States, as much official information as possible is made public or is at least guaranteed to be available through the Freedom of Information Act.[15]

Clearly, no one has discovered exactly how to balance the competing and valid claims of freedom of information and governmental secrecy. As the former director of the Central Intelligence Agency, Stansfield Turner, has asked, "how much does a congressional committee need to know to be sure nothing illegal or immoral is being done? Can it know that much without exposing sensitive and necessary operations?" Turner correctly answers that there is no easy way to balance such competing needs to ensure both accountability and the capability of people who maintain secrets to do their jobs.[16]

The dilemma of executive privilege is made even more complex by a number of other factors explored in this study. First, in popular culture, journalism, and even scholarship, there is a long-standing glorification of the strong presidency. Presidents are encouraged from all these venues to achieve "greatness" through activist policy agendas and bold leadership gestures. Less admiration is reserved for presidents who act cautiously in the exercise of their powers. Nonetheless, presidents also are expected to conform to the letter of the law in exercising their powers. Presidents who attempt to achieve their goals through the use of prerogative powers often find that they are in conflict with legislators who wish to share in the exercise of such powers themselves or who have enacted legal restrictions on presidential authority. History is replete with examples of presidents who, out of some real or perceived necessity, acted beyond the strict letter of the law. Some got away with it and are honored by scholars as "great" presidents (e.g., Jefferson, Lincoln, the two Roosevelts); others did not and are scorned by scholars (e.g., Nixon, Reagan).

Second, even among those who agree that presidents possess independent prerogative powers, there is little agreement regarding the circumstances under which such powers can be exercised legitimately. As Daniel P. Franklin has written, "prerogative powers are difficult to discuss, let alone define, in a society that cannot agree about how much liberty should be sacrificed for the sake of security."[17]

Third, the Constitution is silent on the question of executive branch secrecy. Does this mean that the Framers intended to exclude the exercise of that power forever? Or does it mean that secrecy in the executive branch is such an obvious necessity that no one thought of putting it in the Constitution?

Fourth, the Supreme Court has never recognized an absolute "right to know" or "right to receive information." At most, the First Amendment may recognize a right to receive ideas.[18]

Fifth, the issue of executive privilege concerns questions of both foreign and domestic policy. Nonetheless, the presumption in favor of executive privilege has always been strongest in areas of national security and foreign policy. Yet, if there is a necessity to hold leaders accountable for their actions, how can Congress's and the public's need for information be less valid in some policy areas than in others?

Sixth, often there are demands that withheld information be released without delay. From the perspective of those who claim a need to know, the issue of timeliness of information may be of utmost concern. Those who withhold information often make the case that the cause of democratic accountability is not necessarily better served by immediate disclosure of information as opposed to later disclosure, when the need for secrecy is not so compelling.

Seventh, different views on executive privilege generally reflect different institutional perspectives. Presidents see themselves as imbued with worldwide responsibilities and as the representatives of the national interest. They may perceive members of Congress who demand to play an active role in setting foreign policy or in scrutinizing executive branch foreign policy actions as meddling in areas where legislators do not belong. Members of Congress believe that they have the duty not only to play an active role in the policy process but also to investigate all areas of executive branch activity. Louis Henkin has observed that "if the Framers provided no guidance as to where to find the powers of the federal government in international matters, of course they provided no guidance as to how such unenumerated federal authority is allocated between Congress and the president."[19]

Different institutional perspectives may also be reinforced by different partisan ones. Certainly that has often been the case during periods of divided government. During the Reagan-Bush years, Republicans most often defended presidential powers and prerogatives, while Democrats vigorously challenged presidential authority. During the first two years of the Clinton presidency, the Democratic Party majority did not seriously investigate executive branch activities, despite much evidence of potential wrongdoing. Once the Republican Party achieved majority status in Congress in 1995, a cycle of continuous investigations of the Clinton White House and even of prepresidential activities began. During the early months of the George W. Bush presidency, a GOP-led House committee continued its investigation of Clinton-era scandals, despite opposition from the Justice Department and Attorney General John Ashcroft. Additionally, there was some serious congressional pushback against some of Bush's executive privilege claims by a GOP-led Congress in the first two years of his first term. But not surprisingly, legislative investigations and executive privilege clashes with Bush became much more pronounced after the Democrats became the majority party in 2007.

Chapter 1 reviews the leading arguments against the legitimacy of executive privilege. These arguments are that (1) there is no constitutional grant of executive privilege, (2) the Framers' fear of tyranny prevented such a power from being granted, (3) the public and the coordinate branches of government have a right to know what the executive branch is doing, and (4) presidents have abused the power of executive privilege.

Chapter 2 argues for the legitimacy of executive privilege. The defense of a properly constrained executive privilege is based on (1) its theoretical and constitutional underpinnings; (2) the historical precedents for its exercise; (3) the demands of national security; (4) the need for candid, internal White House deliberations; (5) limitations on the congressional power of inquiry; (6) historical necessities; and (7) the widely accepted secrecy practices of the coordinate branches of government.

Chapter 3 looks at the most crucial turning point for the modern exercise of executive privilege—the Richard M. Nixon years. Nixon's abuse of presidential powers undermined the exercise of executive privilege by his successors. In brief, he gave executive privilege a bad name by invoking that doctrine to withhold embarrassing and incriminating—not vital—information. As far as executive privilege is concerned, the post-Watergate presidents have had to operate in Nixon's shadow.

Chapters 4–7 review and analyze executive privilege controversies in the post-Watergate era. They use White House and congressional documents to analyze the development of executive privilege in the Ford, Carter, Reagan, Bush, Clinton, Bush, and Obama administrations. These chapters examine and analyze each administration's official policy toward executive privilege. Clearly, executive privilege has fallen out of favor in the post-Watergate years, due in part to misuse of that power by presidents, but also to the successful efforts of opponents of executive branch secrecy to portray nearly every attempt to withhold information as a Nixonian ploy to deceive or to conceal wrongdoing. No post-Watergate president has rejected the legitimacy of executive privilege. Nonetheless, because of the taint of Watergate, some modern presidents have crafted strategies to withhold information without resorting to executive privilege. President Bill Clinton tried to reestablish the viability of executive privilege but ultimately failed through the inappropriate use of that power in his administration. President George W. Bush also tried to reestablish executive privilege, but he, too, ran into strong opposition due to having overreached his authority. Early in his presidency, President Barack Obama directly repudiated some of Bush's secrecy actions and promised a more transparent administration. Importantly, one of Obama's first presidential actions was to repeal the controversial Bush executive order that had vastly expanded the scope of executive privilege.

The conclusion proposes a way to resolve the dilemma of executive privilege. The post-Watergate history of executive privilege is one of presidents either withholding information while denying the use of executive privilege or trying to reestablish this constitutional power in inappropriate contexts. In retrospect, it is easy to understand the modern presidential difficulties associated with exercising executive privilege. Immediately after Watergate, presidents wanted to avoid any hint of the taint associated with Nixon's abuse of executive privilege; the mere mention of the phrase was a powerful reminder of abuses of constitutional powers. By the time of the Clinton administration, many believed that the events of Watergate were far enough in the past to allow a president to reestablish executive privilege. Although Clinton was correct to affirm that there is a proper place for executive privilege in the modern presidency, his administration was beset by scandal and used executive privilege to conceal evidence of wrongdoing. President George W. Bush tried to reestablish executive privilege by denying a GOP-led House committee access to Justice Department documents regarding closed investigations. Bush tried to apply executive privilege to all deliberative materials in the executive branch, even though there is ample precedent for Congress to receive such information. Throughout his two terms in office, Bush made other attempts to expand executive privilege over departmental deliberations and even to conceal testimony before Congress by current and former White House aides. Although he has stated his intention for an open presidency in contrast to his predecessor, President Barack Obama also has signaled his commitment to protect what he considers to be legitimate and necessary presidential powers.

This study rejects the view that executive privilege is a "myth" and an unqualified evil, as well as the view that executive privilege is an unfettered presidential prerogative. Instead, it recognizes that executive privilege is a legitimate, though often controversial, presidential power and that disputes over the withholding of information can best be resolved by the political ebb and flow of the separation of powers system.

1

THE ARGUMENTS AGAINST EXECUTIVE PRIVILEGE

Although numerous presidents have exercised executive privilege in one form or another, critics remain unconvinced of its legitimacy. An oft-cited analogy is that a criminal act does not become lawful after being committed many times, it is still a criminal act. That analogy highlights the most powerful criticisms of executive privilege: that it lacks any constitutional foundation, that the Framers of the Constitution were too fearful of executive branch tyranny to allow such a power, that Congress and the public have a "right to know" and a need to know what the executive is doing, and that the right to withhold information has become a convenient cloak for presidents who abuse their powers.

Lack of a Constitutional Foundation

The beginning point for any critique of executive privilege is the fact that our Constitution nowhere explicitly grants the executive the power to withhold information. Such critics as Raoul Berger maintain that determining the scope of the executive power requires a strict reading of the Constitution. According to this view, there is no implied power of executive privilege. Berger argued that the Framers purposefully excluded the executive power to withhold information. Quite simply, had the Framers intended there to be executive privilege, they would have granted it in Article II. Hence, Berger proclaimed executive privilege "a constitutional myth."[1]

A classic statement of the limited nature of the president's constitutional authority comes from William Howard Taft, a former U.S. president and chief justice of the Supreme Court. Responding to former president Theodore Roosevelt's "stewardship theory" of the presidency—that the chief executive has a broad residuum of authority to act, as he sees fit, in the public interest[2]—Taft wrote the following:

> The true view of the executive function is, as I conceive it, that the president can exercise no power which cannot be fairly and reasonably traced to some specific grant of power or justly implied and included within such express grant as proper and necessary to its exercise. . . .

There is no undefined residuum of power which he can exercise because it seems to him to be in the public interest.[3]

Making a convincing constitutional case against executive privilege requires much more than asserting that such a power is not explicitly granted
in the Constitution. Throughout history, presidents have exercised formidable powers not explicitly granted by the Constitution (e.g., war powers, executive agreements), as has Congress (e.g., the power to investigate, the
creation of independent regulatory agencies). The critics of executive privilege also must show that the Framers clearly intended that such a power not
be exercised by the executive and that the Framers created impediments to
such a power ever being adopted.

One constitutional argument against executive privilege is that the
Framers assigned to Congress either a coequal or a "senior partner" status in
its partnership with the executive in foreign policy.[4] Because most claims of
executive privilege center around national security and foreign policy concerns, this argument potentially undermines a frequently cited justification
for the withholding of information: that the executive has a compelling need
for the full use of his authority, or even the exercise of extraconstitutional
authority, vis-à-vis foreign nation-states.

Some reject the concept of extraordinary or prerogative executive powers.[5]
Harold Hongju Koh writes that "the constitutional system of checks and
balances is not suspended simply because foreign affairs are at issue."[6] Louis
Henkin offers the following view:

> Constitutionalism implies limited government. For our subject, that
> means that the Constitution should be expounded so that there can be
> no extraconstitutional government, that, in principle and in effect, no
> activity of government is exempt from constitutional restraints, not
> even foreign affairs. . . . For us, as for the Framers, no branch of gov-
> ernment has authority that is so large as to be essentially undefined and
> uncircumscribed, that is "plenary," that is not checked, not balanced,
> not even the President in foreign affairs.[7]

By implication, executive privilege—an independent, sometimes
unchecked presidential power—cannot be legitimate. Furthermore, some
critics of executive privilege contend that the president is always accountable
to Congress, yet Congress need not be accountable to the president. An
1860 report of the House of Representatives stated that "the conduct of the
President is always subject to the constitutional supervision and judgment of
Congress; while he, on the contrary, has no such power over either branch of

that body."[8] According to this view, the Framers recognized the need for secrecy in government and placed that power in the hands of Congress.[9] The evidence for this argument is found in Article I, Section 5(3), of the Constitution: "Each House shall keep a Journal of its proceedings, and from time to time, publish the same excepting such parts as may in their judgment require secrecy."

Because no such mention of the right of secrecy is made in the executive articles, Halperin and Hoffman conclude that "the Framers gave the President no privilege to withhold information from Congress."[10] Berger adds that "in the Constitution the Framers provided for limited secrecy by Congress alone, thereby excluding executive secrecy from the public."[11]

A former special counsel to the U.S. attorney general, George C. Calhoun, attributes much of the interbranch conflict over executive privilege to the "belief of many in the government that each branch *owns* the information it develops."[12] According to Berger, Congress owns its own information *and* the executive's. He maintains that the Framers "patently modeled" the U.S. Congress after the British Parliament and thereby made Congress the nation's "grand inquest."[13] Consequently, the president has no constitutional authority to resist Congress's demands for information. As Berger told a congressional committee, "There is no word in the Constitution that expresses any intention whatsoever to curtail the normal attribute of the legislative power . . . [and] there is not a single word in any one of the conventions expressing any intention to curtail the legislative power of investigation."[14]

Executive accountability to Congress also is guaranteed by the Article II, Section 4, provision for impeachment: "The President . . . shall be removed from Office on Impeachment for and Conviction of Treason, Bribery, or other high Crimes and Misdemeanors."

To properly conduct an impeachment proceeding, the House of Representatives must have complete access to executive branch information. An 1843 House report stated the following: "The House has the sole right of impeachment . . . a power which implies the right of inquiry on the part of the House to the fullest and most unlimited extent."[15]

President James K. Polk stated in 1846 that the House of Representatives has the right of access to "*all the archives and papers* of the Executive Department, public or private" in cases of inquiry into misspending of public funds by the executive. Polk added that the House's power of inquiry in such cases "*would penetrate into the most secret recesses* of the Executive Departments."[16] If this interpretation of the extent of the House's power of inquiry is correct, then the case for executive privilege appears substantially weakened. Obviously, the House cannot investigate the executive if the president can, for whatever reason, withhold any information.

Berger argues that the Constitution's provision for the presidential delivery to Congress of information on the state of the Union also repudiates any claim to executive privilege. Article II, Section 3—most often perceived as an executive power—is seen by Berger as a legislative power: "He shall from time to time give to the Congress information of the state of the Union, and recommend to their consideration such measures as he shall judge necessary and expedient."

Berger believes that this constitutional duty of presidents is yet another measure of Congress's absolute power of inquiry. The original provision presented at the Constitutional Convention allowed the president little discretion in determining the kinds of information he could provide to Congress. In the rejected version, the Framers established "his duty to inform the Legislature of the Condition of the U.S. so far as may respect his Department." The final, adopted version, he believes, did not limit the president's duty to supply Congress with information.[17] In fact, the duty to provide information "from time to time," according to Berger, "is the reciprocal of the familiar legislative power to inquire."[18]

Finally, Berger cites the Article II, Section 3, provision that the president "shall take care that the laws be faithfully executed" as evidence that the executive must be accountable to the legislative branch. Berger asks, "who has a more legitimate interest in inquiring whether a law has been faithfully executed than the lawmaker?"[19] Executive privilege must be dubious if Congress has a constitutionally based absolute right of inquiry.

Framers' Fear of Tyranny

Fearing that a strong executive might at some time be transformed into a tyrannical ruler, the Framers who gathered at the Constitutional Convention sought to devise a governmental system of limited powers. Given the colonial experiences under the abuses of King George III, the Framers were determined that our constitutional system would prohibit any chance of an arbitrary and tyrannical executive coming to power. Furthermore, the Framers made the legislature the supreme lawmaking branch of government. Our chief constitutional architect, James Madison, explained in *Federalist 51* that "in a republican form of government, the legislature necessarily predominates." Roger Sherman characterized his preference for the executive as "nothing more than an institution for carrying the will of the Legislature into effect."[20]

According to this view, the Framers so feared executive power that they made the legislative the supreme branch of government in all policy areas—

even foreign affairs. David Gray Adler writes that "the Framers clearly granted the bulk of foreign relations powers to Congress. The president's constitutional authority pales by comparison."[21] Specifically, the Constitution grants to the president two exclusive powers—to receive ambassadors and to act as commander in chief of the armed forces. The president must share with the Senate the treaty-making power and the power to appoint ambassadors. Yet Congress has such formidable powers as declaring war and regulating commerce. These constitutional grants of authority led Adler to conclude that although the Constitution provides for a partnership between the president and Congress in foreign policy making, "perhaps surprisingly, Congress is assigned the role of senior partner."[22]

Berger argues as well that the president cannot be the constitutional director of foreign policy.[23] Both Berger and Adler maintain that the foreign policy–making powers of the modern presidency are the result of a gradual usurpation of legislative authority. Although the past six decades have been characterized by executive domination of foreign policy making, such a state of affairs "represents a dramatic departure from the basic scheme of the Constitution."[24] Adler finds evidence for his argument from *Federalist 75,* written by that ultradefender of a strong executive, Alexander Hamilton:

> The history of human conduct does not warrant that exalted opinion of human virtue which would make it wise in a nation to commit interests so delicate and momentous a kind as those which concern its intercourse with the rest of the world to the sole disposal of a magistrate, created and circumstanced, as would be a president of the United States.

According to Berger, a telling example of presidential usurpation of congressional authority is the treaty-making power. He cites a provision of Article II, Section 2, of the Constitution to substantiate the argument that presidents have been acting unconstitutionally: "He shall have power, by and with the advice and consent of the Senate, to make treaties."

The Senate, according to Berger, has the power to participate in the negotiation and formulation of treaties, as well as in the ratification stage. From his study of the Constitutional Convention, Berger concluded that the Framers intended the treaty-making power to belong to the Senate and that "it was the President . . . who was finally made a participant in the treaty-making process, which had been initially lodged—after the pattern of the Continental Congress—in the Senate alone."[25] Berger believes that there is no presidential privilege to withhold information on the development of treaties with foreign nation-states. Berger explained his position to a congressional committee:

How can you help "make" a treaty if you don't know a thing about how it is being negotiated? How can the Senate "advise" as to the "making" of a treaty if it is kept in the dark? That doesn't mean that you have to play strip poker in full view of the public. The alternative to operation in a gold fish bowl is not necessarily a darkroom.[26]

Despite the Framers' fear of a too powerful executive, and despite their efforts to constrain presidential power, even in foreign policy, the ascendance of the president in foreign policy making has become widely accepted. Nonetheless, former senator J. William Fulbright (D-Ark.) once countered that "usurpation is not legitimized simply by repetition, nor is a valid power nullified by failure to exercise it."[27] His comment was reminiscent of former justice Felix Frankfurter's statement that "illegality cannot attain legitimacy through practice"[28] and former chief justice Earl Warren's comment, "that an unconstitutional action has been taken before surely does not render that action any less unconstitutional at a later date."[29]

Indeed, the critics of executive privilege maintain that presidents have usurped such authority, in contravention of the constitutional scheme. How could the Framers—who sought to limit and control executive authority—possibly have accepted such a broad-based, independent power as the right to withhold information? Logically, a chief executive who is subservient to the will of the legislature has no such right.

The "Right" and the Need to Know

A democratic society places a premium on open government and freedom of information. Critics of executive privilege are concerned with the need to foster those values. From their perspective, executive privilege is antithetical to core democratic values. It is, in a word, antidemocratic. More specifically, these critics maintain that, for our democracy to properly function, both Congress and the public must be fully informed of what the executive branch is doing. Congress must have adequate information to carry out its primary functions, and a well-informed citizenry cannot be kept in the dark about its government's actions.

Without a doubt, the executive branch is an essential source of information for Congress. In order to know how best to appropriate funds for the military and assistance to foreign governments, to oversee the bureaucracy, and to review treaties and executive agreements, Congress needs access to executive branch information. Without adequate information, members of Congress are unable to weigh alternatives, estimate costs and benefits, and develop strategies to improve government policies. As former senator Sam Ervin (D-N.C.) explained, "the refusal to make information available to the Congress *when needed for its legislative functions* is inimical to the power of the Congress to fulfill its legislative duties."[30]

Congress often must rely on executive branch information to determine whether public policies are being executed faithfully. To adopt Berger's language, the "Grand Inquest" of the nation can never legitimately be denied access to executive branch information. Former senator Stuart Symington (D-Mo.) agreed: "The Executive Branch of our Government . . . is, or should be, the best source of information to which the Congress can turn to if it is to know how and whether the laws and policies which it approved are, in fact, being carried out."[31]

There is constitutional support for Symington's view. In one leading Supreme Court case, *McGrain v. Daugherty* (1927), Justice Willis Van Devanter offered the following judgment: "In actual legislative practice, power to secure needed information by such [investigatory] means has long been treated as an attribute of power to legislate. It was so regarded in the British Parliament and in the Colonial Legislatures before the American Revolution."[32]

From the perspective of some critics of executive privilege, congressional access to executive branch information is not only a practical necessity; it is legally required. Furthermore, members of Congress are capable of maintaining secrets.[33] The assumption, therefore, is that the executive branch never really loses "control" over secret information because (1) it does not own that information, and (2) Congress can be trusted with secrets.

Members of Congress frequently argue that executive branch information must be made available to them in a timely fashion. Most legislators want timely information so that they can play a substantive role in the early stages of decision making. To be precise, they prefer being "consulted" to being merely "informed."[34] Divulging previously withheld information after a decision has been made does little to advance Congress's role in the policy process. A 1981 House of Representatives report on Congress and foreign policy making stated the dilemma well: "Unless consultation is timely, it loses a good deal of its impact and 'effective' relations are of only symbolic value."[35]

From the congressionalist perspective, a particularly strong argument against executive privilege is that decision makers benefit from being exposed to numerous viewpoints. Irving Janis's classic study *Groupthink* makes it clear that from a policy maker's perspective, it is important to avoid conformity, to seek out different opinions, and to resist isolation from outside opinions. Janis illustrates the disastrous consequences of decisions made by like-minded groups of individuals who resist different points of view.[36] Consequently, an executive may at his peril withhold information from people he knew would disagree with his position. Members of Congress believe that they are particularly well situated to provide the executive with diverse opinions. James MacGregor Burns agrees that leaders benefit from such outside input, in that they can make more informed decisions than when they are secluded from opposing arguments.

> A more effective way to handle choice . . . is to use conflict deliberately to protect decision-making options and power, and, even more, to use conflict to structure [the] political environment so as to maximize "constructive" dissonance, thus allowing for more informed decision-making. Perhaps the chief means of doing this is to create a system of "multiple advocacy" around the decision-maker.[37]

The 1981 House report noted an important obstacle to the executive seeking out diverse viewpoints: a lack of trust in Congress. The report quoted a White House official who agreed that presidents need constructive advice from Congress but then complained that some members of the legislative branch cannot be trusted with secrets.[38] Hence, members of Congress contend that they have a right to—and a need for—executive branch information, but the executive is often reluctant to divulge certain kinds of information out of fear of public disclosure.

Many critics of executive privilege disregard the president's fear of public disclosure of sensitive information. The public, they believe, has a "right to know" everything about the operations of the executive branch in a democratic system of government. From this perspective, executive privilege hinders the free flow of information and ideas. Sam Ervin eloquently stated that

> the practice of executive privilege . . . is clearly in contravention of the basic principle that the free flow of ideas and information and open and full disclosure of the governing process is essential to the operation of a free society. Throughout history, rulers have invoked secrecy regarding their actions in order to enslave the citizenry. When the government operates in secrecy its citizens are not informed and their ignorance breeds oppression. In contrast, a government whose actions are completely visible to all of its citizens is a government which best protects the freedom which the Founding Fathers attempted to embody in the Constitution.[39]

Executive privilege appears difficult to accommodate in a governing system based on the concept of accountability. How can leaders be held accountable for their actions when the public and Congress do not know what these leaders are doing? Bruce Miroff writes that "the American people cannot judge what they do not know."[40] He offers the following assessment of the problem: "Secret action . . . permits a president to persist in a course of policy even if that policy lacks support from, or is strongly opposed by, majorities in Congress and among the American people. . . . Secrecy also encourages contempt for democratic procedures and democratic values."[41]

Perhaps most ironic is the following quotation from former president Richard M. Nixon, just three months prior to the Watergate break-in: "When information which properly belongs to the public is systematically withheld by those in power, the people soon become ignorant of their own affairs, distrustful of those who manage them, and—eventually—incapable of determining their own destinies."[42]

Executive privilege appears to be contrary to the Freedom of Information Act, passed by Congress in 1966 to allow for the fullest possible public disclosure of government actions.[43] Executive privilege also appears antithetical to the principle of a free press. Former *New York Times* writer Hanson W. Baldwin argued that government censorship or control of information "impairs the constitutional rights of a free press, and hence poses a potential danger to our form of democratic and representative government." Furthermore, "no free people can be really free if its press is spoon-fed with government pap, or if the news which provides a democracy with the rationale for its actions is so controlled, restricted, managed, or censored that it cannot be published."[44]

David Wise explains that many authorities believe that there must be a balancing test between national security claims and the principle of a free press. He rejects any such test in favor of an unfettered free press. In his view, because of the First Amendment guarantee of a free press, there can be no limits on the right to publish information about the government's activities, "no matter what the potential harm to an officially defined 'national security.' The risks of repression are greater."[45] As Wise maintains, "a democratic system requires a public informed about the decisions and actions of its political leaders."[46] That public cannot be so informed when the press is unable to obtain and report information about governmental activities.

Misuses of the Privilege

Presidents and their staffs may invoke executive privilege to cover up illegal or unethical governmental activities. They may use executive privilege to hide embarrassing information or to maintain an advantage in policy debates with congressional opponents. Former congressman John E. Moss (D-Calif.) commented that executive branch officials withhold information "to avoid criticism rather than for reasons of national safety."[47] Former Senator Edward M. Kennedy (D-Mass.) argued that

> government secrecy breeds government deceit, that executive privilege nurtures executive arrogance, that national security is frequently the cover for political embarrassment, and that the best antidote to official malfeasance, misfeasance, and nonfeasance is the sunshine and fresh air of full public disclosure of official activities.[48]

Underlying such arguments against executive privilege is a profound distrust of government power. Thomas I. Emerson writes that "to the extent that information is withheld from a citizen the basis for government control over him becomes coercion, not persuasion."[49] Wise adds that "the secrecy system facilitates official lying."[50] In Wise's view, the president may use the excuse of secrecy to distort reality for self-serving purposes.

> Frequently the press and public, unable to check the events independently, can only await the appearance of the president on the television screen to announce the official version of reality, be it the Bay of Pigs, Tonkin Gulf, or Laos, or Cambodia, or Vietnam. . . . The government's capacity to distort information in order to preserve its own political power is almost limitless.
>
> If information is power, the ability to distort and control information will be used more often than not to preserve and perpetuate that power.[51]

Wise acknowledges a leading reason given for government secrecy: the need to conceal information from enemies abroad. Nonetheless, he concludes that there is no moral or philosophical basis for that reason and that the threat of enemies abroad is merely an untruthful justification for keeping people at home uninformed.[52]

Concerns about government misuse of powers such as executive privilege are certainly well founded. Indeed, there are numerous examples of executive branch officials concealing information of minimal security value to cover up governmental misconduct. Under the Nixon administration alone, the Securities and Exchange Commission in 1972 refused to provide pertinent information on the International Telephone and Telegraph investigation to the House Interstate and Foreign Commerce Subcommittee; the

Department of Defense in 1972 refused to supply documents to the House Armed Services Committee during hearings on the firing on General John Lavelle, who was reported to have conducted unauthorized raids over Vietnam; the president refused to allow his secretary of state, William Rogers, to comply with an August 1971 Senate Foreign Relations Committee demand for information on foreign military assistance; and the president used executive privilege to cover up the Watergate scandal. Nixon believed that he had an absolute power of executive privilege—one that could be claimed on behalf of the entire executive branch of government.

President Bill Clinton also abused executive privilege by claiming to be protecting the presidency and U.S. interests abroad while attempting to cover up a scandal. Like Nixon during Watergate, Clinton, during the so-called Lewinsky scandal, claimed that attempts to undermine his use of executive privilege were attacks on the institution of the presidency itself and on his unique ability to protect U.S. interests in the world. Clinton's successor, George W. Bush, made a number of groundless claims of executive privilege that further inflamed the national debate over this presidential power.

Given Nixon's, and then later Clinton's and George W. Bush's abuses of executive privilege, it is no wonder that many critics are suspicious of any such claim of presidential power.[53] Halperin and Hoffman summarize what they perceive as the core dangers of executive privilege:

> Not only has secrecy undermined the constitutional prerogatives of Congress and the electorate, it has also led directly to substantial infringements of civil liberties. . . . We permitted our constitutional system of checks and balances to be eroded, our civil liberties to be infringed, because we believed that secrecy was necessary to our national security.[54]

For many critics of executive privilege, the evils of nondisclosure clearly outweigh any potential evil that might result from executive disclosure of sensitive information. Thus, for those who accept the need for a balancing test, the scale tips decisively in favor of candor and openness. Stuart Symington believes that "it is now clear that the risk of failure of executive branch policies and programs occasioned by their revelation to the Congress is much to be preferred as against the risk of vital damage inflicted on a democratic system because of failure to disclose the truth."[55] The leading critic of executive privilege, Raoul Berger, adds that "against the debatable assumption that fear of disclosure to Congress may inhibit 'candid interchange' there is the proven fact that such exchanges have time and again served as the vehicles of corruption and malversation."[56] But perhaps none other than

Richard Nixon stated the case against executive branch secrecy so clearly. In 1961, the then recently defeated presidential candidate criticized President John F. Kennedy's exercise of secrecy during the Bay of Pigs fiasco. "The concept of a return to secrecy in peacetime demonstrates a profound misunderstanding of the role of a free press as opposed to that of a controlled press. The plea for secrecy could become a cloak for errors, misjudgments, and other failings of government."[57]

Critics of executive privilege maintain that there is no constitutional support for the exercise of such a power. Furthermore, the frequent use of executive privilege in presidential administrations constitutes the repetition of a criminal act. Finally, critics of executive privilege describe such a power as antithetical to a democratic system, a convenient cloak to avoid accountability. From this perspective, the dilemma of executive privilege and democratic accountability is resolved in favor of complete openness in governmental activity.

2

THE ARGUMENTS IN FAVOR OF EXECUTIVE PRIVILEGE

The opponents of executive privilege persuasively argue that government secrecy is undemocratic and leads to abuses of power, but they often overstate their case. For example, it is true that the Framers wanted to preserve liberty by restricting power, but they certainly never set out to cripple executive power. Any power can be used to do right or to do wrong. The Framers sought to devise institutional mechanisms to counterbalance the abuse of power, but they never intended to destroy power altogether as a means of protecting our liberties.

When exercised under the appropriate circumstances, executive privilege has clear constitutional, political, and historical underpinnings. The American separation of powers system provides for executive privilege, but not without limitations. The exercise of that power is always open to challenge by those with compulsory power. Many claims of executive privilege fail the balancing test because, in a democratic system, the presumption generally should be in favor of openness. Unfortunately, one defense of executive privilege is based on the false claim that this power is an absolute, unlimited prerogative. This claim clearly is as misguided as the belief that the Framers rejected for all times and under all circumstances any such exercise of presidential power. Rather, the Framers provided the president with a general grant of power that would enable him to take the actions he deemed necessary, primarily to protect the national security.

Underpinnings of Executive Privilege

Theories of Constitutionalism

As part of their preparation for the Philadelphia Convention of 1787, the Framers studied political theory and history. James Madison, for example, prepared a history of republican governments. The ideas of leading European philosophers weighed on the minds of the American constitutional Framers. An assessment of the Framers' intentions therefore requires an examination of the ideas of the most influential thinkers of modern constitutionalism: John Locke and Baron de Montesquieu.

The neglect, as well as the misunderstanding, of these leading constitutional thinkers has been a source of confusion over the Framers' intentions regarding executive branch secrecy. Archibald Cox, for example, argues that Locke's and Montesquieu's notions of the separation of powers are not germane to the executive privilege debate because "they had no need to concern themselves with problems involving two or more branches that required exact definition of the boundaries of each."[1] Harold Laski writes that our political system, "in its ultimate foundation, is built upon a belief in weak government. It must never be forgotten that the Constitution is the child of the eighteenth century; that the influence of Locke and Montesquieu is written deeply into its clauses."[2] And Raoul Berger concluded from his reading of Montesquieu that "history delineates a virtually unlimited legislative power to demand information from the executive branch."[3]

A careful reading of Locke and Montesquieu reveals that neither of these thinkers advocated weak government or a subordinate executive power at all times. Certainly, they emphasized restrained governmental powers and individual rights more than their predecessors did, which has much to do with their appeal to the Framers. Locke's and Montesquieu's views on executive power must be placed in the proper context of modern political theory.

Political theorists today generally trace the origins of modern political thought to Niccolo Machiavelli. To simplify the distinction, the ancient philosophers focused on the need to create regimes that fostered citizen virtue and community. The modern thinkers, beginning with Machiavelli, concerned themselves with establishing regimes that controlled social and political strife and enabled people to cultivate their own interests without living constantly in fear of one another.

The regimes envisioned by the modernists required some form of executive power. In *The Prince*, Machiavelli advised a ruler on the cruel necessities of executive power during the founding of a regime. Machiavelli believed that to gain control over a principality and get the respect of its subjects the ruler had to establish absolute authority through the exercise of often cruel measures. Only in such a way can order and authority be maintained, Machiavelli reasoned. Machiavelli, therefore, did not advocate an overbearing executive power for its own sake. His masterly work *The Discourses* goes to great lengths to show that there should be inherent limits on the executive power in the postfounding era. Machiavelli feared that an executive who is given enormous powers during the founding period might resist forfeiting such authority during normal times. Hence, he proposed the eventual establishment of a "mixed regime" composed of aristocratic, democratic, and monarchic elements, in which power checks power.

Thomas Hobbes's *Leviathan* proposed that the sovereign power be granted extraordinary authority as the only means of overcoming civil strife. In Hobbes's regime, individuals sacrifice almost all their liberties to the sovereign power in return for the relative comfort bestowed by the absolute dictator. The sovereign has absolute authority but uses it to promote peaceful coexistence in the community.

Machiavelli and Hobbes thus established the necessity of executive power for a stable regime. The chief task of the modern constitutionalists—Locke and Montesquieu—was to create the conditions for such a stable regime while moderating the harsher prescriptions of Machiavelli and Hobbes. Whereas Machiavelli and Hobbes imagined circumstances under which citizens had to forfeit basic liberties to the sovereign power, Locke and Montesquieu sought to create regimes characterized by both strength and liberty. They believed that the way to ensure such a regime was through a system of institutionally separated governmental powers.

John Locke, in his *Second Treatise of Government,* offers a threefold distinction among governmental powers: the legislative, the executive, and the "federative." Although on the surface Locke's emphasis on legislative supremacy seems unequivocal, he invests a considerable amount of power in the executive branch. For example, he places the federative power—the power to make war, peace, treaties, and alliances—solely within the realm of the executive. Locke's chapter "Of Prerogative" is the most revealing. In times of emergency, when the legislature is not in session or when the laws are silent, he proposes giving the executive "the power of doing public good without a rule." For Locke, the "supreme law" of the land is preservation of society. Only the executive can act with power and "despatch" in times of emergency. Whereas the legislative branch has supreme lawmaking powers during normal times, the executive branch has the power to take extraordinary, even extralegal actions in times of emergency.

Accordingly, it is not correct to argue that Locke advocated either weak government or a subordinate executive power. Locke's "executive" is, in many ways, as powerful as Hobbes's "sovereign." The most important difference is that Hobbes takes the exception—civil strife and the need to overcome it through extraordinary executive power—and makes it the rule.[4] Locke's unique contribution to the American experience is showing us how to maintain a strong executive while moderating and checking this power at the same time.

Like his predecessors, Montesquieu also was concerned with the problem of reconciling freedom and coercion. Yet he more clearly formulated the proposition that power can be checked only by power. The liberty of the citizenry, he wrote, can best be protected by preventing any one power from holding the authority to formulate and to execute the laws. He devised a governmental triad—legislative, executive, and judicial powers—as a means of preventing any one arm of the government from becoming tyrannical. In Book II of *The Spirit of the Laws,* he wrote, "Constant experience shows us that every man invested with power is apt to abuse it, and to carry his authority as far as it will go. . . . To prevent this abuse, it is necessary from the very nature of things that power should be a check of power."

Although Montesquieu set forth a separation of powers system to limit governmental power as a means of enhancing individual liberty, he did not advocate weak government. Montesquieu empowers the executive—the "monarch"—to act with a degree of discretion necessary in times of emergency, even if such actions are not specifically granted by the legislature. In the end, Montesquieu allows for a strong executive, independent of direct pressures from the "popular will," capable of acting with force and discretion.

This brief examination of the major thinkers on modern constitutionalism points out the difficulties associated with the conclusion of many writers: that the Framers, taking their cues from Locke and Montesquieu, sought to devise a weak governmental system with a subordinated executive power. Laski and Berger are correct in asserting that earlier constitutional theorists profoundly influenced the Framers, but their interpretations of these thinkers are problematic. Berger and other critics of the privilege have looked to the founding as a time when the Framers sought to preserve liberty to the exclusion of all other values. It cannot be emphasized enough that the Framers sought to preserve both liberty *and* power in devising our constitutional scheme. In fact, in the *Federalist Papers,* Publius makes it clear that efficient, effective government is most conducive to the maintenance of liberty. The notion of checks and balances and the doctrine of separation of powers were devices intended to enhance liberty while maintaining "energy" in the executive. As Paul Peterson asserts, "The doctrines of separation of powers and checks and balances allowed the advocates of a strong executive to carry the day and allowed them to construct an energetic executive within a framework of republican liberty."[5]

Unlike Cox, Laski, and Berger, constitutional scholar Edward S. Corwin wrote that Locke and Montesquieu understood executive power as "a broadly discretionary, residual, power available when other governmental powers fail."[6] Consequently, he concluded that "the Framers had in mind [their] idea of a divided initiative in the matter of legislation and a broad range of autonomous executive power or 'prerogative.'"[7] The Framers may have looked to earlier thinkers for guidance, but these constitution makers also wrote extensively about the role of executive power in republican government. The following evidence clarifies the broad range of discretionary authority vested in the president by the Framers.

The Constitutional Period

Critics of executive privilege point to the Framers' fear of tyranny as proof that the Constitution provides for a subordinate executive power. These critics identify the colonial experiences under King George III as the key point of reference for the Framers in creating the executive power.

The argument that the Framers sought to devise a regime characterized by liberty and weak executive power neglects the true point of reference for these constitution makers: the governing experiences under the Articles of Confederation. During that period, most of the states had extraordinarily weak governors, with terms of office as brief as six months or one year, no reeligibility, and no powers independent of the state legislatures. The most telling exception was New York, which had an independent executive with full administrative powers, a three-year term of office, and unlimited reeligibility. Of the state governments during the Articles of Confederation period, New York could claim the most efficient, competent administration.

At the national level, no single executive existed under the Articles of Confederation. A deliberative assembly, the Continental Congress, had authority for governing the separate states. The failures of governance under this system precipitated the 1787 Constitutional Convention at Philadelphia, where the Framers set forth a new governing plan. Because of the inability of the separate sovereign states to raise a national militia, carry out interstate commerce, and conduct a coherent foreign policy, the Framers established a new constitutional system that included an independent, single-member executive with substantial powers.

Before discussing the Framers' views of executive power—an important foundation for establishing the legitimacy of executive privilege—it is helpful to note that the delegates conducted the Constitutional Convention in secret. They did not officially record the debates of the convention. The official journal of the convention listed only the formal motions and roll-call votes by state, and only the delegates had access to that journal. Delegates had the windows of the building sealed so that no one could overhear the proceedings. The delegates' insistence on secrecy was intended to protect the proceedings from outside pressures. James Madison later attested that "no Constitution would ever have been adopted by the Convention if the debate had been made public."[8] Former chief justice Warren Burger echoed that statement years later when he noted that the convention delegates "were under a pledge to protect the secrecy of the proceedings without which, I think we must know now there would never have been a Constitution coming out of that meeting."[9] In fact, Burger's opinion for a unanimous Court in *U.S. v. Nixon* (1974)—the case that formally recognized the legitimacy of executive privilege—cites the convention delegates' secret proceedings as clear evidence of the Framers' recognition of the need for governmental secrecy.[10]

Contrary to Raoul Berger, the fact that executive privilege is not mentioned in the Constitution does not preclude the legitimate exercise of that presidential power. Recall his interpretation that Article I, Section 5(3), of the Constitution provides for an exclusive legislative privilege to keep secrets. No comparable provision exists in Article II, leading Berger to conclude that the Framers intentionally excluded the president from exercising secrecy.

This narrow reading of the Constitution is not credible. First, Berger fails to note important differences between the legislative and the executive articles of the Constitution. For example, the legislative article, unlike the executive one, contains the words "herein granted" in referring to the legislature's powers and specifies that branch's most important duties (e.g., declaring war, raising and supporting armies, providing and maintaining a navy, regulating commerce, appropriating funds). The executive article provides a general grant of power with relatively few specifics. Many of the president's powers are not defined or enumerated, allowing the chief executive to exercise a broad scope of responsibilities under various circumstances. Under their general grant of authority—"The Executive Power shall be vested in a President of the United States of America"—presidents historically have exercised numerous powers not specified in the Constitution (e.g., issuing proclamations, making executive agreements with foreign nation-states, removing executive officials from office, adopting emergency measures in wartime). Congress too has implied powers (e.g., conducting investigations, issuing subpoenas, holding executive officials in contempt), but it lacks the broad range of discretionary authority invested in the executive.

Second, judging from the writings of the leading Framers who frequently stressed the need for "secrecy" and "despatch" in government, it is hard to imagine that these same people believed that secrecy was so evil that it had to be excluded from the executive article. The Framers understood secrecy as so obvious an executive power—and a judicial one as well—that there was no need for a specific grant of that power in the Constitution. Perhaps the Framers specified such a grant of power in Article I because secrecy could not be assumed to reside in a legislature. Two passages from the *Federalist Papers* support executive branch secrecy. The classic statement is found in Alexander Hamilton's *Federalist 70:* "Decision, activity, secrecy and despatch will generally characterize the proceedings of one man in a much more eminent degree than the proceedings of any great number; and in proportion as the number is increased, these qualities will be diminished." John Jay, who served as the secretary of foreign affairs under the Articles of Confederation, wrote in *Federalist 64* that "secrecy" and "despatch" are characteristic of the executive branch. He recognized the inability of a deliberative assembly to be entrusted with diplomatic secrets:

> There are cases where the most useful intelligence may be obtained, if the persons possessing it can be relieved from apprehensions of discovery. Those apprehensions will operate on those persons whether they are actuated by mercenary or friendly motives; and there doubtless are many of both descriptions who would rely on the secrecy of the President, but who would not confide in that of the Senate, and still less in that of a large popular assembly.

Jay's *Federalist 64* also contradicts Berger's interpretation of the Senate's role in treaties. From the Article II, Section 2, "advice and consent" clause, Berger concludes that the Framers precluded the exercise of executive privilege because the Senate cannot give advice on matters about which it is not informed. But Jay maintained that there are circumstances in which a president may have to resort to secret measures in treaty making. Berger assigns the Senate the preeminent role in treaty making, whereas Jay portrayed the president and the Senate as making substantial contributions of their own based on their particular institutional strengths:

> Although the president must in forming them [treaties], act by the advice and consent of the Senate, yet he will be able to manage the business of intelligence in such manner as prudence may suggest. . . . So often and so essentially have we heretofore suffered from the want of secrecy and despatch that the Constitution would have been inexcusably defective if no attention had been paid to those objects. . . . Thus we see that the Constitution provides that our negotiations for treaties shall have every advantage which can be derived from talents, information, integrity, and deliberative investigations, on the one hand, and from secrecy and despatch on the other.

Hamilton's *Federalist 75* also appears to refute the belief that the Constitution assigns to the Senate the preeminent role in treaty making. Hamilton wrote that "to have intrusted the power of making treaties to the Senate alone, would have been to relinquish the benefits of the constitutional agency of the president in the conduct of foreign negotiations."

Nonetheless, a president who includes the Senate in the negotiation stage acts prudently; otherwise, he risks rejection of the treaty. Still, to suggest that presidents should involve the Senate at each stage of the treaty-making process is not to conclude that such action is required in every case. There are occasions when presidents must deliberate with foreign leaders in secret over the development of treaties. Executive privilege may support the exercise of such secretive negotiations in certain circumstances. Refusing a Senate request for information on the development of a treaty may be exceptional and may even be imprudent in most cases, but notwithstanding the latter, such a refusal is not illegal.

Central to the opponents of executive privilege is the view that the Framers made Congress preeminent in foreign policy making. Logically, the subordinate branch of government cannot keep secrets from the preeminent branch. The evidence, however, supports a different view. The key members of the Committee of Style at the Constitutional Convention—Alexander Hamilton, Rufus King, Gouverneur Morris—shaped the language of Article II to allow the executive to exercise vast powers. The vesting clause, the lack of any enumeration of duties in the commander-in-chief clause, and the silence about war powers, diplomatic powers, and control over executive departments all leave the president with a vast reserve of unspecified authority. Political theorist Michael Foley explains that the U.S. Constitution contains many such silences—what he calls "constitutional abeyances"—that allow for the discretionary exercise of authority according to circumstances.[11] Constitutional scholar Jack W. Peltason writes that Article II "gives the president a power that has never been defined or enumerated and, in fact, cannot be defined since its scope depends largely on circumstances."[12]

Although not assigned to the Committee of Style, James Wilson played a prominent role in the drafting of Article II. He served on the Committee of Detail and wrote the final version of the first draft of Article II. When it came to the subjects of executive power and secrecy, Wilson was unequivocal in his support. In his law lecture notes, Wilson expresses the view that in emergencies, "secrecy may be as necessary as dispatch," and deliberation among numerous leaders of different views may be very costly.[13] Chief Justice John Marshall wrote in the famous *Marbury v. Madison* (1803) case that "the president is invested with certain important political powers, in the exercise of which he is to use his own discretion, and is accountable only to his country in his political character, and to his own conscience."[14]

Critics of executive privilege reject the argument that under certain circumstances, especially those pertaining to foreign policy, the president has vast discretionary authority. They often cite James Madison's observation that the legislature predominates in republican government.[15] Yet Paul Peterson observes that this descriptive statement "is in fact a warning from Madison about the dangers of such supremacy and a warning that republican regimes are particularly susceptible to legislative tyranny."[16]

Because of what he perceives as a system based on legislative supremacy, Berger sees no constitutional basis for executive privilege. Recall that he cites the Article II, Section 4, provision for impeachment as proof of this position. Berger believes that the Framers "patently modeled" the U.S. Congress after the British Parliament. He points out that, historically, both the colonial legislatures and the British Parliament were able to compel disclosure of executive information.[17] For Berger, "history, the traditional index of constitutional construction, discloses that a sweeping power of legislative inquiry had been exercised by the Parliament and by the colonial legislatures."[18] Berger concludes that the modern Congress must have the same limitless power of inquiry as that entrusted to the British Parliament.[19]

The problem with Berger's argument is the assumption that the power of the executive in a presidential system can be equated with that in a parliamentary system. As James W. Ceaser writes, "Under a presidential system the essential executive force is never extinguished or in doubt; under a parliamentary system the executive force cannot be guaranteed (and in practice has not been)."[20]

Berger's argument also rests on the belief that the power of inquiry in a governmental system based on separation of powers is as unquestioned and extensive as the power of inquiry in a system that rejects the concept of separation of powers. As Gary Schmitt argues, the Framers established the separation of powers system "to help foreclose the possibility of legislative supremacy." Furthermore, this system resulted "in a more limited conception of the impeachment power" than Berger envisioned.[21] Although Congress indeed needs information to conduct impeachment inquiries, the Supreme Court has ruled that the congressional power of inquiry has limits.[22] The Court has also determined that in cases of inquiry into possible criminal actions, the executive has to release pertinent information.[23] Congress does not possess a complete, unlimited power of inquiry; nor does the executive possess an unfettered power to withhold any and all information from Congress.

Congress has a very strong claim to any germane executive branch information in cases of impeachment and investigation into executive corruption. But this strong presumption in favor of Congress's demand for information in these circumstances does not bolster the argument that the legislative power of inquiry is absolute. It merely means that the balancing test usually shifts decisively in Congress's favor.

Berger's interpretation of Article II, Section 3, of the Constitution—"He shall from time to time give to the Congress information of the state of the Union, and recommend to their consideration such measures as he shall judge necessary and expedient"—is misleading. Referring to the original version proposed at the Constitutional Convention—rather than the just-recited adopted version—Berger argues that the Framers intended to limit the discretion of the president to present information in the state of the Union address. Therefore, Berger's argument rests on the dubious assumption that historians should look primarily to the original version of Article II, Section 3, introduced at the convention to understand the meaning of that provision in its adopted form. The adopted version means the opposite of what Berger suggests. As Schmitt observes, the president "has the discretion both in determining what he shall say and when he shall say it."[24] In practice, presidents historically have used the state of the Union address to present information they want to reveal to Congress, not information Congress compels them to present. Schmitt reports that in response to an 1808 congressional resolution requesting military information from the president, members of Congress agreed that they had "no power to coerce information" and that Article II, Section 3, made the president the sole judge of what he could communicate.[25]

Executive Privilege in History

The philosophical and constitutional underpinnings of executive privilege are substantial, and evidence of the frequent use of executive privilege supports the legitimacy of that presidential power. It is true that a criminal act does not become legal through repetition, but there is much evidence to indicate that executive privilege is a legitimate, not a usurped, power. The numerous exercises of presidential authority create a strong presumption of validity, especially when the legitimacy of such authority has been accepted by the coordinate branches of government.

Early Years of the Republic

The Framers' view of executive branch secrecy is best understood by examining governmental decision making in the early Republic. The intentions of the Framers are illuminated by what these men did when they put constitutional principles into practice. As Berger writes, an analysis of the early years of the Republic is "more nearly contemporaneous with the forging of the Constitution."[26]

The first presidential administration established the most important precedents for the exercise of executive power. George Washington understood the crucial role he played in establishing precedents for the future. As he wrote on 5 May 1789 to James Madison, "as the first of everything, *in our situation will serve to establish a precedent,* it is devoutly wished on my part, that these precedents may be fixed on true principles."[27] As president, Washington acted in accordance with a Hamiltonian view of executive power. Glenn A. Phelps offers the following perspective:

> From the outside it is clear that Washington had a constitutional agenda as President—and that much of that agenda was predicated upon establishing a national government (and Presidency) independent of and superior to the states. His administration was replete with attempts—some successful, some not—to circumvent the barriers of separation in the name of unity, energy, and efficiency.[28]

Washington established important precedents for executive privilege. The first such action concerned a congressional request to investigate the failure of a November 1791 military expedition by General Arthur St. Clair against American Indians. The House of Representatives established an investigative committee on 27 March 1792 "to call for such persons, papers and records, as may be necessary to assist their inquiries."[29] The investigating committee asked the president for documents regarding St. Clair's expedition.

Washington convened his cabinet to determine how to respond to this first request for presidential materials by a congressional committee.[30] The president wanted to discuss whether any harm would result from public disclosure of the information and, most pertinently, whether he could rightfully refuse to submit documents to Congress. Along with Alexander Hamilton, General Henry Knox, and Edmund Randolph, Thomas Jefferson attended the 2 April 1792 cabinet meeting, and he later recalled the group's determination.

> We had all considered, and were of one mind 1. that the House was an inquest & therefore might institute inquiries. 2. that they might call for papers generally. 3. that the Executive ought to communicate such papers as the public good would permit & ought to refuse those the disclosure of which would injure the public. Consequently were to exercise a discretion. 4. that neither the [committees] nor House has a right to call on the Head of a [department], who & whose papers were under the [President] alone, but that the [committee should] instruct their chairman to move the House to address the President.[31]

Washington eventually determined that public disclosure of the information would not harm the national interest and that it was a necessary action to vindicate General St. Clair. Although Washington chose to negotiate with Congress over the investigating committee's request and to turn over relevant information, he took an affirmative position on the executive branch's

right to withhold information. Adam Breckenridge writes that "this beginning of the executive privilege indicates . . . the president could refuse documents because of their secret nature, a category insisted upon by subsequent
presidents ever since."[32]

Importantly, Washington determined that he had the right to withhold
information if disclosure would injure the public. He did not believe that it
was appropriate to withhold embarrassing or politically damaging information. Unfortunately, this distinction between exercising secrecy in the public
interest as opposed to doing so out of self-interest would be lost on some of
Washington's successors.

On 17 January 1794, the U.S. Senate advanced a motion directing Secretary of State Edmund Randolph "to lay before the Senate the correspondence
which have been had between the Minister of the United States at the Republic of France [Morris], and said Republic, and between said Minister and
the Office of Secretary of State."[33] The Senate later amended the motion to
address the president instead of Minister Morris. The amended version also
"requested" rather than "directed" that such information be forwarded to
Congress.[34] Believing that disclosure of the correspondence would be inappropriate, Washington sought the advice of his cabinet. On 28 January 1794,
three of Washington's cabinet members expressed their opinions.

> General Knox is of the opinion, that no part of the correspondence
> should be sent to the Senate. Colonel Hamilton, that the correct mode
> of proceeding is to do what General Knox advises; but the principle is
> safe, by excepting such parts as the president may choose to withhold.
> Mr. Randolph, that all correspondence proper, from its nature, to be
> communicated to the Senate, should be sent; but that what the presi-
> dent thinks is improper, should not be sent.[35]

Attorney General William Bradford wrote separately, "it is the duty of the
Executive to withhold such parts of the said correspondence as in the judgment of the Executive shall be deemed unsafe and improper to be disclosed."[36]

On 16 February 1794, Washington responded as follows to the Senate's
request:

> After an examination of [the correspondence], I directed copies and
> translations to be made; except in those particulars, in my judgment,
> for public considerations, ought not to be communicated. These copies
> and translations are now transmitted to the Senate; but the nature of
> them manifest the propriety of their being received as confidential.[37]

Washington allowed the Senate to examine some parts of the correspondence, subject to his approval. He believed that information damaging to the "public interest" could constitutionally be withheld from Congress, and the Senate never challenged his authority to withhold that information.[38]

In 1796, John Jay completed U.S. negotiations with Great Britain over unsettled issues from the American Revolution. Because many considered the settlement unfavorable to the United States, Congress took a keen interest in the administration's actions in the negotiations. Not only did the Senate debate ratification of the Jay treaty, but the House set out to conduct its own investigation. On 24 March 1796, the House passed a resolution requesting information concerning Washington's instructions to the U.S. minister to Britain regarding the treaty negotiations. That resolution raised the issue of the House's proper role in the treaty-making process. Washington refused to comply with the House request and replied:

> The nature of foreign negotiations requires caution, and their success must often depend on secrecy; and even when brought to a conclusion a full disclosure of all the measures, demands, or eventual concessions which may have been proposed or contemplated would be extremely impolitic; for this might have a pernicious influence on future negotiations, or produce immediate inconveniences, perhaps danger and mischief, in relation to other powers. The necessity of such caution and secrecy was one cogent reason for vesting the power of making treaties in the President, with the advice and consent of the Senate, the principle on which that body was formed confining it to a small number of members. To admit, then, a right in the House of Representatives to demand and to have as a matter of course all the papers respecting a negotiation with a foreign power would be to establish a dangerous precedent.

Washington explained that "the boundaries fixed by the Constitution between the different departments should be preserved, a just regard to the Constitution and to the duty of my office . . . forbids a compliance with your request."[39]

The House debated the propriety of Washington's action[40] but took no substantive action other than to pass two nonbinding resolutions: one asserting that Congress need not stipulate any reason for requesting information from the executive, and the other proclaiming that the House has a legitimate role in considering the expediency to which a treaty is being implemented.[41] Chief constitutional architect James Madison disagreed in part with Washington's action and defended the House's "right" to request information from the president. Madison also proclaimed, however, "that the Executive had a right, under a due responsibility, also, to withhold information, when of a nature that did not permit a disclosure of it at the time."[42]

During the ratification stage, the senators voted to keep the treaty secret because, as Hamilton wrote, "they thought it the affair of the president to do as he thought fit."[43] The Senate minority opposed to ratification listed seven objections to the treaty. None cited Washington's decision not to seek advice from the Senate.[44]

The Jay treaty controversy is the least clear-cut precedent for executive privilege from the Washington administration. As in the earlier disputes, Washington acted to solidify the constitutional standing of the president to withhold information from Congress when he believed it in the public interest to do so. Nonetheless, Washington implied that the case for House access to the disputed information was weakened by the lack of a constitutional role for the lower chamber in devising treaties. Yet the fact is that many members of the House wanted access because the lower chamber does have a constitutional role in providing funds to implement a treaty. Thus, in the course of this dispute, the House passed a resolution making the point that its members have the constitutional authority and responsibility "to deliberate on the expediency or inexpediency of carrying such Treaty into effect, and to act thereon, as, in their judgment, may be most conducive to the public good."[45] Thus the House made it clear that it could refuse to appropriate funding for or to implement a treaty if the president did not cooperate in providing information that members considered vital to carrying out their constitutional duties.[46]

President John Adams asserted a right to withhold information from Congress during the 1798 XYZ affair. In brief, Adams had secretly dispatched three diplomats to France to negotiate a treaty of international cooperation and trade. The French—through three agents of the Directoire—demanded a bribe from the United States as a condition for the negotiations. Republicans in the House demanded that the Federalist president make public the French correspondence. On 3 April 1798, Adams partially complied with the House request by making the XYZ correspondence public but omitting some information to protect his diplomats abroad.[47]

The Nineteenth Century

Even the ultradefender of popular sovereignty Thomas Jefferson recognized the legitimacy of executive branch secrecy. As president, he classified his correspondence as either public or secret, and he withheld correspondence deemed secret from both the public and Congress.[48] For example, in 1807, President Jefferson denied a congressional request to provide information about the Aaron Burr conspiracy. Burr had been involved with a secessionist conspiracy, resulting in treason charges.[49] Most relevant to the executive privilege debate was a January 1807 House resolution requesting that the president "lay before this House any information in the possession of the Executive, except such as he may deem the public welfare to require not to be disclosed."[50] Congress clearly acknowledged the president's right to exercise a discretion to withhold information. Jefferson replied to the congressional resolution by announcing Burr's guilt and asserting a need to withhold information about the other alleged conspirators. "In this state of the evidence, delivered sometimes, too, under the restrictions of private confidence, neither safety nor justice will permit the exposing names, except that of the principal actor, whose guilt is placed beyond question."[51] Jefferson also wrote to the U.S. district attorney conducting the Burr prosecution that it was "the necessary right of the President of the [United States] to decide, independently, what papers coming to him as President, the public interest permit to be communicated, & to whom."[52]

Germane to the executive privilege controversy are Jefferson's views on presidential prerogative and foreign policy powers. Jefferson, who had conducted secret negotiations over the purchase of the Louisiana Territory, wrote that "a strict observance of the written laws is doubtless *one* of the high duties of a good citizen, but it is not *the highest.* The laws of necessity, of self-preservation, of saving our country when in danger, are of a higher obligation."[53] Jefferson also wrote the following: "The transaction of business with foreign nations is executive altogether. It belongs, then, to the head of that department except as to such portions of it as are strictly submitted to the Senate. *Exceptions are to be construed strictly.*"[54]

The subsequent exercises of presidential secrecy in the nineteenth century are so numerous that an analysis of each one is not possible. Nonetheless, it is possible to provide a concise historical overview to convey the point that numerous presidents exercised what later became known as executive privilege, lending credibility to the constitutionality of that power.

James Madison withheld information from Congress during his presidency. He purposefully withheld information about French trade restrictions against the United States, which eventually led to widespread support for war against Great Britain.[55] Madison and later James Monroe withheld information from Congress regarding the U.S. takeover of the Florida territory.[56] On 16 February 1816, the Senate Committee on Foreign Relations issued a report stating the following:

> If it be true that the success of negotiations is greatly influenced by time and accidental circumstances, the importance to the negotiative

authority of acquiring regular and secret intelligence cannot be doubted. The Senate does not possess the means of acquiring such intelligence. It does not manage the correspondence with our ministers abroad nor with foreign concerns here. . . . The President . . . manages our concerns with foreign nations and must necessarily be most competent to determine when, how and upon what subjects negotiation may be urged with the greatest prospect of success.[57]

In 1825, the House of Representatives requested from President Monroe information concerning the "Steward incident," except any details that the president determined were not in the public interest to disclose.[58] Monroe refused to comply and responded that submitting the requested materials "might tend to excite prejudices" and "would not comport with the public interest nor with what is due to the parties concerned."[59]

Although President Andrew Jackson established, for his time, an unprecedentedly close relationship with the public, he did not shy away from exercising, on numerous occasions, the presidential power to withhold information. In 1832, the House requested information pertaining to U.S. negotiations with the Republic of Buenos Aires, and Jackson responded that it would "not be consistent with the public interest to communicate the correspondence and instructions requested by the House so long as the negotiation shall be pending."[60] In 1833, he refused to divulge information to the Senate pertaining to negotiations with Great Britain over the northeastern boundary of the United States.[61] Later that year, when the Senate requested documents pertaining to the removal of money from the Bank of the United States, the president refused and replied that Congress could not "require of me an account of any communication, either verbally or in writing, made to the heads of Departments acting as a Cabinet council." Jackson protested that the Senate could not compel him to reveal "the free and private conversations I have held with those officers on any subject relating to their duties and my own."[62] In 1835, the president refused to provide to the House certain requested documents pertaining to U.S.-French correspondence.[63] Jackson also refused a Senate request for information pertaining to the removal of U.S. Surveyor General Gideon Fitz and stated that "this is another of those calls for information made upon me by the Senate which have, in my judgment, either related to the subjects exclusively belonging to the executive department or otherwise encroached on the constitutional powers of the Executive."[64]

President John Tyler also frequently asserted a presidential discretion to withhold information. In February 1842, he wrote to Congress that he could not divulge information concerning U.S.-British negotiations over the northeastern boundary because "in my judgment no communication could be made by me at this time on the subject of its resolution without detriment or danger to the public interests."[65] The following month, Tyler refused a House request for information about applicants to executive branch offices on the ground that such information was confidential and strictly an executive branch matter.[66] In June of that year, the House requested from Tyler, "so far as may be compatible with the public interest," information regarding a European treaty on the suppression of the slave trade. Tyler responded that divulging the information "would not be compatible with the public interest."[67] Two months later, Tyler refused a Senate request for information about possible U.S. efforts to get Mexico to recognize claims of U.S. citizens.[68] In December of that year, Tyler told the Senate that he "did not deem it consistent with the public interest" to communicate information about U.S. negotiations with Great Britain over the northwest boundary.[69]

The most celebrated case of executive branch secrecy in the Tyler administration concerned the government's investigation into fraud against the Cherokee Indians. Tyler refused to divulge such information to the House because of ongoing negotiations to settle the Indian claims and because the investigative reports contained possibly incriminating statements by implicated individuals. The president made clear his right to assert a discretion over executive branch documents:

> The injunction of the Constitution that the President "shall take care that the laws be faithfully executed," necessarily confers an authority, commensurate with the obligation imposed to inquire into the manner in which all public agents perform the duties assigned to them by law. To be effective, these inquiries must often be confidential. They may result in the collection of truth or of falsehood, or they may be incomplete and may require further prosecution. To maintain that the President can exercise no discretion as to the time in which the matters thus collected shall be promulgated . . . would deprive him at once of the means of performing one of the most salutary duties of his office. . . . To require from the Executive the transfer of this discretion to a coordinate branch of the Government is equivalent to the denial of its possession by him and would render him dependent upon that branch in the performance of a duty purely executive.[70]

President James K. Polk refused an 1846 House request for information pertaining to the foreign policy expenditures of his predecessor, John Tyler. Polk believed that "it might become absolutely necessary to incur expenditures for objects which could never be accomplished if it were suspected in advance that the items of expenditure and the agencies employed would be made public."[71] In 1848, in response to a House request for information pertaining to the return of President General Lopez de Santa Anna to Mexico, Polk released documents deemed "compatible with the public interests to communicate."[72] Polk then elaborated a strong defense for confidentiality in diplomatic endeavors, based on precedent and necessity. As precedent, he cited George Washington's 30 March 1796 message to the House of Representatives refusing to release certain documents considered "improper to be disclosed."[73] Furthermore, Polk maintained that his own case for protecting confidentiality was particularly compelling, given that full disclosure of the requested information during a war would have resulted in "serious embarrassment in any future negotiation between the [United States and Mexico]." Polk concluded, "I regard it to be my constitutional right and my solemn duty under the circumstances of this case to decline a compliance with the request of the House contained in their resolution."[74]

In July 1848, Polk refused a House request for information concerning his instructions to diplomats who had negotiated the U.S. treaty with Mexico. He reported that, "as a general rule applicable to all our important negotiations with foreign powers, it could not fail to be prejudicial to the public interest to publish the instructions of our ministers until some time had elapsed after the conclusion of such negotiations."[75] Several months later, Polk released the requested documents to the House but iterated his earlier position that he had the right to withhold information when it was in "the public interest" to do so.[76]

President Millard Fillmore withheld diplomatic information from the Senate on several occasions in 1851–1852 when he believed that transmitting such information was not in the public interest.[77] President James Buchanan refused an 1859 Senate request for law enforcement information regarding the illegal landing of a slave ship on the Georgia coast.[78]

President Abraham Lincoln exercised the most extensive prerogative powers of any U.S. president. Given the extraordinary actions adopted by Lincoln to prosecute the federal war effort, it is hardly surprising that he exercised a discretion to withhold information when he deemed secrecy to be in the public interest. In 1861, Lincoln refused a House request for information about the arrests of Baltimore police commissioners at Fort McHenry.[79] In 1862, Lincoln refused a Senate request for information pertaining to the arrest of Brigadier General Stone.[80] In 1863, the House requested from the secretary of state, "if not in [his] judgment incompatible with the public interest," information on U.S. negotiations with New Grenada. Lincoln replied that it would not be in the "public interest" to comply with the request.[81]

Lincoln's successor, Andrew Johnson, refused on several occasions in 1866 to release requested information to Congress.[82] In 1876, Ulysses S. Grant refused a House request for information about his presidential actions away from the nation's capital on the ground that such information had no bearing on Congress's constitutional duties.[83] In 1887, President Grover Cleveland refused a Senate request for information regarding the sale of an American schooner and resignation of the U.S. minister to Mexico.[84] In April 1892, in response to a Senate request for information about a proposed international conference on silver, President Benjamin Harrison said that "it would not be compatible with the public interest" to divulge the information at that time.[85] In his second term, President Cleveland refused an 1896 House request for all information pertaining to U.S. affairs in Cuba, but he did release selected information.[86] That same year, Cleveland withheld from the Senate some requested information about official U.S. correspondence with the government of Spain.[87]

The Twentieth Century

In 1901, President William McKinley refused to divulge to the Senate information on a War Department investigation of expenditures of Cuban funds.[88] President Theodore Roosevelt replied to a January 1909 Senate resolution requesting information from the attorney general on whether proceedings had been instituted against a company for possible Sherman Antitrust Act violations:

> I have instructed the Attorney General not to respond to that portion of the resolution which calls for a statement of his reasons for nonaction. I have done so because I do not conceive it to be within the authority of the Senate to give directions of this character to the head of an executive department, or to demand from him reasons for his action. Heads of the executive departments are subject to the Constitution, and to the laws passed by the Congress in pursuance of the Constitution, and to the directions of the President of the United States, but to no other direction whatever.[89]

The Senate Judiciary Committee cleverly responded by issuing a subpoena for the same documents to the head of the Bureau of Corporations. Roosevelt secured the papers for himself and then told Congress that it would get the documents only by impeaching him.[90] The president explained that "these facts . . . were given to the government under the seal of secrecy and cannot be divulged, and I will see to it that the word of this government to the individual is kept sacred."[91]

In April 1924, President Calvin Coolidge refused a Senate request for information on companies being investigated by the Bureau of Internal Revenue. Coolidge maintained that the information was confidential and not germane to Congress's constitutional duties.[92]

In July 1930, the Senate Foreign Relations Committee requested from President Herbert Hoover's secretary of state copies of correspondence concerning the London Naval Treaty. The president responded that many communications had been provided in confidence and that he had a duty not to violate the trust that negotiators had placed in him. The president did not provide all the requested documents.[93]

President Franklin D. Roosevelt withheld documents requested by Congress on a number of occasions. For example, in 1941, FDR instructed his attorney general to withhold certain Federal Bureau of Investigation (FBI) papers from a House committee. In 1943, FDR's director of the Bureau of the Budget refused a House investigative committee subpoena to testify, because the president had instructed that bureau files remain confidential. That same year, the president directed the acting secretary of war not to divulge to Congress documents pertaining to the Departments of War and Navy. In 1944, a House investigative committee requested information from the FBI director and issued him a subpoena to testify. The director refused to testify and would not divulge the contents of a presidential memorandum requiring him not to testify. The attorney general wrote to the committee that communications between the president and department heads were privileged.[94] That same year, the chairman of the Select House Committee investigating the Federal Communications Commission acknowledged that "for over 140 years" an exemption from testifying before Congress "has been granted to the executive departments, particularly where it involves military secrets or relations with foreign nations."[95]

President Harry S Truman also asserted a discretion to maintain secrecy on numerous occasions. In 1948, the House Un-American Activities Committee attempted to probe allegations of disloyalty in the Truman administration, so the president issued an executive order ensuring the confidentiality of loyalty files in the administration.[96] The president also made it clear that he would not turn papers over to the committee.[97] That same year, Truman would not permit a presidential assistant who had been subpoenaed by the House Committee on Education and Labor to appear before the committee,[98] which wanted to obtain information about the assistant's conversations with the president. The resulting committee minority report asserted that "I cannot believe that any congressional committee is entitled to make that kind of investigation into the private conferences of the president with one of his principal aides."[99] In 1950, the president di-

rected his secretary of state, attorney general, and chairman of the Civil
Service Commission not to comply with a Senate subcommittee subpoena
of files pertaining to the loyalty of State Department employees. Truman
cited his 1948 executive order,[100] but he eventually backed down after learning that the same documents had already been made available to Congress.[101] During Senate hearings in 1951 over Truman's firing of General
Douglas MacArthur, General Omar Bradley refused a request to testify
about conversations he had had as an adviser to the president. Truman considered his conversations with Bradley to be confidential.[102] The chairman
of the Senate Committee on Armed Services, Senator Richard Russell, ruled
that Bradley had the right to hold confidential conversations with the president, and the committee subsequently upheld Russell's ruling by a vote of
eighteen to eight.[103] In 1952, the chairman of a special subcommittee of the
House Judiciary Committee requested government agencies to provide any
information on "cases referred to the Department of Justice or U.S. Attorneys for either criminal or civil action."[104] Truman instructed agency and department heads not to comply with the request, which he considered too
broad—"a dragnet approach to examining the administration of the laws"—
and extremely costly to the government.[105] Finally, that same year, Truman
defended his decision to maintain the confidentiality of the activities of the
Loyalty Security Program.[106]

The presidency of Dwight D. Eisenhower represents an important development in the doctrine of executive privilege. The term *executive privilege*
originated in the Eisenhower administration, which invoked that doctrine
on more than forty occasions. The most important controversy over executive privilege during the Eisenhower years concerned the Army-McCarthy
hearings. During testimony, army counsel John Adams mentioned that he
had had a conference with top White House aides in the attorney general's
office, and congressional investigators sought information on what had transpired in those conversations between high-ranking officials. Eisenhower in-
tervened with a letter on 17 May 1954 to Secretary of Defense Charles
Wilson instructing employees of that department not to testify.

> Because it is essential to efficient and effective administration that em-
> ployees of the Executive Branch be in a position to be completely can-
> did in advising with each other on official matters, and because it is not
> in the public interest that any of their conversations or communica-
> tions, or any documents or reproductions, concerning such advice be
> disclosed, you will instruct employees of your Department that in all of
> their appearances before the Subcommittee of the Senate Committee
> on Government Operations regarding the inquiry now before it they

are not to testify to any such conversations or communications, or to produce any such documents or reproductions. This principle must be maintained regardless of who would benefit by such disclosures.[107]

Other executive branch officials used Eisenhower's letter to justify their refusal to testify before Congress. United Nations Ambassador Henry Cabot Lodge, for example, refused to testify before Congress about the Army-McCarthy affair on the ground that he was a White House adviser. Eisenhower replied affirmatively: "The position you propose to take is exactly correct. I would be astonished if any of my personal advisors would undertake to give testimony on intimate staff counsel and advice. The result would be to eliminate all such offices from the presidential staff. In turn, this would mean paralysis."[108]

Eisenhower adopted an uncompromising stand on executive privilege. He told a group of Republican legislative leaders that "any man who testifies as to the advice he gave me won't be working for me that night." Eisenhower elaborated his position: "Those people who have a position here in this government because of me, those people who are my confidential advisors are not going to be subpoenaed. . . . Governor Adams's official job is really a part of me and he's not going up on the Hill."[109] Senator Joseph McCarthy (R-Wis.) denounced Eisenhower's order as an "iron curtain" and exclaimed, "This is the first time I've ever seen the executive branch of government take the fifth amendment."[110] Despite some other criticism of the president for defining executive privilege too broadly—possibly allowing every executive branch officer to assert that prerogative—the *Washington Post* agreed that the president's constitutional authority to withhold information from Congress "is altogether beyond question."[111]

There are too many other cases of executive privilege in the Eisenhower administration to cover here. It is most important to recognize that Eisenhower's 17 May 1954 letter established a precedent for the exercise of executive privilege in the modern presidency. For example, Eisenhower's Democratic successor, John F. Kennedy, did not shy away from executive privilege.

Kennedy's view of executive privilege fit comfortably within his understanding of presidential power. As a presidential candidate in 1960, Kennedy told the National Press Club that a president "must be prepared to exercise the fullest powers of his office—all that are specified and some that are not."[112] In his first presidential press conference, Kennedy responded to a reporter's question on executive privilege: "But I must say that I do not hold the view that all matters and all information which is available to the Executive should be made available at all times, and I don't think any member of the press does."[113] Kennedy also explained his view of executive privilege as follows:

Since the early days of the Republic, Americans have also recognized that the Federal Government is obliged to protect certain information which might otherwise jeopardize the security of the country. That need has become particularly acute in recent years as the United States has assumed a powerful position in world affairs, and as world peace has come to depend in large part on how that position is safeguarded. We are also moving into an era of delicate negotiations in which it will be especially important that governments be able to communicate in confidence.

Clearly, the two principles of an informed public and of confidentiality within the Government are irreconcilable in their purest forms, and a balance must be struck between them.[114]

In 1962, a special Senate subcommittee investigated military Cold War education and speech-review policies. The president wrote letters to his secretary of defense instructing him not to comply with a request for the names of individuals who wrote or edited speeches. Kennedy specifically instructed the secretary "not to give testimony or produce any documents which would disclose such information." Kennedy's letter further stated that "it would not be possible for you to maintain an orderly Department and receive the candid advice and loyal respect of your subordinates if they, instead of you and your senior associates, are to be individually answerable to the Congress, as well as to you, for their internal acts and advice."[115] The chairman of the subcommittee, Senator John Stennis (D-Miss.), ruled in favor of Kennedy's claim of executive privilege, and the full committee upheld that ruling.[116]

In practice, Kennedy permitted administrative officers to exercise executive privilege, but in principle, he supported a less expansive use of that prerogative than did the Eisenhower administration. The chairman of the House Subcommittee on Government Information, John E. Moss (D-Calif.), vigorously opposed the use of executive privilege by presidential administrations. When Moss requested clarification of Kennedy's official policy toward executive privilege, the president emphasized that such authority "can be invoked only by the president and will not be used without specific presidential approval." Kennedy expressed agreement with the need for Congress to have "the widest public accessibility to governmental information."[117] Nonetheless, Kennedy used executive privilege to prevent legislative oversight of foreign policy. The president ordered his military adviser, General Maxwell Taylor, to refuse to testify before a congressional committee examining the Bay of Pigs fiasco.[118]

Moss later requested clarification of President Lyndon B. Johnson's policy on executive privilege. The president replied that, following Kennedy's policy, "the claim of 'executive privilege' will continue to be made only by the president."[119] Again, this presidential policy was not followed. In 1968, the Department of Defense refused a request by the Senate Foreign Relations Committee for a copy of the Command Control Study of the Gulf of Tonkin incident.[120] That same year, the Senate Judiciary Committee requested that Treasury Undersecretary Joseph W. Barr, Associate Special Counsel to the President DeVier Pierson, and Secretary of Defense Clark Clifford testify in the hearings on the nomination of Abe Fortas for chief justice of the Supreme Court. Barr refused to testify on the basis that he had

> participated in meetings with representatives of the White House and discussed the matter directly with the President. Based on long-standing precedents, it would be improper for me under these circumstances to give testimony before a Congressional committee concerning such meetings and discussions. Therefore, I must, with great respect, decline your invitation to appear and testify.[121]

Clifford requested to be excused from testifying because of other pressing responsibilities.[122] Pierson did not testify for the following reasons:

> As Associate Special Counsel to the President since March of 1967, I have been one of the "immediate staff assistants" provided to the President by law. (3 U.S.C. 105, 106.) It has been firmly established, as a matter of principle and precedents, that members of the President's immediate staff shall not appear before a Congressional committee to testify with respect to the performance of their duties on behalf of the President. This limitation, which has been recognized by Congress as well as the Executive, is fundamental to our system of government. I must, therefore, respectfully decline the invitation to testify in these hearings.[123]

Although the Kennedy and Johnson administrations did not exercise executive privilege as extensively as the Eisenhower administration did, they clearly accepted the validity of this presidential power. The modern exercise of executive privilege, however, reached its most expansive stage during the Nixon years, which were also a major stage in the development of the executive privilege controversy. Nixon attempted to transform executive privilege from a widely accepted constitutional principle to an absolute, unfettered presidential power. Nixon's excesses eventually served to partially discredit executive privilege, and with the exceptions of Bill Clinton and George W.

Bush, most of Nixon's successors have been cautious about claiming executive privilege.

Because Nixon's presidency represents such a crucial turning point in the executive privilege controversy, the following chapter deals with the Nixon years in some detail. It is important to recognize that presidents historically have exercised what is now known as executive privilege. The widespread use of this power by presidents lends validity to the claim that executive privilege is constitutional. But beyond an examination of the uses of executive privilege, it is necessary to present the various justifications for this presidential power.

In Defense of Executive Privilege

Although numerous presidents have exercised executive privilege, not all have done so judiciously. As with all other grants of authority, the power to do good is also the power to do bad. The only way to avoid the latter—and consequently eliminate the ability to do the former—is to strip away authority altogether. William Rehnquist once defended the need for executive privilege as follows:

> While reasonable men may dispute the propriety of particular invocations of executive privilege by various presidents during the nation's history, I think most would agree that the doctrine itself is an absolutely essential condition for the faithful discharge by the executive of his constitutional duties. It is, therefore, as surely implied in the Constitution as is the power of Congress to investigate and compel testimony.[124]

The evidence for executive privilege in many cases is convincing, and the reasons for its exercise are compelling. Critics of executive privilege take too narrow a view of the Constitution and have an unrealistic understanding of how our governing system should work. Executive privilege is not only constitutional; it is also occasionally necessary to the effective discharge of the president's duties.

National Security

Congress's and the public's "right to know" must be balanced with the requirements of national security. Although the Framers recognized the importance of secrecy, unity, and dispatch to governing, the need to enhance those values in the modern era—particularly with regard to foreign policy making—is even more compelling than it was over two centuries ago. Many, if not most, of the crises faced by modern governments cannot be dealt with through open, lengthy, national deliberations. The heightened pace of contemporary international events places a premium on rapid and decisive decision making. The presidency possesses the institutional capacities uniquely suited to responding to crisis situations. The leading Framers recognized that, being one, rather than many, the president is much more capable than Congress of acting with unity, secrecy, dispatch, and resolve. As Paul Peterson has written, "it is the executive power that most lends itself to energy. . . . To speak of energy in the legislative or judicial branches would be something akin to an oxymoron."[125] The courts have recognized the executive's preeminence in national security and foreign policy making on a number of occasions.[126] A. Stephen Boyan, Jr., writes that in the area of national security concerns, a review of cases shows that,

> while the courts rhetorically support the separation of powers, in varying degrees they accept presidential characterization of the disputed matter without challenge and they permit the president to act without clear legislative authorization. . . . Moreover, while national security cases typically involve civil liberties issues, the courts have refused to apply the constitutional doctrines which they would apply if the same issue arose in a non–national security context.[127]

Foreign policy typically has been conducted on less democratic principles than has domestic policy making. The classic constitutional statement of that position is Justice George Sutherland's highly controversial opinion, writing for the majority in *U.S. v. Curtiss-Wright Corporation*.[128] Sutherland notes that it is important to "consider the differences between the powers of the federal government in respect of foreign or external affairs and those in respect of domestic or internal affairs. That there are differences between them, and that these differences are fundamental, may not be doubted."[129] This Court opinion lends further support to the position that the chief executive has a discretion in foreign affairs to act beyond what the law allows.[130] Sutherland went so far as to declare that the "very delicate, plenary and exclusive power of the president as the sole organ of the federal government in the field of international relations [is] a power which does not require as a basis for its exercise an act of Congress, but . . . must be exercised in subordination to the applicable provisions of the Constitution."[131]

There are serious difficulties with the Sutherland opinion, much of which was dictum. In misusing John Marshall's famous "sole organ" phrase,

Sutherland implies that the president always has the exclusive authority to make foreign policy. That was not Marshall's position, nor is it an accurate description of presidential foreign policy powers. It is one thing to argue that the president has a prerogative power to act independently of Congress during emergencies, and quite another to suggest that the president can routinely act in foreign affairs without any congressional involvement.

Nonetheless, in any discussion of governmental secrecy, the different institutional orientations of the executive and legislative branches must be acknowledged. Congress usually deliberates in public; official actions behind closed doors are the exception there. The executive branch deliberates outside of the public view; open deliberations are the exception there.

In the national security realm, an important matter of presidential concern is the potential effect of public revelations of policy discussions. Such openness, for example, could lead to demands for the executive branch to act before it is prepared to do so. Consequently, the ability to deliberate carefully over time and to weigh options before making decisions could be compromised. In national security policy making, it is often important to be somewhat removed from time and partisan pressures that may affect policy decisions.

The courts have generally provided broad discretionary authority to the president in national security and foreign affairs. In *Zemel v. Rusk* (1965), the Supreme Court decided that "Congress—in giving the president authority over matters of foreign affairs—must of necessity paint with a brush broader than that it customarily wields in domestic affairs."[132] The courts have agreed that it is neither constitutionally proper nor prudent for Congress to tie the hands of the president in foreign affairs during an emergency situation.[133] The Supreme Court has struck down important legislative control devices, further expanding the scope of the president's powers.[134] Finally, the Court has determined that secrecy is a necessary condition for the president to carry out many of his constitutional duties, especially in foreign affairs. In *Chicago and Southern Airlines v. Waterman Steamship Corporation* (1948), the Court held the following: "The president, both as Commander-in-Chief and as the nation's organ for foreign affairs, has available intelligence services whose reports are not and ought not to be published to the world. It would be intolerable that courts, without the relevant information, should review and perhaps nullify actions of the Executive taken on information properly held secret."[135]

The strongest judicial defense of executive branch secrecy in national security affairs is *U.S. v. Reynolds* (1953). The Supreme Court held that "it may be possible to satisfy the Court, from all the circumstances of the case, that there is a reasonable danger that compulsion of the evidence will expose military secrets which, in the interest of national security, should not be divulged."[136] The *Reynolds* case also held that department heads could exercise a discretion to withhold information.[137]

Since these two important cases, Congress has enacted statutory grants of authority to the federal courts to decide national security cases.[138] Thus, the courts need not automatically defer to the executive branch in such cases, although that has been the pattern for decades.

Some advocates defend executive privilege on the grounds that Congress is ill suited to handling sensitive national security information and is not capable of decisive foreign policy making. Indeed, under U.S. law, the power to classify information is given to the executive, not the legislative, branch. The congressional decision-making process is purposefully slow. And although it is unlikely in the modern era, Congress may be out of session when foreign policy problems arise. In addition, there have been cases in which Congress failed to maintain secrecy. Once sensitive information is turned over to members of Congress, there is no guarantee that some member will not divulge materials for policy or partisan reasons.

Nonetheless, Congress is not unique in that regard. The executive branch also leaks information, probably far more often than does Congress. To suggest that one branch of the federal government is virtuous and another highly suspect with regard to maintaining secrecy is to seriously distort reality. However, executive privilege may be necessary in some instances to substantially limit the circle of individuals with access to sensitive information, including members of Congress, especially when national security is at stake.

Although the right to exercise executive privilege is a necessary precondition for the chief executive to protect the national security, merely uttering the words *national security* does not in itself justify a claim of executive privilege. The threat to national security must be real. Lacking such a threat, the case for executive privilege must stand on some other grounds. For example, executive privilege also recognizes that the chief executive needs sound staff advice, and the quality of his counsel depends ultimately on the degree of candor.

Candid Advice

Former consultant to the National Security Council Michael A. Ledeen makes a distinction between two kinds of openness. "One refers to candor, the other to the number of participants. We need candor, but we do not need large meetings or a large number of participants, or a full public debate *at every stage* of the policy process, or even of every aspect of the policy."[139]

The president's constitutional duties necessitate his being able to consult with advisers, without fear of public disclosure of their advice. If officers of the executive branch believed that their confidential advice could eventually be disclosed, the quality of that advice would be seriously damaged. Indeed, it would be difficult for advisers to be completely honest and frank in their discussions if their every word might someday be disclosed to partisan opponents or to the public. Averell Harriman testified to Congress, "The president is entitled to receive the frank views of his advisers and therefore must be able to protect the personal or confidential nature of their communications with him."[140] William P. Bundy also testified, "If officers of an administration should come to feel that their confidential advice would be disclosed, short of a period of many years, I do believe that the consequences in terms of honesty, candor, courage, and frankness within the executive branch could be very serious indeed."[141]

The White House Office, created in 1939, established a presidential enclave of advisers and assistants in whom the chief executive had personal confidence. Then, as now, many considered it commonsensical that the president should be able to have candid interchanges with his closest advisers. Executive privilege recognizes this commonsense notion. Unfortunately, because President Nixon invoked executive privilege to protect incriminating candid interchanges, he gave executive privilege a bad name. Theodore H. White made the important distinction:

Executive privilege is a matter of vital importance to the conduct of the American Presidency. Unless the President can talk frankly, and listen to frank advice, he cannot think clearly enough to act effectively. Whoever invades this privacy weakens the presidency. It was Richard Nixon's misfortune and guilt to invoke executive privilege, not to protect the Presidency, but to protect himself.[142]

Indeed, in *U.S. v. Nixon,* the Supreme Court recognized not only the constitutionality of executive privilege but also the necessity of executive branch secrecy to the operation of the presidency:

The valid need for protection of communications between high government officials and those who advise and assist them in the performance of their manifold duties . . . is too plain to require further discussion. Human experience teaches that those who expect public dissemination of their remarks may well temper candor with a concern for appearances and for their own interests to the detriment of the decision-making process. . . . The confidentiality of presidential communications . . . has constitutional underpinnings. . . . The privilege is fundamental to the operation of government and inextricably rooted in the separation of powers under the Constitution.[143]

In 1979, the Court iterated its support of executive privilege based on the need for candid interchange among advisers. "Documents shielded by executive privilege remain privileged even after the decision to which they pertain may have been effected, since disclosure at any time could inhibit the free flow of advice, including analysis, reports and expression of opinions."[144]

The Court has recognized that the need for candid interchange is an important basis for executive privilege. Although it is well recognized that Congress needs access to executive branch information to carry out its oversight and investigative duties, it does not follow that Congress must have full access to the details of every executive branch communication. Congressional inquiry, like executive privilege, has limits. This is not to suggest that presidents can use the need for candid advice to restrict any and all information. In fact, Congress's power of inquiry trumps a claim of executive privilege unless the president can make a showing of a need for secrecy.

Limits on Congressional Inquiry

Congress's power of inquiry, though broad, is not unlimited.[145] Berger's claim that the Constitution grants to Congress the power to be the "Grand Inquest" of the nation is unfounded, as there is nothing in Article I, or anywhere else in the Constitution, that substantiates that claim. The debates at the Constitutional Convention and at the subsequent ratifying conventions provide little evidence that the Framers intended to confer such authority on Congress. The legitimacy of the congressional power of inquiry is indeed unquestioned,[146] but the argument that this power is unlimited goes too far.

Regarding the power of inquiry, a distinction must be drawn between sources of information generally and those necessary to the legislative branch to perform its legislative and investigative functions.[147] There is a strong presumption of validity to a congressional request for information that is clearly relevant to these functions. The presumption weakens in the case of a congressional "fishing expedition"—a broad, sweeping quest for any and all executive branch information that is of interest to Congress for no specified reason.

To be sure, the courts have ruled that the congressional power of investigation is available even for pursuit down "blind alleys." Yet in a balancing test between a seemingly strong presidential claim to executive privilege and a blind congressional pursuit, the inquiry power of Congress may have to yield to the executive branch.

Congress itself has recognized that there are limits on its power of inquiry and that the executive branch needs confidentiality. In some cases, the legislative branch has even gone too far in stating the limits of inquiry. For example, in 1879, a House Judiciary Committee report stated that neither the legislative nor the executive branch has compulsory power over the records of the other.[148]

Berger nonetheless believes that Congress has an absolute, unlimited power to compel disclosure of all executive branch information. His view has been echoed by Representative John Dingell (D-Mich.), who said that members of Congress "have the power under the law to receive each and every item in the hands of the government."[149] This expansive view of congressional inquiry is as wrong as the belief that the president has the unlimited power to withhold all information from Congress. There are inherent institutional limits on the powers of the respective governmental branches. The common standard for legislative inquiry has been whether the requested information is vital to Congress's lawmaking and oversight function. It is ironic that Berger maintains that executive privilege lacks validity because it is not specifically granted by the Constitution and then argues that Congress possesses an absolute, unlimited inquiry power despite a similar lack of such a constitutional grant.

Congress has given statutory authority to some forms of executive branch withholding of information. Congress recognized the necessity of protecting intelligence sources when it enacted the "sources and methods proviso" of the 1947 National Security Act and when it enacted the 1949 implementing provision of the Central Intelligence Agency (CIA) Act. The judicial branch has ruled that the proviso is a proper basis for the secrecy agreement of CIA employees.[150] The proviso and the implementing provision are recognized as nondisclosure statutes in cases of Freedom of Information Act (FOIA) requests.[151] In the 1966 Freedom of Information Act, Congress permitted executive branch withholding of information. The FOIA stipulates nine conditions under which access to government documents may be denied.

The argument for executive branch secrecy in cases of congressional inquiry is generally stronger in foreign than in domestic affairs. This is not to suggest that claiming a foreign policy necessity automatically settles an informational dispute in favor of the executive. But generally, executive privilege claims are easier to sustain when foreign policy issues—especially those pertaining to national security—are at stake.

The case against an absolute congressional inquiry power is made stronger by the problem of potential leaks. The trouble with leaks is not merely that sensitive information is made public. There is also the complicated nature of maintaining the trust of allies abroad. Michael Ledeen notes that foreign leaders purposely withhold vital information from the United States when they believe that the U.S. government is unable to keep secrets. Exposure of secrets by Congress has deprived the United States "of the honest thoughts of foreign leaders, and their knowledge as well." Ledeen concludes that "secrecy actually encourages the free flow of information and candid expression, while exposure limits the flow of knowledge and forces top officials to speak guardedly, if at all."[152] Benjamin R. Civiletti presented a similar view when he wrote that "secrecy . . . is an essential element of effective intelligence gathering. . . . If we reveal the information obtained, we will not only lose our advantage and risk changes in the required plans, but we will also jeopardize or perhaps destroy our sources and methods of gathering information."[153]

Historical Necessity

Numerous historical incidents—too many to cover here—have also confirmed that there are good reasons for withholding information. For example, World War II, the crises over Berlin and Cuba, the long Cold War, the war against Iraq, and the war against terrorism have all confronted the United States with situations requiring rapid responses, as well as secret negotiations, thereby precluding full disclosure to Congress of military and diplomatic plans. William Rehnquist offers a commonsensical view:

> The need for extraordinary secrecy in the field of weapons systems and tactical military plans for the conducting of hostilities would appear to be self-evident. At least those of my generation and older are familiar with the extraordinary precaution taken against revelation of either the date or the place of landing on the Normandy beaches during the Second World War in 1944. The executive branch is charged with the responsibility for such decisions, and has quite wisely insisted that where lives of American soldiers or the security of the nation is at stake, the very minimum dissemination of future plans is absolutely essential. Such secrecy with respect to highly sensitive decisions of this sort exclude not merely Congress, but all but an infinitesimal number of the employees and officials of the executive branch as well.[154]

Prior to U.S. involvement in World War II, due to an increasingly unstable international environment, President Franklin D. Roosevelt frequently overrode the legislative decision-making process. Through the use of the executive agreement (which does not require congressional consent),[155] the president effectively bypassed the isolationist majority in Congress on a number of occasions. Roosevelt concluded an alliance with Great Britain in

1940, ignoring the congressional neutrality laws. As Richard Pious writes, the president "was wise to bypass Congress."[156] In the end, presidential discretion was vindicated and congressional performance discredited. Three months prior to the bombing of Pearl Harbor, Congress nearly repealed the Selective Service Act; Congress also blocked funds for the construction of vital naval facilities and turned down administration requests for the procurement of advanced arms. Not until the end of 1941 did Congress repeal neutrality legislation. Pious concludes that "Congress demonstrated no foresight, courage, or common sense."[157] Congressional decision making during the emergence of the nation's gravest crisis proved to be wholly inadequate. Therefore, a major defense of the executive privilege rests on the proposition that Congress often does not discharge its duties in the national security realm with wisdom, and that legislative involvement in international negotiations may have deleterious effects on the nation's security in crisis situations. In his concurring opinion in *New York Times v. United States* (1971), Justice Potter Stewart expressed this view:

> Yet it is elementary that the successful conduct of international diplomacy and the maintenance of an effective national defense require both confidentiality and secrecy. Other nations can hardly deal with this Nation in an atmosphere of mutual trust unless they can be assured that their confidences will be kept. And within our own executive departments, the development of considered and intelligent international policies would be impossible if those charged with their formulation could not communicate with each other freely, frankly, and in confidence. In the area of basic national defense the frequent need for absolute secrecy is, of course, self evident.[158]

Exercise of Confidentiality in the Other Branches

Finally, executive privilege can be defended on the basis of accepted practices of secrecy in the other branches of government. Members of Congress receive candid, confidential advice from committee staff and legislative assistants.[159] Congressional committees meet on occasion in closed session to "mark up" legislation. Congress is not obligated to disclose information to another branch, and a court subpoena will not be honored except with a vote of the legislative chamber concerned. Members of Congress enjoy a constitutional form of privilege that absolves them from having to account for their official behavior, particularly regarding speech, anywhere but in Congress. As with the executive, this privilege does not extend into the realm of criminal conduct.

Secrecy is also found in the judicial branch. It is difficult to imagine more secretive deliberations than those that take place in Supreme Court conferences. David M. O'Brien refers to secrecy as one of the "basic institutional norms" of the Supreme Court. "Isolation from the Capitol and the close proximity of the justices' chambers within the Court promote secrecy, to a degree that is remarkable. . . . The norm of secrecy conditions the employment of the justices' staff and has become more important as the number of employees increases."[160] Members of the judiciary claim immunity from having to respond to congressional subpoenas. The norm of judicial privilege also protects judges from having to testify about their professional conduct.

It is inconceivable that secrecy, so common to the legislative and judicial branches, should not be exercised by the executive branch.[161] The executive branch is regularly engaged in a number of activities that are secret in nature. George C. Calhoun explains that the executive branch

> presents . . . matters to grand juries; assembles confidential investigative files in criminal matters; compiles files containing personal information involving such things as census, tax, and veterans information; and health, education and welfare benefits to name a few. All of these activities must, of necessity, generate a considerable amount of confidential information. And personnel in the executive branch . . . necessarily prepare many more confidential memoranda. Finally, they produce a considerable amount of classified information as a result of the activities of the intelligence community.[162]

In the cases of legislative, judicial, and executive branch secrecy, a common purpose is being served: to arrive at more prudent policy decisions than those that would be arrived at through an open process. In each case, the end result is what will be subject to scrutiny. Indeed, accountability is built into secretive decision-making processes. The elected public officials must justify the end result at some point.

Conclusion

Executive privilege clearly has substantial constitutional underpinnings, historical precedents, and compelling arguments in its favor. Despite the evidence, executive privilege remains a constitutional doctrine mired in controversy. Much of the controversy can be attributed to the fact that—as with other constitutional powers—not every president has exercised executive privilege prudently or properly. Executive privilege became most controversial during the Watergate era. Regarding President Nixon's actions, Berger explains that "'confidentiality' was the vehicle for the cover-up of criminal acts and conspiracies by his aides, an instrument he repeatedly employed to the obstruction of justice."[163]

Berger's description of governmental secrecy in the Nixon White House is indisputable, but it is important not to use the abuses of one administration to generalize that all "secrecy in the operations of government is an abomination."[164] It is no more valid to argue against the legitimate exercise of executive privilege because of Nixon's abuse of that power than it is to dismiss the legitimate exercise of legislative inquiry because of the abuses by Senator Joseph McCarthy. Nonetheless, the Nixon years are important in the debate over governmental secrecy because those years represent a turning point in the perceptions and uses of executive privilege.

3

UNDERMINING A CONSTITUTIONAL DOCTRINE: RICHARD NIXON AND THE ABUSE OF EXECUTIVE PRIVILEGE

Although executive privilege is a legitimate power with constitutional underpinnings, it is not an unlimited, unfettered presidential power. Traditionally, presidents who have exercised executive privilege have done so without rejecting in principle the prerogative either of Congress to conduct inquiries or the judiciary to question presidential authority. For the most part, presidents have recognized the necessity of a balancing test to weigh the importance of competing institutional claims. Presidents have weighed in favor of executive privilege to protect the nation's security, the public interest, and the candidness of internal White House deliberations.

President Richard M. Nixon went beyond the traditional defenses of executive privilege. Although he claimed, like his predecessors, to have used executive privilege for the public good, his actions did not evidence public-interest motivations. He invoked executive privilege for purposes of political expediency and used that power as a vehicle to withhold embarrassing and incriminating information.

The Nixon era brought about a fundamental change in the way that executive privilege is perceived and exercised. Prior to Nixon, many presidents confidently asserted this authority, and the coordinate branches of government generally accepted the legitimacy of executive privilege. In the post-Watergate era, most presidents have been reluctant to assert executive privilege, and many members of Congress have characterized all exercises of executive branch secrecy as Nixonian attempts to conceal and deceive. Nixon's exercise of executive privilege has had a profound and lasting impact on the status of that constitutional power.

Nixon's Executive Privilege Policy

Although President Nixon is remembered for his unremitting defense of an absolute executive privilege power during Watergate, he did not always hold such a view. Ironically, as a member of the House of Representatives in 1948, Nixon vigorously objected to President Harry S Truman's refusal to release the text of an FBI letter concerning a prominent scientist accused of disloyalty by the House Un-American Activities Committee. As a member of that committee, Nixon rose on 22 April 1948 to protest the president's assertion of a right to withhold information from Congress:

> The point has been made that the President of the United States has issued an order that none of this information can be released to the Congress and that therefore the Congress has no right to question the judgment of the President in making that decision.
>
> I say that the proposition cannot stand from a constitutional standpoint or on the basis of the merits for this very good reason: that would mean that the President could have arbitrarily issued an Executive order in the Meyers case, the Teapot Dome case, or any other case denying the Congress of the United States information that it needed to conduct an investigation of the executive department and the Congress would have no right to question his decision.
>
> Any such order of the President can be questioned by the Congress as to whether or not that order is justified on the merits.[1]

During the 1968 presidential campaign, Nixon made a statement pledging to conduct an open administration in which there would be a free flow of information from the executive branch to Congress, the media, and the public. Nixon iterated that pledge early in his first term. Just more than one week after Nixon took the oath of office, the chairman of the House Subcommittee on Government Information, John E. Moss (D-Calif.), wrote a letter to the president urging that the new administration reaffirm the Kennedy and Johnson administrations' official policy of allowing only the president—not White House staffers or subordinate officers of the executive branch—to assert executive privilege. Moss previously had solicited, and received, assurances from Nixon's two most recent predecessors that executive privilege would only be asserted by the president.[2] In a 7 April 1969 letter to Moss, Nixon responded affirmatively and attached a copy of a memorandum outlining administration policy on executive privilege that the president had issued to heads of executive agencies. First, Nixon explained to Moss the administration's position on executive privilege:

> I believe, and I have stated earlier, that the scope of executive privilege must be very narrowly construed. Under this Administration, executive privilege will not be asserted without specific Presidential approval.
>
> I want to take this opportunity to assure you and your committee that this Administration is dedicated to insuring a free flow of information to the Congress and the news media—and, thus, to the citizens.

You are, I am sure, familiar with the statement I made on this subject during the campaign. Now that I have the responsibility to implement this pledge, I wish to reaffirm my intent to do so. I want open government to be a reality in every way possible.[3]

Second, Nixon's enclosed memorandum of 24 March 1969, "Establishing a Procedure to Govern Compliance with Congressional Demands for Information," stated the following:

The policy of this Administration is to comply to the fullest extent possible with Congressional requests for information. While the Executive branch has the responsibility of withholding certain information the disclosure of which would be incompatible with the public interest, this administration will invoke this authority only in the most compelling circumstances and after a rigorous inquiry into the actual need for its exercise. For those reasons Executive privilege will not be used without specific Presidential approval.[4]

The memorandum outlined the procedure to be used whenever a question of executive privilege was raised. To summarize, under the official procedure, if a department head believed that a congressional request might concern privileged information, he would consult with the attorney general. The department head and attorney general would then decide whether to release the information to Congress or submit the matter to the president through the counsel to the president. At that stage, the president would either instruct the department head to claim executive privilege with presidential approval or request that Congress give him some time to make a decision.[5]

Nixon's official policy on the use of executive privilege did not diverge fundamentally from the policies of his predecessors. Executive privilege, under Nixon's policy, could be invoked only for the most compelling reasons, and only the president could decide whether it was appropriate to assert executive privilege.

Nonetheless, Nixon's exercise of executive privilege became controversial when many critics charged that the administration had used the constitutional doctrine to shield White House officials from testifying before Congress and to conceal wrongdoing. At an impromptu press conference near the beginning of his second term, the president promised that he would clarify his administration's policy on executive privilege. Several weeks later, on 12 March 1973, the president issued a statement to the press doing just that: "Executive privilege will not be used as a shield to prevent embarrassing information from being made available but will be exercised only in

those particular instances in which disclosure would harm the public interest."[6] Nixon's 1973 statement specifically addressed the question of congressional demands for testimony from executive branch officials, which the
1969 Nixon memorandum had not. To summarize these additional guidelines, any agency official confronted with a congressional request for information or testimony had to follow the 1969 guidelines; the same procedure
applied to cabinet officers and to members of the president's personal staff.
Finally, members and former members of the president's personal staff "normally shall follow the well-established precedent and decline a request for
formal appearance before a committee of the Congress."[7]

On 10 April 1973, Attorney General Richard Kleindienst effectively expanded the administration's definition of executive privilege by stating that
the president had the authority to prevent any federal employee from testifying before Congress, for whatever reason.[8] Nonetheless, the president emphasized in his policy that "reasonable" congressional requests for
documents or testimony would be accommodated. The ultimate determination of reasonableness was left to the attorney general and the president. Under this policy, the president's determination was final and could not be
challenged by another branch of government.

On the surface, Nixon's guidelines on executive privilege appear unusually
broad based, in that they apply to all executive branch officials. Yet the
Nixon guidelines are carefully crafted to appear consistent with the approaches of his predecessors. They mandate presidential approval of any use
of executive privilege and make it clear that, in the normal course of events,
Congress's requests for information and testimony will be honored.

Nixon's formal executive privilege guidelines do not tell the whole story of
his administration's exercise of that power, however. To understand the nature
of the executive privilege controversy during the Nixon years, it is necessary
to examine the administration's actual use of that power and other statements
and actions justifying its approach toward withholding information.

Nixon's Exercise of Executive Privilege

In his 12 March 1973 statement, President Nixon maintained that he had
asserted executive privilege on only three occasions, whereas "hundreds of
administration officials spent thousands of hours freely testifying before
committees of the Congress." Nixon added that "these facts speak not of a
closed administration but one that is pledged to openness and is proud to
stand on its record."[9]

The president's claims were misleading. Prior to Watergate, Nixon exercised executive privilege, directly and indirectly, on more than three occasions. Furthermore, on numerous occasions, agency heads refused requests to either provide information or testify before Congress.

National Security Adviser Henry Kissinger refused numerous requests to appear before congressional committees. Members of Congress believed that the Nixon White House went to extraordinary lengths in permitting agency heads to decide for themselves not to provide information or testify. In fact, Congress held a number of hearings on the matter of whether "agency" or "departmental privilege" was a legitimate exercise of executive branch power. The invocation of executive privilege by numerous subordinate officials in the Nixon administration prompted legislation to curtail such claims of privilege. For example, H.R. 6228, introduced by John N. Erlenborn (R-Ill.), proposed that all executive branch information be made available to Congress and the comptroller general of the United States, "except in cases where the president himself invokes the claim of executive privilege."[10] The purpose of this proposal was to make the president alone accountable for all claims of executive privilege. However, the legislation was opposed both by advocates of a broad definition of executive privilege and by strict opponents of the privilege, who claimed that the proposal would legitimize it. What is telling is that members of Congress thought it necessary to restrict executive privilege exclusively to presidential use, when the official policy of the Nixon administration imposed a similar limitation.

Nixon cleverly sought to restrict congressional access to information and testimony from agency heads by giving them dual responsibilities—in addition to their cabinet positions, some of them were members of the president's personal staff. Recall that Nixon's 12 March 1973 statement emphasized that members of his personal staff could not be compelled to divulge information or to testify before Congress because a president must be assured of confidential interchanges among his most trusted personal advisers. On several occasions, agency heads refused congressional requests for information or testimony based on their responsibilities as White House advisers, even though the issues raised by Congress clearly involved matters of agency responsibility.[11]

The president did not always make it clear whether he, or someone else within the White House, actually made the decision whether to allow an assertion of executive privilege. For example, in 1973, a former air force secretary refused to testify at a Civil Service Commission investigation into his firing of a civilian cost analyst for revealing confidential information about cost overruns on the C-5A aircraft. The air force secretary asserted executive privilege as the basis for not testifying. When asked whether executive privilege had been properly used in this case, President Nixon responded as follows: "In this case, as I understand it—and I did not approve this directly, but it was approved at my direction by those who have the responsibility within the White House—in this case it was a proper area in which the executive privilege should have been used."[12]

Nixon either asserted or approved the use of executive privilege on other occasions as well. In June 1970, the Intergovernmental Relations Subcommittee of the House Committee on Government Operations requested information on certain scientists who had been nominated to serve on advisory boards in the Department of Health, Education, and Welfare (HEW) but then were rejected. Specifically, members of Congress sought access to FBI files used by HEW that allegedly showed that some of the individuals had been active members of the Communist Party U.S.A. The secretary of HEW, Robert Finch, responded that the department could make the files available only with authorization from the investigative agency responsible for the files, in this case, the Department of Justice. The president approved an assertion of executive privilege by Attorney General John Mitchell to withhold the requested documents on the basis that it would not be in the public interest to release confidential FBI reports.[13]

In August 1971, Senator J. William Fulbright (D-Ark.), the chairman of the Senate Foreign Relations Committee, requested from Secretary of State William P. Rogers specific information on the administration's military assistance programs. On 31 August 1971, the president asserted executive privilege, denying Fulbright's request for that information. Neither Fulbright nor the other members of the committee raised this difference of opinion to the level of a constitutional dispute. Rather, they emphasized that Congress needed the information so that it could act more financially responsibly by scrutinizing government spending.[14]

In 1972, while considering the nomination of Richard Kleindienst as attorney general, the Senate Committee on the Judiciary began to look into accusations that the Justice Department had settled three antitrust lawsuits against the International Telephone and Telegraph Company (ITT) in return for an agreement that ITT would cover $400,000 in expenses for the 1972 Republican National Convention. The committee requested the testimony of White House adviser Peter Flanagan, who allegedly had knowledge of ITT's efforts to gain the settlement. The Nixon White House claimed executive privilege and refused to allow Flanagan to testify, citing the president's policy of not allowing members of his immediate staff to testify regarding their official duties. The White House and the committee eventually compromised on the issue, allowing Flanagan to provide limited testimony on an agreed-upon topic pertaining to the Kleindienst nomination but not the ITT controversy.[15]

Another controversy raised the issue of executive privilege even though the president did not invoke the power. At issue was the availability of information on recommendations made to the president about the proposed Amchitka underground nuclear tests. Some members of the House of Representatives had already tried, unsuccessfully, to block the tests through budgetary means. When House members learned that the president had received conflicting advice on whether to carry out the tests, some of them sought access to the agency reports. The president refused, claiming national defense and foreign policy reasons for withholding the information. Thirty-three House members joined as private individuals to take legal action against the president's decision, using the Freedom of Information Act to compel disclosure. The case, *Environmental Protection Agency v. Mink* (1973), eventually reached the Supreme Court.[16]

Germane to the executive privilege controversy is the fact that the Nixon administration claimed the authority to withhold any information that it deemed was in the national interest not to divulge, and that such a claim could not be examined by any other branch of government. The president even denied that the courts had any authority to review the disputed materials in camera, because such review constituted actual disclosure of privileged information. Ultimately, the Supreme Court held in the *Mink* case that the courts can require in camera inspection of documents, and such inspection is not tantamount to revealing vital secrets.[17]

The Watergate scandal stands as the most celebrated case in history of the executive privilege controversy. During the course of that scandal, the president used executive privilege as a shield to prevent the disclosure of embarrassing, legally damaging information. And in his attempt to cover up the scandal, Nixon cited national security concerns as a reason for withholding information vital to the Watergate inquiries.[18]

Throughout much of the Watergate investigation, the president tried to convey a reasonable posture on the question of executive privilege. He claimed to be willing to make unprecedented concessions to demands for information. He even waived executive privilege for staff aides to testify before the Senate Watergate Committee on issues of possible criminal conduct. Nixon instructed White House staff to assert the privilege only as follows:

In connection with the appearance of witnesses before grand juries, judicial proceedings, and congressional committees, I direct that executive privilege be waived in all matters except those involving national security, those involving direct communication to or from the president in any form, written or oral, and those involving communication given or received in any form, written or oral on behalf of the president.[19]

On 16 July 1973, a former assistant to H. R. Haldeman, Alexander But-
terfield, testified before the Senate Watergate Committee that the president
had tape-recorded conversations in the Oval Office and the Executive Office
Building. The Senate Watergate Committee subsequently requested the
tapes, as did Watergate Special Prosecutor Archibald Cox. Nixon claimed
executive privilege and refused to turn over the tapes to either the committee
or Cox. After a number of efforts to secure the tapes, Cox went to federal
court to have a subpoena issued for recordings of specific conversations.
Judge John Sirica issued the subpoena, which Nixon refused to comply with,
again claiming executive privilege. Nixon appealed to the U.S. Court of Appeals in the District of Columbia, which upheld Sirica's ruling. Nixon responded by having Cox fired (the notorious "Saturday night massacre")—an
event that set off such a firestorm of protest that Nixon had to turn the disputed tapes over to Sirica.

In April 1974, the new Watergate special prosecutor, Leon Jaworski, requested sixty-four additional White House tapes, and Nixon again claimed
executive privilege to withhold the tapes. This time, Sirica demanded on 20
May 1974 that the tapes be released to him for in camera inspection. Four
days later, Nixon attorney James St. Clair appealed the Sirica order to the
court of appeals, and Jaworski requested from the Supreme Court a writ of
certiorari prior to the court of appeals ruling.

In *U.S. v. Nixon*,[20] the Supreme Court issued its historic, unanimous decision on the Nixon tapes controversy. During oral argument in the case, St.
Clair presented the president's position in favor of an absolute executive
privilege and maintained that the president did not have to comply with the
special prosecutor's subpoena. Jaworski responded that executive privilege
could not be used to shield criminal conduct and posed a question that addressed the essence of the executive privilege controversy: "Shall the evidence from the White House be confined to what a single person, highly
interested in the outcome, is willing to make available?"[21]

The Court rejected the claim of an absolute presidential power of executive privilege, as well as the claim that the president had ultimate authority
over all executive branch information. Further, the Court reaffirmed the
right of the judicial branch to resolve disputes between the political branches
of government. In this particular controversy, the Court ruled that the president's claim of executive privilege had to be balanced against the special
prosecutor's need for information in a criminal case. Regarding executive
privilege, the Court stated, "to the extent that this interest in confidentiality
relates to the effective discharge of the president's powers, it is constitutionally based."[22] Nonetheless, the Court ruled that the need for information in
this criminal case overruled the president's claim to executive privilege.[23]

The Court determined that to permit a claim of executive privilege that effectively resulted in the withholding of vital evidence "would cut deeply into the guarantee of due process of law and gravely impair the basic function of the courts."[24] With that decision, the president had no recourse but to turn over the incriminating tapes that ended his presidency.

Nixon continued to claim executive privilege, even out of office. As expresident, he sought control over his presidential materials, including the White House tapes. The Court acknowledged in *Nixon v. Administrator of General Services* (1977) that ex-presidents do have authority to claim executive privilege in particular circumstances. Nonetheless, the Court ruled that, in this particular case, the balance tipped in favor of the public's right to have access to presidential materials.[25] Despite this decision, Nixon continued to press his claims.

Nixon's Defense of Executive Privilege

President Nixon offered the most far-reaching, comprehensive definition of executive privilege imaginable under our constitutional system. He argued that (1) the president has an unlimited power of executive privilege; (2) under the separation of powers system, no other branch of government can question the president's constitutional authority in this area; (3) executive privilege belongs to all executive branch officials; (4) he had to strongly assert executive privilege during the Watergate investigations to protect the office of the presidency, but not himself; and (5) any breach of the president's absolute power of executive privilege would threaten the national security.

Unlimited Power of Executive Privilege

Nixon tried to make the case that there can be no limitations on the president's use of executive privilege, that only the president himself has the authority to limit the use of executive privilege. In *Senate Select Committee on Presidential Campaign Activities v. Nixon* (1973), the president's defenders adopted this absolute executive privilege claim in their statement that "such a privilege, inherent in the constitutional grant of executive power, is a matter of presidential judgement alone."[26] In the brief in opposition to the special prosecutor's demand for White House tapes, Nixon's defenders maintained that

the privilege is not confined to specific kinds of subject matter . . . nor to particular kinds of communications. Reason dictates a much broader concept, that the privilege extends to all of the executive power vested in the president by Article II and that it reaches any information that the president determines cannot be disclosed consistent with the public interest and the proper performance of his constitutional duties.[27]

After leaving office, Nixon went so far as to argue that there are no limits on presidential power generally. Nixon most clearly presented that view in his televised interviews with journalist David Frost. When questioned on 19 May 1977 by Frost about the limits on presidential power, Nixon replied, "when the president does it, that means it is not illegal."[28] Such a statement implies that there are no limits on presidential authority, including the power to withhold information; all that is required is presidential approval of an action. In a clear refutation of the more common constitutional view that no person is above the law, Nixon argued that presidential actions have higher standing than the law itself. For example, Nixon justified the burglary of Daniel Ellsberg's psychiatrist's office as a legitimate presidential action, not subject to limitation. While asserting that he did not know of the burglary in advance, Nixon responded that, if told, "I would have said, 'Go right ahead.'" Nixon added, "I didn't want to discredit the man as an individual. I couldn't care less about the punk. I wanted to discredit that kind of activity, which was despicable and damaging to the national interest."[29] Nixon added that such normally illegal activities become lawful when sanctioned by the president. The causes for sanctioning such activities are varied and may, Nixon asserted, include the "national interest" or "national security."

Separation of Powers

During his presidency, Nixon adopted the view that Congress and the courts lack the authority to question or contest claims of executive privilege. In Nixon's understanding of the separation of powers, the president stands supreme and may unilaterally determine the scope and limits of his own powers. Nixon believed that whenever a dispute between the political branches over executive privilege occurs, the president's claim of privilege resolves the dispute. In a sense, this view of the president in the separation of powers system elevates his role to that of participant *and* referee in a political struggle, because even the judiciary cannot referee disputes over executive privilege. In a revealing quote, President Nixon stated during the Watergate controversy that "the manner in which the president exercises his assigned executive powers is not subject to questioning by another branch of the government."[30]

In the president's brief in opposition to the special prosecutor's demand for White House tapes, Nixon's attorneys offered the following view:

In the exercise of his discretion to claim executive privilege the president is answerable to the Nation but not to the courts. The courts, a co-equal but not a superior branch of government, are not free to probe the mental processes and the private confidences of the president and his advisers. To do so would be a clear violation of the constitutional separation of powers. Under that doctrine the judicial branch lacks power to compel the president to produce information that he has determined it is not in the public interest to disclose.[31]

The president personally responded in the same vein to Judge Sirica. In expressing his reasons for refusing to comply with the subpoena of White House tapes, Nixon stated, "the president is not subject to compulsory process from the other branches of government." He provided the following reasons: "The independence of the three branches of our government is at the very heart of our constitutional system. It would be wholly inadmissible for the president to seek to compel some particular action by the courts. It is equally inadmissible for the courts to seek to compel some particular action from the president."[32] During oral argument in *U.S. v. Nixon,* the president's attorney candidly rejected the right of the judiciary to contest presidential claims of privilege. The following exchange between the Court's justices and James St. Clair revealed the president's view that although the Court could declare the law, the president still had the final word:

QUESTION: You are submitting this matter to the Court . . .
ST. CLAIR: To this Court under a special showing on behalf of the president . . .
QUESTION: And you are still leaving it up to this Court to decide it.
ST. CLAIR: Yes, in a sense.
QUESTION: In what sense?
ST. CLAIR: In the sense that this Court has the obligation to determine the law. The President also has an obligation to carry out his constitutional duties.
QUESTION: Well, do you agree that this is what is before this Court, and you are submitting it to this Court for decision?
ST. CLAIR: This is being submitted to this Court for its guidance and judgment with respect to the law. The President, on the other hand, has his obligations under the Constitution.
QUESTION: Are you submitting it to this Court for this Court's decision?
ST. CLAIR: As to what the law is, yes.[33]

During testimony before Senate committees, Kleindienst argued that

Congress has no right even to seek information on criminal activities in the executive branch if the president claims executive privilege. Furthermore, he asserted that the attorney general alone determines what information Congress can receive from the Department of Justice.[34] Kleindienst also maintained that the doctrine of executive privilege could be used to withhold information sought by Congress in an impeachment hearing.[35]

In Nixon's view of executive privilege, the president's authority to exercise such power is absolute, unfettered by any actions that the other branches of government might take to compel disclosure or settle disputes over withheld information. Nixon also extended this vast power to members of his staff and, effectively, to the entire federal bureaucracy.

Staff and Departmental Privilege

Nixon not only argued that the president's actions to protect the national interest cannot be unlawful; he also said that the activities of members of the executive branch are exempt from normal legal limitations if conducted on the president's behalf. "If the President, for example, approves something, approves an action because of the national security or . . . because of a threat to internal peace and order of significant magnitude, then the President's decision in that instance is one that enables those who carry it out to carry it out without violating a law."[36]

To Nixon, executive privilege was not a power possessed only by the president and selected White House insiders. Rather, in his view, executive privilege could be invoked by the president on behalf of *all* executive branch officials. Just as the president's exercise of power could not be questioned by the other branches of government, the president's aides could not be questioned. Nixon maintained that "if the president is not subject to such questioning, it is equally inappropriate that members of his staff not [*sic*] be so questioned, for their roles are in effect an extension of the president."[37]

Nixon applied this reasoning not only to his White House staff but also to the entire executive bureaucracy. Attorney General Kleindienst asserted on behalf of the president that Congress lacked the authority to call any employee of the federal government to appear before it if the president decided to bar such testimony.[38] Kleindienst further maintained that the president could invoke executive privilege to bar congressional testimony by White House staff in an impeachment proceeding: "If you are conducting an impeachment proceeding based upon high crimes and misdemeanors and you want to subpoena someone from the president's staff to give you information, I believe that, based upon the doctrine of separation of powers, the president would have the power to invoke executive privilege with respect to that information."[39]

Nixon initially tried to prevent John Dean, counsel to the president, from testifying before the Senate Watergate Committee. In a 15 March 1973 news conference, the president maintained that it was proper to prevent Dean from testifying because "he has, in effect, what I would call a double privilege." The so-called double privilege consisted of the lawyer-client privilege and "the presidential privilege."[40] Dean maintained that he could testify because he would not be discussing matters of national security. Although, on the surface, the lawyer-client privilege appears to be a sound reason to prevent the counsel to the president from testifying before Congress, in this case, Dean would be testifying about a criminal conspiracy between the attorney and the client. Neither the lawyer-client privilege nor the presidential privilege can be used to shield criminal conspiracies.

By extending the executive privilege to White House staff, the president defined the constitutional doctrine in a way that was compatible with historical precedent. What made Nixon's action in this regard extraordinary was his use of executive privilege to shield wrongdoing by himself and his staff. When Nixon effectively extended executive privilege to the entire federal bureaucracy, he acted without precedent. As noted earlier, because of the Nixon administration's unprecedentedly broad use of executive privilege, debates arose in Congress over the exercise of "agency" and "departmental privilege." Congress and the courts also tried to subpoena information from the Nixon White House to investigate criminal conspiracy charges, and both met with resistance. Nixon claimed that he had to take these actions to protect the presidency, given his "constitutional responsibility to defend the principle of separation of powers."[41]

Protecting the Presidency

In refusing to disclose information to Congress and the judiciary during the Watergate investigations, Nixon argued that in no sense was he acting merely to protect himself. Instead, he insisted, he was obligated to protect the presidency from improper encroachments on its constitutional prerogatives. During a question-and-answer session at a 17 November 1973 conference of the Associated Press Managing Editors Association in Orlando, Florida, the president responded to a query about his view of executive privilege. Nixon asserted that he had waived executive privilege for himself and his staff "voluntarily," so as "to avoid a precedent that might destroy the principle of confidentiality for future presidents." The president then cited what he called the "Jefferson rule" of presidential refusal to disclose information to the courts and Congress to protect the powers of the presidency. Referring to the Burr conspiracy case, Nixon explained as follows:

Now why did Jefferson do that? Jefferson didn't do that to protect Jefferson. He did that to protect the presidency. That is exactly what I will do in these cases. It isn't for the purpose of protecting the President; it is for the purpose of seeing that the presidency, where great decisions have to be made, and great decisions cannot be made unless there is very free flow of conversation, and that means confidentiality, I have a responsibility to protect that presidency.[42]

On 26 November 1973, when Nixon submitted seven of the presidential tapes to Judge Sirica, he included a number of claims of executive privilege with regard to certain material in the tapes, presumably to protect the confidentiality of White House deliberations. Although presented as a conciliatory gesture to try to end the demand for White House tapes, the tactic merely fueled the controversy and led to demands for more tapes.

In the brief in opposition to the special prosecutor's demand for the White House tapes, Nixon's defenders asserted that he had refused the order to protect the president's constitutional powers and ability to provide the nation with "informed and vigorous leadership."[43] The president's brief made the following argument for protecting the presidency:

If the special Prosecutor should be successful in the attempt to compel disclosure of recordings of presidential conversations, the damage to the institution of the presidency will be irreparable. The character of that office will be fundamentally altered and the total structure of government—dependent as it is upon the separation of powers—will be impaired.

The consequence of an order to disclose recordings or notes would be that no longer could a president speak in confidence with his close advisers on any subject. The threat of potential disclosure of any and all conversations would make it virtually impossible for President Nixon or his successors in that great office to function. Beyond that, a holding that the president is personally subject to the orders of a court would effectively destroy the status of the Executive Branch as an equal and coordinate element of government.

There is no precedent that can be said to justify or permit such a result. On the contrary, it is clear that while courts and their grand juries have the power to seek evidence of all persons, including the president, the president has the power and thus the privilege to withhold information if he concludes that disclosure would be contrary to the public interest.[44]

The president articulated similar arguments in two letters to the chairman of the Senate Watergate Committee, Sam J. Ervin (D-N.C.). First, in response to a letter from Ervin requesting personal testimony from the president, as well as access to presidential papers, Nixon wrote on 6 July 1973:

> In this letter I shall state the reasons why I shall not testify before the committee or permit access to presidential papers.
>
> I want to strongly emphasize that my decision, in both cases, is based on my constitutional obligation to preserve intact the powers and prerogatives of the presidency and not upon any desire to withhold information relevant to your inquiry. . . . The pending requests . . . would move us from proper presidential cooperation with a Senate Committee to jeopardizing the fundamental constitutional role of the presidency. This I must and shall resist.

Nixon went on to say that the president cannot function in an environment in which the candor of his staff is threatened by public disclosure of presidential papers and materials. He added that "the duty of every president to protect and defend the constitutional rights and powers of his office is an obligation that runs directly to the people of this country."[45]

Second, in response to the Senate committee's subpoena of presidential materials, Nixon responded in a 4 January 1974 letter to Ervin:

> To produce the material you now seek would unquestionably destroy any vestige of confidentiality of presidential communications, thereby irreparably impairing the constitutional functions of the office of the presidency. Neither the judiciary nor the Congress could survive a similar power asserted by the executive branch to rummage through their files and confidential processes. Under the circumstances, I can only view your subpoena as an overt attempt to intrude into the executive to a degree that constitutes an unconstitutional usurpation of power. . . . I take this position to protect the office of the president against incursions by another branch, which I believe, as have my predecessors in office, is of utmost constitutional importance. Accordingly, in order to protect the fundamental structure of our government of three separate but equal branches, I must and do respectfully decline to produce the materials called for in your subpoenas.[46]

Preserving National Security

Finally, President Nixon asserted traditional national security concerns as justification for his use of executive privilege during the Watergate scandal. He argued that without the protection of executive privilege, "our military security, our relations with other countries, our law enforcement procedures, and many other aspects of the national interest could be significantly damaged and the decisionmaking process of the executive branch could be impaired."[47]

Once again, the president's brief in opposition to the special prosecutor's demand for information stated the argument in favor of executive privilege:

> Disclosure of information allegedly relevant to this inquiry would mean disclosure as well as [*sic*] other information of a highly confidential nature relating to a wide range of matters not related to this inquiry. Some of these matters deal with sensitive issues of national security. Others go to the exercise by the president of his constitutional duties on matters other than Watergate.[48]

In announcing Executive Order 11652, dealing with security classification, on 8 March 1972, Nixon stated:

> the federal government is obliged to protect certain information which might otherwise jeopardize the security of the country. The need has become particularly acute in recent years as the United States has assumed a powerful position in world affairs, and as world peace has come to depend in large part on how that position is safeguarded. We are also moving into an era of delicate negotiations in which it will be especially important that governments be able to communicate in confidence.

Ironically, Nixon declared the need for a balance between the public's right to know and government secrecy and argued that the security classification system should not be used to conceal mistakes "or to prevent embarrassment to [government] officials." In contrast to his arguments in favor of an absolute executive privilege power, Nixon stated, "Fundamental to our way of life is the belief that when information which properly belongs to the public is systematically withheld by those in power, the people soon become ignorant of their own affairs, distrustful of those who manage them, and— eventually—incapable of determining their own destinies."[49]

Abuse of the Constitutional Doctrine

President Nixon's view of executive privilege lacks constitutional and historical validity. In the unanimous *U.S. v. Nixon* decision, the Supreme
Court made it abundantly clear that executive privilege is not an unlimited,
unfettered presidential power. The Court strongly rejected the argument
that, under the separation of powers system, the president's exercise of
power cannot be questioned by the coordinate branches of government. Indeed, the Court reaffirmed its own authority to determine what the law is
and to challenge the presidential exercise of power. Nixon's claim that only
the president can determine the scope and limits of his own constitutional
authority was indefensible.

There is no doubt that, under appropriate circumstances, national security is a sound basis for defending executive privilege. For Nixon, the problem was that he used the national security argument to cover up White
House wrongdoing. In a 21 March 1973 conversation among Nixon,
Haldeman, and Dean, the president proposed using national security concerns as a Watergate defense:

PRESIDENT: What is the answer on this? How can you keep it out? I
don't know. You can't keep it out if Hunt talks. You see the point is irrelevant. It has gotten to this point . . .
DEAN: You might put it on a national security basis . . .
PRESIDENT: With the bombing thing coming out and everything coming out, the whole thing was national security.
DEAN: I think we could get by on that . . .
PRESIDENT: Bud [Krogh] should just say it was a question of national
security, and I was not in a position to divulge it. Anyway let's don't go
beyond that.[50]

Nixon persisted in claiming that his actions had been motivated by national security—even after publication of the White House transcripts revealed the sham, and even after he was forced to resign the presidency. In his
1977 interview with David Frost, Nixon recited Abraham Lincoln's words as
supportive of the view that normally unconstitutional actions become constitutional when undertaken by the president to preserve the nation. Frost
protested that "there was no comparison was there between the situation you
faced and the situation Lincoln faced." Nixon did not back down. "This nation was torn apart in an ideological way by the war in Vietnam, as much as

the Civil War tore apart the nation when Lincoln was president." Nixon insisted that his actions must "be understood in the context of the times. The nation was at war. Men were dying." Further, he argued, "keeping the peace at home and keeping support for the war was essential in order to get the enemy to negotiate." Hence, Nixon defended the infamous Huston Plan, which advocated infiltration of antiwar groups through wiretappings, burglaries, mail openings, and other techniques.[51] He also defended FBI wiretaps of National Security Council staff members and White House wiretaps of news reporters on the basis of national security. Nixon told Dean that the wiretaps were legal and covered by the doctrine of executive privilege.[52]

The facts make it unarguably clear that Nixon did not use executive privilege during the Watergate scandal to protect the presidency—he did so to protect himself. Like his predecessors, Nixon claimed that he had to exercise executive privilege for the public good, but his actions betrayed that claim. The major result of Nixon's use of executive privilege was to politically discredit a legitimate, necessary constitutional power of the presidency. Even though *U.S. v. Nixon* was a defeat for Nixon and a victory for executive privilege, that doctrine has not yet recovered from Nixon's abuse of power. Nixon's actions undermined his successors' ability to exercise this constitutional power and lent credibility and stature to such anti–executive privilege absolutists as Raoul Berger. Presidents Ford, Carter, Reagan, Bush, Clinton, Bush, and Obama have had to deal with this particular legacy of Watergate.

Nixon and the opponents of executive privilege have something important in common: they all believe in absolute, unambiguous answers to a complex constitutional controversy. One argues that the president has an absolute, unlimited power of executive privilege that cannot be challenged by the other branches of government. The other maintains that the president never, under any circumstance, has the authority to assert executive privilege and that Congress can compel the executive branch to hand over any information that it wants.

Before presenting the argument for a properly limited executive privilege, it is necessary to examine the more recent history of that constitutional power. Executive privilege suffered as a result of Watergate, in part because its opponents tried to characterize every use of presidential secrecy as a Nixonian cover-up. Although post-Watergate presidents, Republican and Democrat alike, have accepted the constitutional legitimacy of executive privilege, most have been reluctant to exercise this power. And it is no coincidence that those presidents who served closest in time to the Nixon years were most reticent regarding executive privilege.

4

THE POST-WATERGATE YEARS I: THE "OPEN" PRESIDENCIES OF GERALD FORD AND JIMMY CARTER

The Watergate crisis brought executive privilege to the forefront of public discourse in the United States. Although the constitutional doctrine had been a matter of some controversy for many years, no single event had ever brought executive privilege to such a prominent place in national political discussion.

The Nixon administration's actions discredited a constitutional doctrine that had been used judiciously by many previous administrations. Nixon's successors have had to deal with this legacy of his presidency, including the fact that Congress has become much more aggressive in challenging presidential exercise of executive privilege. Most of Nixon's successors have thus been reluctant to exercise, or make a case for, executive privilege.

Although executive privilege has fallen out of favor, Nixon's successors have continued to exercise secrecy. In some cases, they adopted strategies of withholding information without citing executive privilege, relying instead on statutory authority or some other power. Despite these creative efforts to maintain secrecy and confidentiality, Congress generally has been able to compel disclosure of executive branch information by resorting to various political and legal maneuvers. In the post-Watergate years most administrations have usually backed down from their claims of executive privilege in the face of legislative challenges. Even the Reagan administration, which adopted unprecedented secrecy measures, never made a strong case for executive privilege and chose, instead, to accommodate its short-term political needs by time and again conceding to Congress disputed information.

The ways in which post-Watergate presidents have handled executive privilege have weakened that power substantially, resulting in (1) creative presidential efforts to achieve the ends of executive privilege, without citing it as the source of authority; (2) congressional attempts, largely successful, to demean every use of executive privilege as a ploy to deceive or to conceal wrongdoing; and (3) the undermining of a legitimate presidential power that often is necessary to the conduct of the presidency. The following evidence makes it clear that executive privilege must be reestablished in the political branches as a necessary executive power. But none of the post-Watergate presidencies has taken the proper steps to do so.

73

GERALD R. FORD, 1974–1977

The Ford years represent an important transitional stage in the modern presidency. As the first post-Watergate president, Ford experienced vigorous challenges to his authority and veracity—challenges certainly more suited to his predecessor—by Congress and the media. To be sure, his candor and efforts to lead an open presidency did much to move the nation beyond the cynicism and rancor of the Nixon years. Nonetheless, many members of Congress and many political commentators believed that an important lesson of the Nixon years was that power in the hands of the executive leads to abuses of authority. Congress thus embarked on an unprecedented reform effort to invigorate its own authority and to limit the exercise of presidential powers. It also undertook unprecedented investigations into the activities of the U.S. intelligence community.

It was against this backdrop that a number of executive privilege controversies arose during the Ford years. President Ford never adopted a formal policy on executive privilege, but he did exercise that power on several occasions, with varying degrees of success.

Ford's Executive Privilege "Policy"

Unlike his predecessor, President Ford never issued a formal memorandum or executive order specifying his administration's policy on executive privilege. A review of White House documents reveals that certain members of the Ford administration raised the subject of developing procedures for handling executive privilege controversies, and certain members of Congress sent letters to the president requesting that such a set of procedures be issued. The White House even composed a draft executive order on executive privilege, but Ford never issued the order. If there was any Ford White House strategy on executive privilege, it was to avoid controversy as much as possible by not issuing a formal policy, by avoiding the use of the phrase *executive privilege* in favor of other terms for decisions to withhold information, and, when possible, by citing statutory authority to deny requested information. Ford believed that the president possessed the authority of executive privilege, and he exercised that power himself on just a few occasions to protect what he considered vital national security information.

Within one week of Ford's inauguration, Congressman John E. Moss sent a letter to the president requesting that Ford adopt a formal policy on executive privilege in which that power could be "invoked only by the president or with specific presidential approval in each instance." Moss noted that he had received commitments from Presidents Kennedy, Johnson, and Nixon to limit the use of executive privilege to personal claims by the president. Consequently, Moss expected a similar response from Ford.[1] But Ford never directly responded to the Moss letter, breaking the precedent established by his three predecessors. Only the deputy assistant to the president, Max L. Friedersdorf, responded to Moss's letter and assured the congressman that the letter would be shared with the president's advisers.[2]

Ford also received a letter on executive privilege from Congressmen John N. Erlenborn and William S. Moorhead on 13 August 1974, and another joint letter on executive privilege from Senators Sam Ervin, William V. Roth, and Edmund S. Muskie on 22 August 1974. Friedersdorf acknowledged the Erlenborn letter, and Assistant to the President William E. Timmons acknowledged the senators' letter.[3] No formal action was taken on the matters raised in these letters.

The White House continued to receive pressure to adopt a policy on the use of executive privilege. On 19 September 1974, the general counsel to the Office of Management and Budget (OMB), Stanley Ebner, expressed his concern to the counsel to the president, Philip W. Buchen, that "President Ford has taken no public position on the issue of executive privilege." Ebner noted that the OMB had to deal with numerous "requests for information or records from the Congress and from outside government." He recalled President Nixon's memorandum on executive privilege and concluded, "you will no doubt want to give some consideration to the question of a possible reaffirmation or modification of this policy by the president on his own initiative."[4]

Timmons advised Buchen on 23 September 1974 to "research the issue [of executive privilege] and get guidance from the president on how he plans to handle this ticklish problem when it is raised." Timmons noted that members of Congress would press for disputed information on Watergate, the Nixon pardon, and other matters, making it imperative that the president set some guidelines on the use of executive privilege.[5]

That same day, Timmons and Friedersdorf proposed a meeting between the president and Representatives Erlenborn and Moorhead to discuss pending legislation on executive privilege.[6] The meeting was held for fifteen minutes on 10 October 1974 at the Oval Office. There is no record of what was said in the meeting, but a White House background paper for the meeting identified "talking points" for the president. The talking points noted that Ford should emphasize his desire to run an open administration and that he would value the "views and recommendations" of the congressmen on the topic of executive privilege.[7] The legislative proposal on executive privilege that was the basis for the meeting failed to pass Congress.

The Ford White House continued to use an ad hoc group, formed during the Nixon administration, to make recommendations on information policy issues, including those pertaining to the Freedom of Information Act (FOIA) and executive privilege. A 24 September 1974 memorandum from the executive director of the Domestic Council on the Right of Privacy, Doug Metz, to Buchen outlined several recommendations and presidential options on the topic of executive privilege. Metz made it clear that Ford's options on executive privilege were limited because that subject was "inextricably bound up with Watergate." The memorandum advised Ford to meet with members of Congress on the subject, to affirm the intention to conduct an "open presidency," to avoid an outright defense of the constitutional prerogative of executive privilege, and to issue an executive order on the subject "affirming the traditional commitment to prudence in the exercise of the privilege." It was accompanied by a discussion draft of an executive order entitled "Establishing a Procedure for Determining Whether Executive Privilege Should Be Invoked." Also included was a proposed draft letter on executive privilege for the president to issue to all federal employees.[8] The intention of the executive order and the letter was to formalize a presidential position on executive privilege, but Ford never issued either one.

A 25 September 1974 memorandum from Associate Counsel Dudley Chapman to Buchen summarized executive privilege issues faced by the administration and offered recommendations for handling them. Echoing the Metz memorandum, Chapman stated that "the unfavorable connotations of executive privilege and the present mood of Congress dictate a sharp break from traditional practice." Chapman too recommended that Ford adopt a formal policy on executive privilege rather than try to deal with each controversy on a case-by-case basis. Chapman believed that Ford needed to acknowledge the legitimacy of Congress's various requests for information and should meet with the congressmen who had written letters urging the adoption of legislation to limit the use of executive privilege.[9]

In November, Chapman followed up with another executive privilege memorandum. This one noted the difficulty posed by the new personalities in Congress who were requesting executive branch information and who "no longer give up when they are told no." Chapman maintained that "many of the requests we are now getting cannot be resolved through traditional compromise because the purpose of the request is to test the principle." Chapman offered suggestions for getting around executive privilege controversies: (1) cite exemptions from the FOIA as the basis for withholding information, "rather than executive privilege"; (2) use executive privilege as a last resort—even avoid the use of the term in favor of "presidential" or "constitutional privilege," "confidential working papers," and so forth; and (3) issue formal guidelines on the use of executive privilege. Chapman noted that congres-

sional requests for a formal presidential declaration on executive privilege remained unanswered.[10]

The issue of how the White House should treat executive privilege controversies remained unresolved throughout the Ford years. On 4 April 1975,
a discussion of how to handle such controversies was held at the office of the
deputy counsel to the president, and the discussion summary makes it clear
that the administration lacked a set of guidelines.[11]

In late November 1975, Buchen sent a memorandum to all senior White
House staff and members of the cabinet summarizing access-to-information
controversies before the administration. The memorandum cited the use of
statutory bases for refusing information in some cases, compliance with
congressional requests in a number of cases, and the use of executive privilege as a basis to withhold information in a few cases. Part III of the memorandum was entitled "Procedures for Asserting Executive Privilege," and it
summarized the procedures adopted by some of Ford's predecessors. It
identified no such procedures for the Ford administration, however. In fact,
the only mention of Ford in this section was the fact that the president, in
response to a question, had told Congress that he believed in the principle
of executive privilege and in the right of confidentiality for each branch of
government.[12]

A November 1975 memorandum on executive privilege from the Office of
the Attorney General noted the need to approach the subject when it arises
"in a systematic fashion." The memorandum was "intended to facilitate the
construction of a framework for future actions" and suggested categories of
areas in which executive privilege could be asserted and the levels of priority
to be granted to the stated purposes for withholding information.[13]

What is most telling about all these memoranda and letters is how much
effort the Ford administration devoted to discussing how to handle this controversial issue, yet despite all this discussion, the president never adopted a
formal policy on the use of executive privilege. His administration dealt with
executive privilege controversies on a case-by-case basis.

To understand Ford's handling of this subject, the political context of the
period must be acknowledged. Adopting a formal, and hence public, position on executive privilege would have invited an avalanche of public protest
and congressional condemnation of Ford's action, even if the president had
adopted a reasonably restrictive policy toward the exercise of such power. To
many in the public and in Congress, "executive privilege" and "Watergate"
were intertwined. Ford's decision not to adopt a formal policy on executive
privilege—given that the only one conceivable at the time would have severely weakened the constitutional doctrine—was prudent, considering the
difficult environment in which he governed.

Ford's Exercise of Executive Privilege

In the wake of Watergate, President Ford projected a willingness to accommodate the needs of Congress. On 12 August 1974, three days after taking the oath of office, Ford addressed members of Congress from the House chambers. He made it clear that he intended to be very different from his predecessor.

> As president . . . my motto toward the Congress is communication, conciliation, compromise and cooperation. This Congress, unless it has changed, will be my working partner as well as my most constructive critic. I am not asking for conformity. . . . I do not want a honeymoon with you. I want a good marriage. . . . My office door has always been open, and that is how it is going to be at the White House. . . . There will be no illegal tapings, eavesdropping, buggings or break-ins by my administration. There will be hot pursuit of tough laws to prevent illegal invasion of privacy.[14]

Ford's speech drew an enormously favorable response from the legislators. In retrospect, it seems remarkable that members of Congress would feel moved to applaud with such enthusiasm a presidential pledge not to break the law or abuse power. But this response must be understood within the context of the times. Members of Congress were delighted to be rid of Nixon, and they saw in Ford—a former congressman—hope for the beginning of an era of presidential-congressional cooperation. A *New York Times* reporter wrote that the legislators were so overjoyed with Ford that "they probably would have cheered if he had read them a page from the telephone book."[15]

Ford's pledge of cooperation, along with his promise to run an "open presidency," certainly created high expectations in Congress. Nonetheless, regarding the doctrine of executive privilege, some members of Congress wanted to test how far Ford would go in exercising that presidential power. And despite his pledge to cooperate with Congress, Ford never conceded that the legislature had the right of access to all executive branch information.

The Nixon Pardon

The unpopular presidential pardon of Richard M. Nixon on 8 September 1974 set back much of the progress Ford had made in establishing a relationship with Congress based on trust. Many members of Congress reacted angrily not only to the decision itself but also to the secretive manner in which Ford considered and then issued the pardon. The way that Ford handled the pardon decision, dropping it on an unsuspecting country one Sunday morning "like Pearl Harbor," as Deputy Press Secretary John W. Hushen described it, also fueled speculation that Nixon and Ford had struck an unseemly deal: the White House for a pardon.[16]

To determine whether any such deal had taken place, some members of Congress sought to compel testimony from Ford's legal counsel Philip W. Buchen and other White House staffers. These requests for congressional testimony from the White House staff led to the first executive privilege controversy during Ford's presidency. The president ended the controversy on 30 September 1974 when he agreed to appear before Congress to answer questions about his decision to pardon Nixon.[17] During his 17 October 1974 nationally televised appearance before the House Subcommittee on Criminal Justice, Ford said that "the right of executive privilege is to be exercised with caution and restraint." He explained, "I feel a responsibility, as you do, that each branch of government must preserve a degree of confidentiality for its internal communications."[18] In effect, Ford projected a conciliatory tone while affirming presidential authority to assert executive privilege.

Aid to South Vietnam

During his brief term in office, Ford went to unusual lengths to provide information to Congress in areas where previous presidents had been reluctant to cooperate with legislative inquiries. The president agreed to furnish Congress with requested information on the activities of the Central Intelligence Agency (CIA) and the Federal Bureau of Investigation (FBI). For example, Ford turned over to Congress previously withheld information that was relevant to inquiries into alleged CIA complicity in assassination schemes.

Nonetheless, Ford drew the line on certain requests for information. In 1975, the Senate Judiciary Subcommittee on Separation of Powers requested the release of correspondence between President Nixon and South Vietnamese President Nguyen Van Thieu regarding promises of U.S. aid to South Vietnam in the event that North Vietnam did not honor the Paris Peace Accords. On 1 May 1975, Ford declared that he would not release any of the disputed documents and letters. The subcommittee declared Ford "adamant in his refusal" to release the materials, but it could do little more than hold hearings on the issue of congressional access to executive branch information.[19]

Request for Survey of Hospitals

Because of the controversial nature of executive privilege in light of Nixon's actions, the Ford White House adopted a strategy of occasionally citing statutory authority to withhold information.[20] Two cases in particular show that the strategy to substitute statutory law for executive privilege as the basis for withholding information from Congress did not work.

In the first case, on 23 October 1975, John Moss, chairman of the House Subcommittee on Oversight and Investigations of the Committee on Interstate and Foreign Commerce, requested from secretary of the Department of Health, Education, and Welfare (HEW), F. David Mathews, information on surveys of hospitals conducted by the Joint Commission on Accreditation of Hospitals. On the advice of counsel, Mathews refused the request and cited the Social Security Act's confidentiality provision (Section 186a). The subcommittee challenged Mathews and issued a subpoena for the information. On 12 November 1975, Attorney General Edward Levi advised Mathews that the confidentiality provision of the Social Security Act was not a strong enough basis for an executive branch official to withhold information requested by Congress. The provision pertained only to not making information public. Subsequently, Mathews ended the controversy by turning the requested information over to Congress.[21]

Confidential Export Reports

In the second case, on 10 July 1975, Chairman Moss requested from the Department of Commerce's director of the Office of Export Administration copies of all quarterly reports filed by exporters under the Export Administration Act of 1969.[22] Moss's subcommittee was investigating the extent to which U.S. companies had been requested by Arab countries not to do business with Israel. On 24 July 1975, the secretary of the Department of Commerce, Rogers C. B. Morton, sent Moss a summary of Israel boycott information reported by U.S. companies. Morton refused to submit the requested quarterly reports and based his authority for such a refusal on Section 7(c) of the Export Administration Act:

> No department, agency, or official exercising any functions under this Act shall publish or disclose information obtained hereunder which is deemed confidential or with reference to which a request for confidential treatment is made by the person furnishing such information, unless the head of such department or agency determines that the withholding thereof is contrary to the national interest.[23]

The subcommittee responded on 28 July 1975 by issuing a subpoena for the documents. On 4 September 1975, Attorney General Levi issued an opinion to Morton that Section 7(c) of the Export Administration Act did apply to Congress and that it was therefore proper to withhold the disputed documents. Morton appeared before the subcommittee on 22 September 1975 and informed its members of the attorney general's opinion. Morton offered to provide Congress with summaries of the information in the reports, but the subcommittee members insisted on having access to the actual reports, which contained the names of companies participating in the boycott of Israel.[24]

The subcommittee held hearings on this controversy on 11 and 12 October 1975 and heard testimony from legal scholars. On 11 November 1975, the subcommittee passed a resolution to hold Morton in contempt of Congress. The Interstate and Foreign Commerce Committee scheduled a meeting to discuss the contempt resolution, but the day before the meeting, Morton agreed to show the disputed documents to Chairman Moss, with the understanding that the information would not be made public. The committee dropped the contempt of Congress proceedings against Morton, as Congress had finally achieved the result it desired.

House Select Committee on Intelligence Subpoenas

On 6 November 1975, the House Select Committee on Intelligence, chaired by Otis Pike (D-N.Y.), served seven subpoenas on the Ford administration.[25] Five of those subpoenas were issued to the National Security Council (NSC). On 11 November 1975, Lieutenant General Brent Scowcroft, deputy assistant to the president for national security affairs, responded to the subpoenas by forwarding the available documents to the committee and promising to furnish the remaining materials when they became available. The NSC did not claim executive privilege with regard to any of the documents.

The committee issued one subpoena to the CIA. On 11 November 1975, the special counsel to the CIA, Mitchell Rogovin, responded with a letter to the committee providing the requested information. The CIA did not claim executive privilege either.

The last subpoena was issued to Secretary of State Henry Kissinger to compel disclosure of all documents pertaining to Department of State recommendations to the NSC on covert activities for the period 20 January 1965 forward. In this case, President Ford formally directed Kissinger to assert executive privilege over the documents. On 14 November 1975, the State Department legal adviser informed the committee of Ford's decision. That same day, the committee cited Kissinger for contempt and recommended that the Speaker of the House certify the report of the Select Committee as to the contumacious conduct of Henry A. Kissinger, as Secretary of State, in failing and refusing to produce certain pertinent materials in compliance with a subpoena duces tecum of said Select Committee . . . , under the seal of the House of Representatives to the United States Attorney for the District of Columbia, to the end that Henry A. Kissinger, as Secretary of State, may be proceeded against in the manner and form provided by law.[26]

In a 19 November 1975 letter to Pike, the president wrote that "in addition to disclosing highly sensitive military and foreign affairs assessments and evaluations, the documents revealed to an unacceptable degree the consultation process involving advice and recommendations to Presidents Kennedy, Johnson and Nixon, made to them directly or to committees composed of their closest aides and counselors."[27] A White House memorandum from Buchen reveals a number of bases for the assertion of executive privilege in this case. In particular, he cites *U.S. v. Nixon* and instances in the Eisenhower and Kennedy administrations of "presidential directives to Cabinet members not to release certain information to Congress."[28] Eventually the administration and Congress reached a compromise whereby committee members and staff would attend an oral briefing on the information contained in the disputed materials. The committee recommitted its report recommending a citation of contempt for Kissinger before the House of Representatives had an opportunity to vote on the measure.

Electronic Surveillance Controversy

The most controversial case of presidential withholding of information during the Ford administration occurred in 1976 and resulted in a complex series of interbranch negotiations and legal disputes over a two-year period that extended into Jimmy Carter's term of office.[29] This controversy involved the use of warrantless wiretaps on citizens for national security purposes. In brief, the FBI had sent letters to the American Telephone and Telegraph Company (AT&T) requesting that certain individuals be placed under electronic surveillance. The House Committee on Interstate and Foreign Commerce subpoenaed the letters and other documents on behalf of the Subcommittee on Oversight and Investigations. The subcommittee wanted to investigate the extent of wiretapping activity, the names of individuals subject to surveillance, whether the wiretaps truly were for national security reasons, and whether these activities were being carried out in accordance with existing laws.

The president refused to divulge the requested letters and documents, claiming national security concerns. Ford offered a compromise in which he would supply the committee with the attorney general's memoranda citing the reasons for the surveillance, as well as a sample list of surveillances with the individuals' names deleted. The subcommittee rejected the compromise, maintaining that Ford had not offered enough information to determine whether abuses had actually taken place.

AT&T decided that it should comply with the congressional subpoena and supply the requested materials to the subcommittee. The Department of Justice sued AT&T to prohibit the company from turning over the materials. Ford maintained that the company had an obligation "as an agent of the United States" not to comply with the subpoena.[30] The district court sided with Ford and enjoined AT&T from releasing the disputed materials. The district court determined that because the controversy concerned a national security matter and disclosure of the disputed materials to the subcommittee could lead to public disclosure of sensitive information, there must be deference to the executive.[31]

Subcommittee Chairman Moss appealed the case on behalf of the House of Representatives. The court of appeals rejected the district court decision to defer to the executive branch but nonetheless upheld the injunction against AT&T. The court of appeals remanded the dispute to the district court for further negotiation between the political branches.[32] When negotiations failed to resolve the dispute, the case again went to the court of appeals.[33] The appeals court still refused to side with either branch and encouraged further negotiation and compromise, suggesting procedures for the sampling of disputed materials and in camera inspection by the district court.[34] Eventually, the executive and legislative branches agreed on a procedure whereby committee counsel received certain intelligence memoranda. The committee thus achieved its goal in gaining access and subsequently determined that there had been no abuse of surveillance authority. In December 1978, both parties to the dispute agreed to dismiss the case.

In this dispute over information, the judicial branch served as a facilitator of negotiations between the political branches. The court of appeals acknowledged the executive's legitimate national security claims and the legislature's legitimate need for information in order to conduct investigations. Rather than decide completely in favor of either side, the court of appeals worked to get the two parties to compromise. Although the resolution to this controversy does not stand as an affirmation of either the executive or the legislative position, it does stand as testimony to Congress's ability to get disputed information from the executive when it is motivated to do so.

Executive Privilege in the Ford Administration

The preceding review illustrates just how sensitive an issue executive privilege became immediately after Watergate. Ford never rejected the legitimacy of that power, but, given the post-Watergate environment, he was in no position politically to vigorously defend it. Ford never issued a formal policy on his administration's use of executive privilege, and he avoided personally responding to congressional inquiries regarding his administration's policy on it. In the spirit of an open administration, Ford gave Congress unprecedented access to information about the activities of the CIA and the FBI. To the extent possible, his White House avoided using the phrase *executive privilege* and cited other legal bases for withholding information (e.g., statutory law, separation of powers doctrine). Although administration members held extensive discussions about how to handle executive privilege controversies, the president avoided taking any public position on the issue that was more specific than support in principle for the doctrine. Ford understood the nature of the post-Watergate environment and did not wish to unnecessarily stir up controversy over an issue so closely linked to the Nixon presidency as executive privilege.

JIMMY CARTER, 1977–1981

Candidate Jimmy Carter promised an open government and a fundamental change from the Nixon era, but as president, he never rejected the power of executive privilege. Nonetheless, Carter did not make much use of that constitutional power, even when circumstances appeared to justify such action. Carter never issued any formal policy on his administration's use of executive privilege, and he avoided personally responding to congressional inquiries on the subject. When his administration sought to withhold information, it generally did so without raising executive privilege as a constitutional basis for such action.

Carter's response to executive privilege was very similar to Ford's. The thirty-ninth president often avoided the phrase *executive privilege,* and his administration often couched decisions to withhold information in terms of "separation of powers" or the need to protect "free and open" exchanges within the White House. Clearly, Carter's advisers understood that because of his promise to run an open presidency, the use of executive privilege would result in substantial criticism of the administration.

An examination of the Carter administration's handling of executive privilege makes it clear that the doctrine was still controversial. As it had during the Ford years, during Carter's tenure, Congress took an aggressive posture toward gaining access to executive branch information. The Carter White House tried to protect confidentiality, keep the pledge of an open presidency, and satisfy congressional demands for information, all at the same time.

Carter's Executive Privilege "Policy"

Like his predecessor, President Carter never issued a formal memorandum or executive order specifying his administration's policy on executive privilege. A review of White House documents reveals that certain members of the Carter administration raised the subject of developing a formal policy on executive privilege on a number of occasions. Some members of Congress sent inquiries to the Carter White House requesting a commitment from the president that only he would assert executive privilege, if such a power had to be exercised at all. And certain Carter White House staffers wrote a proposed executive order on executive privilege that met congressional resistance and that the president never issued.

Carter's approach to executive privilege controversies must be considered within the context of his promise to conduct an open presidency. Although Carter believed in the presidential power of executive privilege, he exercised that authority sparingly.

In keeping with the precedent established by Moss, the chairman of the Government Information and Individual Rights Subcommittee of the House Committee on Government Operations, Richardson Preyer (D-N.C.), and the ranking minority party member, Paul N. McCloskey, Jr. (R-Calif.), wrote a letter to Carter on 13 June 1977 requesting a formal statement of policy on the use of executive privilege. The congressmen noted that Presidents Kennedy, Johnson, and Nixon had personally responded to such requests by affirming that "executive privilege can be invoked only by the president and would not be used without specific presidential approval." Preyer and McCloskey explained that a Carter deputy attorney general had already shown reluctance to turn over to the Senate Rules Committee an internal Department of Justice memorandum and had seemed confused over whether executive privilege had been invoked. The controversy, they wrote, "underscored the confusion among new administration officials about the guidelines for such a claim."[35]

Carter followed the post-Watergate precedent established by Ford—he never responded to the letter. Preyer and McCloskey nonetheless persisted in their efforts to get Carter to commit, in some manner, to an official policy limiting executive privilege to presidential use only. In May 1978, Preyer and members of his staff met with counsel to the president Robert J. Lipshutz and members of his staff to discuss a variety of issues germane to the work of the Subcommittee on Government Information and Individual Rights. Although there is no White House record of what transpired in that meeting, Lipshutz apparently told the participants that the White House policy on executive privilege was that the president must assert that authority. Preyer sought more than a verbal assurance of Carter's policy and wrote the following to Lipshutz soon after the meeting:

> I was especially encouraged to learn that it is your policy that only the president can invoke a claim of "executive privilege" and that so far this administration has been able to negotiate successfully all the disputes in regard to conflicts over requests for information between Congress and the Executive branch. Such accommodation encourages a lasting comity between co-equal branches of government.
>
> In this regard I think it would be helpful both to Congress and to the Executive branch if the president would publicly reaffirm his policy of openness. Traditionally this has taken the form of a letter to this subcommittee briefly stating the president's intention in this area.[36]

Preyer added that he planned to write another letter to Carter to reiterate his request for a policy statement on executive privilege. Nearly four months later, Preyer and McCloskey wrote to Carter:

> On June 13, 1977, this subcommittee, following a long tradition dating back to the presidency of John Kennedy, requested from you a statement of your administration's policy regarding the use of the claim of "executive privilege." Since writing we have been in contact with your Counsel, Robert F. [sic] Lipshutz, on this matter and were happy to discover that it is your practice that only the president is authorized to invoke a claim of "executive privilege." We also were pleased to ascertain that thus far your administration has been able to negotiate successfully all of the disputes between Congress and the Executive branch without the use of this concept.
>
> The members of our subcommittee, however, still believe it would be helpful if you would publicly affirm this policy. In the past this has been accomplished by a letter to the subcommittee briefly stating the president's intentions in this area. Such a public affirmation, we believe, would materially aid both the Congress and the Executive branch in its day-to-day relationships.[37]

Preyer and McCloskey received acknowledgment of their request from the assistant to the president for congressional liaison, Frank Moore.[38] The president did not respond personally and never issued any statement of policy on executive privilege.[39]

In the first year of Carter's term, there were a good many internal administration discussions and correspondences concerning the issue of executive privilege,[40] and they focused on the need to establish a formal administration policy.[41] The Office of Counsel to the President developed a draft executive order on the use of executive privilege by departmental agencies. Heads of the various executive departments then had the opportunity to respond to the proposed executive order.[42] The draft emphasized the administration's goal of cooperation with congressional requests for information, a belief in the use of executive privilege under only the most compelling circumstances, and the requirement of "specific presidential approval" for any use of executive privilege. The draft executive order stated formal procedures for the use of executive privilege.[43]

John Moss reviewed the proposed executive order and wrote to Carter urging that the directive not be issued. Moss vigorously objected that the proposed executive order would "create an imbalance" of power between the executive and legislative branches. He argued that the proposal was too broad and that it would allow certain executive branch personnel "to play a substantive role in determining the application of executive privilege to congressional requests for information."[44]

Because Carter never issued the proposed executive order and never conveyed any guidelines on how to handle executive privilege controversies, members of the administration did not know how to respond to such controversies. As late as 1979, a controversy arose over requested congressional testimony from White House staff, prompting a memorandum from Lipshutz. The memorandum made it clear that "the personal staff of the president is immune from testimonial compulsion by Congress." Lipshutz further emphasized the importance of "frank and candid discussions between the president and his personal staff."[45]

It was not until the week before election day in 1980 that the Carter administration established official procedures for the use of executive privilege. In early 1980, the new counsel to the president, Lloyd Cutler, requested an intradepartmental memorandum on the use of executive privilege. Doug Huron and Barbara Bergman of the Office of Counsel to the President produced a memorandum summarizing the history of the doctrine, legal principles, congressional enforcement mechanisms, and procedures for invocation. The memorandum stated that, under Carter, no official procedures on the use of executive privilege had been established, and the administration had adopted de facto the procedures of the Nixon administration.[46]

Because of a trade conflict with Mexico that resulted in a White House debate over how to handle certain internal documents, Cutler wrote to special trade representative Reubin Askew on 22 October 1980: "I am concerned that a uniform policy regarding assertion of executive privilege be applied throughout the Executive Office of the President." Cutler explained that presidential advisers could not waive executive privilege without presidential approval. This memorandum constituted the first official statement on executive privilege procedures in the Carter White House.[47]

Cutler further developed the procedures in a 31 October 1980 memorandum to all White House staff and heads of units within the Executive Office of the President. That memorandum established that the concurrence of the Office of Counsel to the President must be sought by those considering the use of executive privilege. The memorandum also emphasized that only the president had the authority to waive executive privilege. Cutler expressed concern that the decision by senior officials to waive executive privilege over disputed information would "significantly affect the successful assertion of privilege by other advisers to the president and by the president himself."[48] These procedures applied only to the White House staff and the heads of units within the Executive Office of the President. Consequently, Cutler wrote a memorandum that same day to the attorney general requesting some input as to whether "a similar consultation arrangement throughout the executive branch" should be adopted.[49]

Ronald Reagan's election to the presidency made moot these deliberations over developing a uniform executive privilege procedure throughout the executive branch. The discussions turned to outlining for the incoming administration "the pending matters raising executive privilege problems."[50]

Carter's Exercise of Executive Privilege

President Carter did not make extensive use of executive privilege, but he accepted the legitimacy of that presidential power and asserted it on a few occasions.

The first such case concerned the president's controversial decision not to support funding for some water dam projects but to allow other such projects to be completed. The White House refused a congressional request for access to internal White House memoranda relating to this decision on the basis that such materials are privileged. The Audubon Society then filed suit against the administration to compel release of the memoranda. The Audubon Society believed that the president had approved the completion of one dam project and the construction of another in an arbitrary fashion without the benefit of environmental impact statements. In a 30 April 1977 memorandum, Robert Lipshutz and Margaret McKenna outlined three options for the president: produce the documents, claim executive privilege, or negotiate a continuance of the lawsuit. The president approved the claim of executive privilege in this case,[51] but the claim was soon withdrawn because the Audubon Society and the Department of Interior reached an agreement that ended the litigation.[52]

The issue of executive privilege arose in White House deliberations later that year when the chairman of the Subcommittee on Commerce, Consumer, and Monetary Affairs of the House Committee on Government Operations, Benjamin S. Rosenthal (D-N.Y.), requested on 1 November 1977 access to documents relevant to the antiboycott amendments to the Export Administration Act. Secretary of Commerce Juanita M. Kreps wrote a memorandum to the president explaining that certain requested documents should be submitted to Rosenthal and other documents—considered too sensitive—should not. She noted that although executive privilege constituted the only legal ground for withholding information, "because of the connotations this term has acquired since Watergate, it is preferable for us to couch our response in other terms, such as separation of powers."[53] Kreps wrote to Rosenthal to advise him that the Department of Commerce would make certain documents available to the subcommittee and would provide only summaries of information contained in the more sensitive documents.[54] The subcommittee completed its hearings without seeing the disputed documents but—not wishing to set a precedent unfavorable to Congress—formally rejected Kreps's proposal for handling disputed documents.[55] So even though the only legal basis for withholding the documents was executive privilege, the administration resolved the dispute in its favor without asserting the controversial doctrine.

Rosenthal separately requested a broad range of documents from the Department of Treasury regarding the income tax treatment of payments made by U.S. oil companies to foreign nation-states. On 23 November 1977, Lipshutz wrote a memorandum to domestic policy adviser Stuart Eizenstat explaining the sensitive nature of the documents. Apparently, if the payments were reclassified as royalties, rather than foreign taxes, domestic oil companies would be subjected to a much higher tax liability. Lipshutz believed that public disclosure of documents regarding the possible reclassification would disrupt Middle East negotiations, possibly influence the deliberations of the Organization of Petroleum Exporting Countries, and jeopardize the administration's energy legislation.[56] Rosenthal decided not to pursue the documents while the Internal Revenue Service was in the process of advising the Department of Treasury on how to classify the payments. Rosenthal advised the White House that he might raise the access issue again after Congress reconvened the following January. Lipshutz conveyed to Carter that "the 'executive privilege' question has been finessed successfully at least for the next seven weeks."[57]

On 12 July 1978, Rosenthal requested from James Griffin, director of the Office of International Investments at the Department of Treasury, "access to all documents, records and papers relating to the Committee on Foreign Investment in the United States . . . including all letters, memoranda, minutes of meetings and all other documents . . . and to have copies of any of these materials necessary to the conduct of our investigation."[58] Because this request raised, once again, the sensitive matter of foreign investment in the United States, members of the Department of Treasury met with Rosenthal to work out a compromise on the documents. Notes from the meeting indicate that Rosenthal received most of the requested documents from Treasury, but some documents and materials were withheld, and portions of others "had been deleted for foreign policy purposes." Rosenthal refused to accept any limitation on congressional claims to executive branch information and pursued his request for all the documents.[59] Secretary of the Treasury C. Fred Bergsten wrote to Rosenthal to explain that the withheld documents concerned either communications with foreign governments or confidential policy deliberations. He stated that "discussions leading to policy formulation must be free from outside scrutiny lest the full and candid consideration of policy alternatives be harmfully chilled."[60] After a series of negotiations and reconsiderations, Rosenthal gained access to many more disputed materials and did not press claims on other documents thought to be unimportant to his subcommittee's investigation. In the end, only one document was in dispute, prompting the general counsel to the Treasury Department, Robert H. Mundheim, to recommend that, if necessary, the president approve the assertion of "a governmental privilege" if Congress subpoenaed the document.[61] But the president never used executive privilege in this case, because Congress never subpoenaed the document.

In a separate controversy in 1978, a House subcommittee issued a subpoena for disputed administration documents and cited a cabinet secretary for contempt of Congress. The Subcommittee on Oversight and Investigations of the House Committee on Interstate and Foreign Commerce sought from the Department of Health, Education, and Welfare certain documents concerning the processing methods of drug manufacturers. The Department of Justice ruled that the requested documents could not be disclosed to Congress because they contained trade secrets. The subcommittee subpoenaed the documents, and HEW Secretary Joseph A. Califano refused to comply. The subcommittee voted to cite Califano for contempt of Congress and informed the full committee of this decision. But before further action could be taken, Califano worked out a compromise agreement whereby Congress received edited versions of the disputed documents. The White House chose to refrain from asserting executive privilege in this case.[62]

In 1979, a controversy arose over whether Congress could compel testimony from personal aides to the president. Senator Harrison A. Williams (D-N.J.) had invited Sarah Weddington, the special assistant to the president, to testify at hearings on "Women in the Coming Decade" held by the Senate Human Resources Committee. Unaware of any White House prohibition against personal aides testifying on Capitol Hill, Weddington initially accepted the invitation but then canceled her scheduled appearance on 31 January 1979, on the advice of the counsel to the president.[63] The late cancellation angered Williams and prompted press inquiries into whether the White House had used executive privilege to prevent congressional testimony by White House staff. Illustrative of the sensitive nature of the issue was a news conference exhange between a reporter and Press Secretary Jody Powell. The reporter asked if executive privilege had been invoked to prevent Weddington's testimony, to which Powell replied: "Oooh, executive privilege! [Laughter.] That always scares the hell out of the White House when anybody raises executive privilege. [Laughter.] I don't know anything about the thing. I do know that historically senior advisers to the president are not compelled to appear, cannot be compelled to appear."[64]

This controversy prompted Lipshutz to request a draft of proposed guidelines on how White House staff should respond to future requests from Congress.[65] On 8 February 1979, Lipshutz issued the guidelines, which articulated the traditional arguments against compulsory congressional testimony by White House advisers (e.g., the need for "frank and candid discussions," the role of personal advisers as agents of the president). Significantly, Lipshutz did not mention executive privilege as the legal basis for preventing the testimony of White House staff but stated instead that "this immunity is grounded in the Constitutional doctrine of separation of powers."[66]

Two years before, a U.S. senator had requested a copy of draft testimony to Congress by an assistant secretary in the Department of Commerce. The draft testimony contained advice to the president that the White House did not want made public (the actual testimony differed substantially from the draft form). The president agreed to refuse to release the draft testimony to Congress, and a memorandum from Lipshutz and McKenna to Carter stated, "we hope to find a sound legal basis to answer the subpoena without using the term executive privilege."[67]

Nonetheless, in late 1980, the counsel to the president, Lloyd Cutler, wrote a letter to the chairman of the Subcommittee on Investigations of the House Committee on Armed Services, Samuel S. Stratton (D-N.Y.), to inform the congressman that the president had directed a deputy assistant to the president for national security affairs, David Aaron, not to testify before the subcommittee. Cutler's letter stated that "Congress has always respected the privilege of the president to decline requests that the president himself or his immediate White House advisers appear to testify before congressional committees."[68]

A 1980 controversy over access to administration documents illustrates the extent to which Carter sought to avoid the use of executive privilege yet considered that power a possible last resort in a battle with Congress. On 3 April 1980, Carter issued a proclamation imposing a fee on imported crude oil and gasoline.[69] Five days after this unpopular decision, the Subcommittee on the Environment, Energy, and Natural Resources of the House Committee on Government Operations requested all the Department of Energy documents relevant to Carter's decision. The department refused the request on the ground that the White House needed time to review the documents before deciding *not* to invoke executive privilege.[70] The subcommittee responded on 22 April 1980 by voting to subpoena the documents.[71] Department of Energy Secretary Charles Duncan responded the next day by forwarding to the subcommittee some of the requested documents but withholding others to protect free and open deliberations within the administration.[72] The subcommittee voted on 24 April 1980 to subpoena Duncan to appear before the subcommittee with the disputed documents.[73] Duncan appeared on 29 April 1980 but explained that he planned to continue withholding the disputed documents without resorting to the use of executive privilege. Nonetheless, he explained that executive privilege would be used as a last resort, if necessary.[74] The subcommittee voted to hold Duncan in contempt of Congress.[75] The controversy was effectively ended on 13 May 1980 when a district court voided Carter's proclamation, and on the following day, the administration agreed to the subcommittee's offer to review the documents in executive session.[76]

Executive Privilege in the Carter Administration

Following the lead of his predecessor, Gerald R. Ford, Jimmy Carter never issued a formal presidential directive defining his administration's policy toward the use of executive privilege. It was not until near election day 1980 that the counsel to the president issued a set of procedures on the use of executive privilege to White House staff and the heads of units within the Executive Office of the President.

Also in the spirit of the Ford administration, the Carter administration tried, to the extent possible, to avoid the use of executive privilege while still defending the presidential right to withhold information through other sources of authority. White House memoranda reveal that, because of the taint of Watergate, the administration tried to avoid using the phrase *executive privilege* and made concerted efforts to accommodate requests for information without resorting to executive privilege, even when there appeared to be a compelling reason for withholding information. Nowhere in the White House files does any member of the Carter administration suggest that executive privilege should be avoided because its constitutionality is dubious. Carter officials accepted the legitimacy of that presidential power but sought, to the extent possible, to avoid its use—or at least to avoid the use of the phrase—for what they perceived to be politically necessary reasons.

5

THE POST-WATERGATE YEARS II:
RONALD REAGAN, GEORGE H. W. BUSH,
AND THE ERA OF DIVIDED GOVERNMENT

Although Presidents Ford and Carter pledged to conduct open administrations, neither of these chief executives rejected the legitimacy of executive privilege. Both of them sought to avoid informational disputes while protecting presidential secrecy. Their successors—Ronald Reagan and George H. W. Bush—were somewhat more aggressive at pursuing governmental secrecy, although not successful at reestablishing the credibility of executive privilege.

RONALD REAGAN, 1981–1989

To its partisans, the Reagan administration brought about a revival of effective presidential leadership after a sequence of failed presidencies. According to this view, Reagan refuted the political science theories of the "imperiled" presidency and restored workable, active leadership to the executive branch.

In contrast, Reagan's critics maintain that his administration abused power and sacrificed substantive accomplishment for the image of leadership. From this perspective, Reagan's notion of leadership is one in which little credence is given to the legitimate interests of the coordinate branches or of private citizens.

Central to this debate on the Reagan legacy is the controversy over executive branch secrecy. Reagan's partisan defenders and critics alike can certainly agree that his presidency differed substantially on issues of governmental secrecy from the "open" presidencies of Gerald Ford and Jimmy Carter, who mistakenly assumed that, after the Watergate scandal, a policy of openness best suited the demands of presidential leadership. Reagan perhaps better understood that information control, not openness, enhances presidential power.

The Reagan years provide telling commentary on just how far executive privilege had fallen into disrepute and, hence, disuse. The Reagan administration—accused by many critics of being prone to secrecy and deception—showed great reluctance to fully exercise executive privilege. When the administration did invoke the privilege on a few occasions, it eventually backed down in the face of congressional citations for contempt and threats to delay confirmation proceedings. Unsure of his own authority in this area, President Reagan—who had championed proposals for unprecedented strict classification of information, cumbersome impediments on Freedom of Information Act (FOIA) requests, lie detector tests for potential leakers, lifetime censorship for more than 100,000 current and former government employees, and numerous other forms of information control—waived executive privilege for all administration officials called to testify at the Iran-contra hearings and refused advice to assert executive privilege over his personal diaries.

The Reagan administration experience reveals two important facts about executive privilege. First, executive privilege lacks the political support necessary to withstand most congressional demands for information. That is, it lacks support in Congress, so much so that members of the legislature are often unrestrained in their efforts to seek compliance with requests for information. Most of the modern presidents have displayed little will to battle Congress over executive privilege. Furthermore, it is now inherently difficult for presidents who challenge congressional demands for information to make a persuasive public case for governmental secrecy, especially given the media's natural bias in favor of complete openness. A legitimate presidential power has become a victim of the post-Watergate trend toward greater impediments on the chief executive's authority. Second, Congress clearly has the means by which to compel executive disclosure of information. Any attempt to provide a statutory definition of executive privilege, as a way of limiting this presidential power, would be frivolous. As the Reagan experience so clearly demonstrates, the traditional separation of powers system provides Congress all the necessary means by which to combat executive privilege claims.

Reagan's Executive Privilege Policy

Reagan's predecessors, Carter and Ford, did not officially change the policy toward executive privilege set out in Richard Nixon's 24 March 1969 memorandum to department heads. On 4 November 1982, President Reagan issued a redraft of the Nixon memorandum to the heads of executive departments and agencies. Reagan's "Procedures Governing Responses to Congressional Requests for Information" did not fundamentally change the Nixon guidelines.

The Reagan guidelines stated the administration's policy of "comply[ing] with congressional requests for information to the fullest extent consistent with the constitutional and statutory obligations of the executive branch." The memorandum upheld the need for "confidentiality of some communications" and added that executive privilege would be used "only in the most compelling circumstances, and only after careful review demonstrates that assertion of the privilege is necessary." The memorandum emphasized the importance of negotiating with Congress to settle any differences of opinion between the branches and assured that "executive privilege shall not be invoked without specific presidential authorization."

The Reagan memorandum asserted that there are "legitimate and appropriate" uses of executive privilege and established procedures to be followed by agencies in cases of congressional requests for confidential or sensitive information. Under those procedures, congressional requests for information would be complied with unless "compliance raises a substantial question of executive privilege." Such a question would be raised if the information "might significantly impair the national security (including the conduct of foreign relations), the deliberative process of the executive branch or other aspects of the performance of the executive branch's constitutional duties." If a department head believed that a congressional request for information might concern privileged information, he or she would notify and consult with the attorney general and the counsel to the president. The department head, attorney general, and counsel to the president would then decide whether to release the information to Congress or to submit the matter to the president for a decision (the matter went to the president if any one of the three believed that an invocation of executive privilege was necessary). At that stage, the department head would request that Congress await a presidential decision before taking any additional action. If the president chose to use executive privilege, he would instruct the department head to inform Congress "that the claim of executive privilege is being made with the specific approval of the president."[1]

The Reagan memorandum allowed for the protection of various forms of executive branch information, even if that information originated from staff levels far removed from the president. Nonetheless, under Reagan's procedures, the president himself had to approve the use of executive privilege. The Reagan memorandum states more clearly than the 1969 Nixon memorandum the purposes for which executive privilege might be invoked.

The fact that Reagan issued such a memorandum—when Presidents Ford and Carter avoided doing so—is itself a measure of the importance his administration attached to the need for secrecy in certain executive branch activities. The Reagan administration adopted a number of measures to enhance secrecy in government, but it did not vigorously employ or defend executive privilege.

Executive Branch Secrecy under Reagan

Given the administration's expansive efforts to promote secrecy, its inability to make a sustained case for a broad executive privilege power stands out. For example, in issuing Executive Order 12356 in 1982, President Reagan became the first chief executive in four decades to mandate tighter access to information and more classification. Whereas President Carter had mandated (in Executive Order 12065) that there be a balancing test to weigh security interests against the public need to know when classifying documents, Reagan ensured that all such questions would be resolved in favor of secrecy. Reagan's executive order eliminated the requirement that "identifiable damage" to security interests be demonstrated before restricting materials. It also extended the classification period, eliminated automatic declassification of documents after a specified period, and authorized executive branch agencies to reclassify previously declassified documents.[2]

Reagan issued National Security Directive 84 on 11 March 1983 as an addendum to Executive Order 12356. To promote security interests, this directive "imposed prior lifetime censorship, secrecy pledges, and lie-detector tests on *any* government employee with access to classified information."[3] Due to widespread controversy and congressional reaction, the president suspended, but did not withdraw, the requirements for lifetime prior censorship and the use of lie detector tests.[4] Nonetheless, in November 1985, Reagan issued an order authorizing lie detector tests for thousands of government employees dealing with sensitive materials. The order appeared to include cabinet officers, leading Secretary of State George P. Shultz to threaten to resign if forced to take a lie detector test. "The minute in this government I am told that I'm not trusted is the day I leave."[5] Also, more than 120,000 government employees—outside of the Central Intelligence Agency (CIA) and the National Security Administration—had already signed lifetime censorship agreements under a 1981 nondisclosure requirement (Form 4193).[6]

Reagan's Executive Order 12333 authorized domestic surveillance by the CIA.[7] Early in Reagan's term, the CIA ended the long-standing practice of providing background information briefings on intelligence matters to reporters.[8] A Reagan executive order in December 1981 provided a definition of "special activities" that enhanced the CIA's role in pursuing covert operations and made congressional oversight more difficult.[9] The president also promoted and signed into law in October 1984 legislation permitting the CIA director to close "operational files" from public scrutiny under the FOIA, thus creating a new exemption from that act.[10]

One of the most controversial information control efforts by Reagan involved an effort to stop leaks of classified information. On 12 January 1982, Reagan spokesman David Gergen held a briefing for reporters in which he delivered and explained the following presidential statement:

> Unauthorized disclosure of classified information under the jurisdiction of the National Security Council and of classified intelligence reports is a problem of major proportions within the U.S. Government. The Constitution of the United States provides for the protection of individual rights and liberties, including freedom of speech and freedom of the press, but it also requires that Government functions be discharged efficiently and effectively, especially where the national security is involved. As President of the United States, I am responsible for honoring both constitutional requirements, and I intend to do so in a balanced and careful manner. I do not believe, however, that the Constitution entitles Government employees, entrusted with confidential information critical to the functioning and effectiveness of the Government, to disclose such information with impunity. Yet this is precisely the situation we have. It must not be allowed to continue.[11]

As Stephen Hess reported, the presidential statement then specified new policies. For example, "'all contacts' with reporters in which classified information was to be discussed would require the 'advance, approval of a senior official' and must be followed by a memorandum outlining 'all information provided to the media representatives.' Fewer officials would have access to intelligence documents." The administration would also investigate unauthorized disclosures to determine the sources of national security leaks.[12]

Because of a severely negative press reaction, National Security Adviser William Clark issued new procedures on 2 February 1982, superseding the 12 January presidential order.[13] In effect, the more controversial elements of the order—controls on interviews, investigation of leaks by "all legal methods"—were deleted. Nonetheless, the incident further revealed the extent to which the Reagan administration wanted to control access to information.

Other secrecy measures included the Intelligence Identities Protection Act of 1982, which prohibited intentional disclosure of the identities of covert agents and specified punishment for offenders.[14] The administration imposed costs on FOIA requests, in part to discourage such requests. The fees could be waived only if the request clearly met a "public interest" standard based on several qualifying criteria.[15] The administration sought to exempt certain materials from FOIA requests by maintaining that the Privacy Act of 1974 precluded the release of those materials.[16]

The administration's invasion of Grenada resulted in widespread criticism of excessive secrecy. During the early stages of the invasion, journalists could move only as close as Barbados—160 miles northeast of Grenada. Two days passed before the military escorted a group of journalists to Grenada. Reporters fumed that they had been "left in the dark" and denied due access to the military action.[17] The administration credibly argued that it did not want to endanger the military operation or the lives of journalists by escorting reporters to the attack. Critics of the policy maintained that the administration actually intended to cover up embarrassing information about the operation.

In the view of leading journalists, the Reagan administration went to unprecedented lengths to maintain and promote secrecy about its actions. *Newsday* managing editor Anthony Marro wrote that Reagan's administration went "well beyond other recent administrations in its attempts to bottle up information, to prevent public access to government officials and records, to threaten and intimidate the bureaucracy in order to dry up sources of information, and to prevent the press and public from learning how the government is functioning."[18] *Los Angeles Times* Washington bureau chief Jack Nelson complained that Reagan had "set a policy and tone for secrecy in government that exceeds anything since Watergate. In fact, not even during the Nixon years were so many steps taken to establish secrecy as government policy."[19]

Despite a penchant for secrecy, the administration never made a strong case for executive privilege. In an administration that showed no reluctance to control information, the lack of a strong stand on, or defense of, executive privilege is telling. Four cases of executive privilege in the Reagan administration demonstrate why this constitutional doctrine fared so poorly even during the Reagan years.

Four Cases of Executive Privilege

The Department of the Interior and the Mineral Lands Leasing Act, 1981–1982

The first significant executive privilege controversy during the Reagan administration occurred in the president's first year in office and put Interior Secretary James G. Watt in the national spotlight.[20] In 1981, the Subcommittee on Oversight and Investigations of the House Committee on Energy and Commerce was investigating the Mineral Lands Leasing Act because of a significant number of takeovers of American companies by foreign interests. The cabinet secretary responsible for implementation of the act had control over the documents sought by the subcommittee. Secretary Watt determined that thirty-one requested documents contained sensitive information and refused to supply them to Congress. The subcommittee responded with a subpoena on 28 September 1981, raising the stakes of the conflict.

The president requested the opinion of Attorney General William French Smith regarding the executive's right to withhold the contested documents. A 13 October 1981 letter from the attorney general to the president cited the necessity of an assertion of executive privilege over the documents. The attorney general offered a standard defense of executive privilege based on the need to protect White House confidentiality and national interests. The letter stated the following: "All of the documents at issue are either necessary and fundamental to the deliberative process presently ongoing in the Executive Branch or relate to sensitive foreign policy considerations."[21] Smith emphasized that internal staff discussions about unsettled issues would be compromised by public release of the documents. Furthermore, the documents contained the views of Canadian government officials expressed in confidence. Smith cited the landmark *U.S. v. Nixon* case as supportive of a claim of executive privilege in this instance. He concluded that "release of these documents would seriously impair the deliberative process and the conduct of foreign policy. There is, therefore, a strong public interest in withholding the documents from congressional scrutiny at this time."[22]

Smith's opinion went beyond a defense of executive privilege based on mere confidentiality and national interest concerns. He maintained that by demanding confidential documents, members of Congress were trying to become participants in executive branch decision-making processes. Perhaps more provocatively, Smith alleged that Congress lacked a strong interest in executive branch information when it was requested merely for investigative purposes:

> The interest of Congress in obtaining information for oversight purposes is, I believe, considerably weaker than its interest when specific legislative proposals are in question. . . . [T]he congressional oversight interest will support a demand for predecisional, deliberative documents in the possession of the Executive Branch only in the most unusual circumstances.[23]

The next day, 14 October, Watt appeared before the subcommittee and submitted a memorandum from the president asserting executive privilege over the thirty-one contested documents. Watt also furnished the subcommittee with a copy of the attorney general's opinion. The interior secretary refused to answer subcommittee members' questions about matters pertaining to the documents. The president refused a subsequent request to release the documents.

The subcommittee did not accept the claim of executive privilege as valid. It solicited and received an opinion of the general counsel to the clerk of the House refuting the attorney general's legal opinion on executive privilege.[24] On 9 February 1982, the subcommittee voted to hold Watt in contempt and referred the conflict to the full committee. On 25 February 1982, the Committee on Energy and Commerce passed a resolution recommending that Watt be cited by the full House for contempt of Congress.

At this stage, the administration had to weigh the importance of protecting the documents against the likelihood of a House citation for contempt and further executive-legislative feuding over the matter. The administration decided to resolve the issue in Congress's favor and on 18 March 1982 made the contested documents available to the subcommittee for review. On 15 September 1982, the Committee on Energy and Commerce unanimously voted not to bring the contempt citation to the full House.

Having made a strong initial case for executive privilege, the administration backed down when pushed by Congress. Despite its claim that confidentiality and national interests were at stake, the administration decided to accommodate the legislature. The Justice Department did not take part in the negotiations resulting in the settlement. Assistant Attorney General Theodore Olson, who had written to the committee chair expressing the administration's position and had appeared with Watt before the subcommittee on 14 October 1981, opposed the settlement terms.[25] The Reagan administration decided to make a short-term political accommodation rather than to defend executive privilege.

The Environmental Protection Agency and Superfund, 1982–1983

The most contentious debate over executive privilege in the Reagan administration concerned the refusal of the Environmental Protection Agency (EPA) to release to Congress certain documents pertaining to the enforcement of hazardous waste laws (particularly Superfund cleanup regulations).[26] Once again, the Oversight and Investigations Subcommittee of the House Committee on Energy and Commerce played a central role in the controversy. In 1982, that subcommittee was investigating the agency's implementation of hazardous waste laws and had become frustrated by delays and nonresponses when requesting data on EPA efforts.

The Subcommittee on Investigations and Oversight of the House Public Works and Transportation Committee had experienced similar difficulties in its own examination of EPA enforcement of hazardous waste laws. A pattern developed whereby the EPA released some requested documents and the Justice Department forbade the release of others. The Justice Department asserted that its duty was to protect the administration from undesired disclosure of sensitive materials by individual agencies. In this case, the Justice Department maintained that law enforcement efforts could be undermined by public disclosure of "enforcement-sensitive" documents, and the department did not want the EPA alone to determine which documents met the criterion of "enforcement-sensitive."

On 21 October 1982, the chair of the House Committee on Energy and Commerce, John Dingell (D-Mich.), issued a subpoena to EPA Administrator Anne Gorsuch,[27] directing her to appear before the committee with certain documents. The second investigating subcommittee, chaired by Elliot Levitas (D-Ga.), subpoenaed Gorsuch on 22 November 1982 to obtain withheld documents.

Despite Gorsuch's protests, the Justice Department urged the president to assert executive privilege over the documents. White House counsel Fred Fielding assured Gorsuch that, unlike in the Watt controversy, the administration would stand solidly behind this claim of executive privilege.

On 30 November 1982, President Reagan sent the EPA a memorandum with an attached copy of a letter to Dingell from the attorney general "setting forth the historic position of the Executive Branch, with which I concur, that sensitive documents found in open law enforcement files should not be made available to Congress or the public except in extraordinary circumstances." The president instructed Gorsuch and her colleagues "not to furnish copies of this category of documents to the Subcommittees in response to their subpoenas."[28]

That same day, the attorney general issued a response to the two subcommittee chairs defending the administration's assertion of executive privilege. In this case, the attorney general did not cite traditional national security or foreign policy concerns as justification for executive privilege. Instead, he emphasized the sensitive nature of "internal deliberations" and the need to keep secret "prosecutorial strategy."[29] The letter also specified the president's official policy toward executive privilege that had been issued on 4 November 1982.[30]

On 2 December 1982, Gorsuch appeared before the Levitas subcommittee and conveyed the president's insistence on asserting executive privilege. The subcommittee responded by voting Gorsuch in contempt. On 10 December 1982, the House Public Works Committee also voted to hold her in contempt. On 16 December 1982, the House of Representatives voted 259–105 to find Gorsuch in contempt of Congress. Within a few moments of that vote, the Justice Department filed suit against the House of Representatives.[31] The U.S. district attorney would not, as specified in the contempt statute, "bring the matter before the grand jury for their action" while the suit against the House was pending.[32]

On 3 February 1983, the district court of the District of Columbia granted the defendants' motion to dismiss the suit. In so doing, the court encouraged the two branches "to settle their differences without further judicial involvement."[33] The court did not address the claim of executive privilege but explained that "if these two co-equal branches maintain their present adversarial positions, the Judicial Branch will be required to resolve the dispute by determining the validity of the Administrator's claim of executive privilege."[34]

Two weeks after the dismissal of the suit, the administration struck a bargain with the Levitas subcommittee, agreeing to allow limited disclosure of certain documents. Gorsuch advocated full disclosure, but the White House disagreed. Dingell did not consider the Levitas agreement acceptable and continued to press for full disclosure of the disputed documents. On 1 March 1982, Dingell wrote a strongly worded letter to the president requesting full disclosure and emphasizing that the investigation would continue until the White House released the disputed documents.

As in the Watt case, in an effort to put the controversy to rest, the White House accepted a compromise to release the disputed documents. On 9 March 1983, Gorsuch resigned her position as EPA administrator, and the White House agreed to release its documents to the Dingell committee in a much less limited form than anticipated by the agreement with the Levitas subcommittee. The U.S. attorney presented the Gorsuch contempt citation to a grand jury, which unanimously decided not to indict her.

Although the administration initially took a strong stand on executive privilege, it backed down in the face of mounting political pressure. But the decision to compromise did not settle the executive privilege controversy. The House Committee on the Judiciary investigated the Justice Department's role in the controversy and concluded that it had misused executive privilege by advocating the withholding of documents that had not been thoroughly reviewed.[35] The committee also alleged that the Justice Department withheld documents to cover up wrongdoing at the EPA.[36] The administration's compromise served as a temporary political expedient that eventually allowed Congress to examine previously withheld documents and draw broader conclusions about the exercise of executive privilege. Reagan may have won a temporary reprieve from political pressures, but he lost ground in his effort to establish the viability of executive privilege.

The Rehnquist Memoranda, 1986

On 17 June 1986, President Reagan nominated Associate Justice of the Supreme Court William H. Rehnquist to replace retiring Chief Justice Warren Burger.[37] Reagan also nominated federal appeals court judge Antonin

Scalia to fill the associate justice position opened up by Rehnquist's move to chief justice.

Although he was eventually confirmed by the Senate, Rehnquist's nomination was controversial. Members of the Senate Judiciary Committee requested Justice Department documents that Rehnquist had written as head of the Nixon administration's Office of Legal Counsel. Rehnquist had no objection to his earlier memos being made available to the Judiciary Committee, but the Justice Department refused to turn them over, and President Reagan invoked executive privilege to protect the documents, which contained confidential legal advice.

With a Republican-controlled Senate, the administration may have felt safe invoking executive privilege in this case. Unfortunately for Reagan, a majority of the Judiciary Committee—eight Democrats and two Republicans—said that they wanted to review the contested documents. It became apparent that the committee had the votes to subpoena the documents and even to delay the Rehnquist and Scalia confirmation proceedings. Members of the Justice Department disagreed on which course of action to follow. Some advocated battling the Judiciary Committee all the way to the judicial branch; others urged accommodation.

After several days of negotiations, the president waived his claim of executive privilege over the documents. The Justice Department and Judiciary Committee agreed on an arrangement in which certain documents would be reviewed by selected senators and staff members. Although the president had again backed away from an executive privilege claim, in this case, he was able to ensure that a fairly narrow range of documents would be made available rather than a comprehensive set of documents from Rehnquist's tenure at the Nixon Justice Department. Judiciary Committee Democrats boasted that they had secured access to the most critical documents, and the Justice Department spokesman also claimed victory for having limited the senators' access to only certain documents.

The controversy ended when senators expressed satisfaction that the Rehnquist memos contained no damaging information that would undermine his confirmation. Reagan may have weakened his claim to executive privilege by turning over specific documents, but he understood the implications of not giving in to the senators opposing his claim: a potentially serious threat to the Rehnquist and Scalia confirmations, as well as another congressional subpoena of executive branch documents.

The President's Diaries, 1987

Although some critics of the Reagan presidency went so far as to compare the Iran-contra controversy to the Watergate scandal, a major difference in the presidential handling of these crises deserves to be acknowledged: whereas President Nixon conspired in a cover-up of executive branch wrongdoing, President Reagan mostly cooperated with the congressional investigation.[38] In all, the Reagan administration furnished over 300,000 White House, State Department, Defense Department, CIA, and Justice Department documents to Congress. The investigating committees deposed numerous executive branch officials, and the president waived executive privilege for those officials who testified before Congress.[39] The president vowed to cooperate fully with the investigations when he stated, "I recognize fully the interest of Congress in this matter and the fact that in performing its important oversight and legislative role, Congress will want to inquire into what occurred. We will cooperate with these inquiries."[40]

The issue of executive privilege surfaced nonetheless when Chief of Staff Donald Regan revealed before the Senate Select Committee on Intelligence that the president kept personal diaries, primarily for the purpose of aiding the writing of his memoirs later on. Committee members raised the issue of access to the diaries, which contained some recollections of the Iran-contra affair. Regan protested that the president's diaries were purely personal and thus not subject to disclosure. Initially, the White House also took the position that a president's diaries were personal and that disclosure of them "would infringe on the privacy of the president and others."[41]

A battle over executive privilege appeared imminent. Senator George Mitchell (D-Maine) declared the privacy issue irrelevant. "The decision ought not to be whether they are personal or not, but . . . whether they are relevant to our investigation, whether they shed light on answers to questions the committee wants."[42]

Assistant Attorney General William Bradford Reynolds offered a strong defense of executive privilege, arguing that acquiescence to congressional demands for information is tantamount to "near abdication" of the executive's constitutional powers.[43] Because Reynolds's comments were made during the controversy over Reagan's diaries, this led to speculation about how the administration would resolve the controversy. Clearly, many members of the Reagan administration had urged the president to take an affirmative stand on executive privilege over his personal diaries.

On 2 February 1987, White House spokesman Marlin Fitzwater said that Reagan's notes were "very personal in nature," leading the White House to favor nondisclosure.[44] "There is a concern for invasion of the president's privacy and the privacy of others," Fitzwater explained. He added that the White House counsel and special counsel had determined that Reagan's notes were not relevant to the congressional inquiries. Soon after making these comments, Fitzwater learned that the president had decided not to assert executive privilege over his diaries. In his second statement, Fitzwater emphasized the White House position of full cooperation with the investigation and added that "the president wants to get to the bottom of the matter and fix what went wrong."[45]

Perhaps no action by Reagan did more to harm the constitutional doctrine of executive privilege than establishing the precedent of turning over his personal diaries. If such materials are not entitled to protection, it is hard to imagine executive privilege being accepted for anything but the most compelling national security information. Even if Congress had subpoenaed the diaries, the courts most likely would have upheld the president's claim of privilege. Although *U.S. v. Nixon* made it clear that a president must supply subpoenaed evidence in a criminal investigation, the law makes no such absolute claim for congressional subpoenas. In this case, as well as the earlier ones, Reagan chose not to defend his prerogatives and instead sought the most expedient solution to his immediate political problems.

Executive Privilege in the Reagan Administration

Although Reagan invoked executive privilege on several occasions, he never fully exercised that power. When confronted by congressional demands for information, he generally followed a pattern of initial resistance followed by accommodation of the request. Reagan never made a concerted effort to defend his prerogative in this area. As a result, he further weakened a constitutional presidential power that had already lost stature because of Watergate. Because of Nixon's use of executive privilege to cover up White House wrongdoing, subsequent efforts to invoke that doctrine became suspect. Consequently, even an administration that went to great lengths to establish secrecy measures was reluctant to make a strong case for executive privilege.

The Reagan experiences also show that any effort to adopt a statutory definition of or limitation on executive privilege would be frivolous. Limitations on the exercise of that power are provided in the traditional separation of powers doctrine, in which each branch employs whatever powers it has to resist encroachments by the other branches. Congress has many means by which it can resist the exercise of executive privilege. For example, it can issue subpoenas, delay confirmation hearings, withhold support for administration programs, issue contempt citations, and even try to impeach the president. As the Reagan examples show, when Congress feels strongly about the disclosure of executive branch information, it can force the president into a very difficult situation.

The president, of course, has the option of further resisting Congress's demands. He can even allow the dispute to rise to the level of a constitutional crisis to be decided at the judicial level. Reagan did not do that. He sought accommodations with Congress that would resolve his short-term political problems. A more vigorous defense of the constitutional doctrine of executive privilege would have to await another presidency.

GEORGE H. W. BUSH, 1989–1993

George Bush's presidency provides an important contrast to Ronald Reagan's. Despite his experience as Reagan's two-term vice president, Bush brought a different leadership style to the White House. Whereas Reagan effectively articulated a philosophy of governance that provided some degree of coherence to his various programs, Bush expressed discomfort with what he called the "vision thing" and never clearly defined his administration's policy goals. Whereas Reagan was content to leave the details of governance to others, Bush practiced a more hands-on approach to presidential leadership. Furthermore, whereas Reagan came to the Oval Office as an outsider committed to change, Bush was the consummate Washington insider who sought to work within the system.

These differences in leadership style had important implications for how each administration tried to manage controversies over executive privilege. Reagan presented a formal memorandum outlining his administration's policy toward executive privilege. When controversies over executive privilege arose, his administration responded by articulating constitutional principles regarding the prerogatives of the presidency. But in the face of opposition from Congress as well as media criticism, Reagan backed down from his principled stands.

By contrast, Bush never issued a formal policy on executive privilege and made no concerted effort to articulate constitutional principles as the bases for his actions. Bush's response to executive privilege controversies was never dogmatic. His response tended to be bureaucratic: find some way to work around the problem without raising the level of conflict. Bush consequently had more success at withholding information than did his predecessor.

Bush's Executive Privilege Policy

The Bush administration never adopted its own formal policy on executive privilege. Instead, the 4 November 1982 Reagan memorandum on executive privilege remained in effect as the official Bush administration procedure. The Bush approach to executive privilege differed substantially from Reagan's, however. Whereas the Reagan administration boldly proclaimed its constitutional prerogative to assert executive privilege and then had to back down in the face of congressional and popular opposition, the Bush administration adopted a much more politically feasible strategy. In theory, Bush maintained the Reagan policy of requiring the president to personally approve the use of executive privilege, but in fact, his administration withheld information from Congress on many occasions without invoking executive privilege—in effect, without calling attention to the controversial doctrine. In brief, Bush's strategy was to further the cause of withholding information by *not* invoking executive privilege.

Perhaps there is no stronger indication of how far the doctrine of executive privilege has fallen into political disrepute than the Bush administration's efforts to secure all the benefits of governmental secrecy without making a case for this presidential power. Bush understood that drawing too much attention to the controversial doctrine would have the same effect his predecessor had experienced: public confrontations with Congress, congressional contempt citations, and critical media coverage of executive branch secrecy.

On many occasions, rather than invoke executive privilege, the Bush administration used other names for justifying the withholding of information or cited some other source of authority for doing so. Among the phrases and justifications used to defend the withholding of information were "deliberative process privilege," "attorney-client privilege," "attorney work product," "internal departmental deliberations," "deliberations of another agency," "secret opinions policy," "sensitive law enforcement materials," and "ongoing criminal investigations." These phrases and justifications are not all original to the Bush administration. Numerous administrations have, for example, withheld documents pertaining to "ongoing criminal investigations" in the Department of Justice without specifically citing executive privilege. What is telling is the extent to which the Bush administration cloaked the use of executive privilege under different names. As the chief investigator for the House Committee on the Judiciary, Jim Lewin, explained, "Bush was more clever than Reagan when it came to executive privilege. You have to remember that Bush really was our first bureaucrat president. He knew how to work the system. He avoided formally claiming executive privilege and instead called it other things. In reality, executive privilege was in full force and effect during the Bush years, probably more so than under Reagan."[46]

The Bush administration further downplayed, and hence weakened, executive privilege by failing to openly articulate or defend any constitutional arguments for its exercise. Bush was content to effectively concede the constitutional issues over executive privilege to its opponents to achieve his short-term political goal of avoiding constitutional conflict while at the same time blocking congressional committees and the public from attaining certain information.

None of this suggests that Bush did not believe in or never personally invoked executive privilege. On a few occasions, Bush resorted to executive privilege when no other option was available to achieve the purpose of withholding information.

Bush's Exercise of Executive Privilege

In keeping with the practice since the Kennedy administration, the chair and the ranking minority member of a subcommittee of the House Committee on Government Operations wrote to Bush to request a statement of the administration's policy on executive privilege.[47] The White House responded by acknowledging the letter ("You may rest assured that your letter is receiving our close attention") and then ignoring the request.[48]

In June 1989, Assistant Attorney General William P. Barr wrote a memorandum describing executive privilege procedures. In addition to describing the operative procedures from the 1982 Reagan memorandum, Barr elaborated certain principles that expanded the Bush administration's potential exercise of executive privilege. For example, Barr determined that an actual use of executive privilege in a dispute with Congress would not occur except in the case of "a lawful subpoena." Therefore, the limits on a president's powers under the principle of executive privilege did not apply to congressional requests for information when no lawful subpoena was issued.[49] That being the case, it is hardly surprising that the Bush administration exercised expansive secrecy powers without much direct use of executive privilege. Furthermore, Barr restated the dubious position first elaborated by Attorney General William French Smith that Congress's interest in getting access to executive branch information for oversight is weaker than in the case of lawmaking.[50]

Although President Bush never established his own formal procedures for using executive privilege, a number of controversies during his presidency bring to light how his administration exercised that power in a crafty, even underhanded, fashion.

The Kmiec Memo, 1989

The first executive privilege statement by the Bush administration did not involve the president and did not result in any substantive policy decision. On 24 March 1989, the assistant attorney general in the Department of Justice's Office of Legal Counsel, Douglas M. Kmiec, issued a memorandum proclaiming that under the doctine of executive privilege, inspectors general are not obligated to provide to Congress "confidential information about an open criminal investigation."[51] Oddly enough, Kmiec did not issue the memorandum in reaction to any specific controversy between the Bush administration and Congress, and nobody from the Bush administration had requested the opinion. In fact, Kmiec offered the opinion as a response to a 3 June 1987 Reagan administration inquiry into how inspectors general should respond to congressional demands for information.[52] It is unclear why Kmiec—who held his position in both the Reagan and the Bush administrations—waited almost two years to respond to the inquiry, after a change in administrations.

The Kmiec memo provided a brief historical justification for the doctrine of executive privilege and stated that "Congress has a limited interest in the conduct of an ongoing criminal investigation and the executive branch has a strong interest in preserving the confidentiality of such investigations. Accordingly, in light of established executive branch policy and practice, and absent extraordinary circumstances, an IG should not provide Congress with confidential information concerning an open criminal investigation."[53]

In terms of influencing Bush administration use of executive privilege, the Kmiec memo amounted to nothing. The general counsel to the clerk of the House, Steven R. Ross, and the deputy general counsel, Charles Tiefer, responded that congressional committees did indeed have the "authority to obtain information on agency waste, fraud, and wrongdoing, from Inspectors General as from other agency officers. The Kmiec memo represents a gratuitous and unjustified break with a clear historic tradition and attempts to put aside explicit statutory language. It should [be] regarded as simply an error."[54] As Tiefer later explained, the Kmiec memo represented nothing more than an "abstract statement" that had no bearing on official policy or administration action. Indeed, during the Bush years, Congress met no resistance from inspectors general in its various requests for information.[55]

The Reagan Diaries, 1990

The Bush administration asserted executive privilege over the personal diaries of Ronald Reagan when former national security adviser John M.

Poindexter sought access to portions of them for use in his Iran-contra trial.[56] Poindexter was attempting to substantiate the claim that Reagan had authorized certain activities in the Iran-contra affair.

On 30 January 1990, federal district court judge Harold H. Greene ordered Reagan to turn over to Poindexter excerpts from the former president's diaries. Reagan's attorneys had been attempting since November 1989 to persuade Greene to cancel a subpoena for the diaries. Greene instead ordered that the diary excerpts be released and gave Reagan's attorneys until 5 February 1990 to challenge that decision with an assertion of executive privilege. Greene had privately reviewed the excerpts and determined "that some but not all the diary entries produced in response to various subpoena categories are relevant to defendant's claim."[57]

On 2 February 1990, the Department of Justice moved in federal court to delay the order that Reagan's diary excerpts be produced for Poindexter's trial. The objective was to keep Reagan's attorneys from having to assert executive privilege. The Justice Department maintained that the court order could become a "significant intrusion into what are probably a president's most personal records," possibly resulting in a "serious constitutional confrontation."[58]

The tactic failed, and on 5 February 1990, Reagan asserted executive privilege over the diaries. In the attorney's brief for Reagan, the former president's lawyer, Theodore B. Olson, wrote that "these materials are the private reflections of the former president prepared for his personal deliberations and touch the core of the presidency."[59] The former president's spokesman maintained that Reagan had decided to invoke executive privilege to protect the privacy of future presidents.[60] In his formal motion to invoke executive privilege, Reagan maintained that he had no other choice, because Judge Greene had refused to disclose Poindexter's written statements of why the diary excerpts were important to the case unless the former president claimed executive privilege.[61] Greene maintained that such a claim of executive privilege would require him to reexamine his earlier decision to compel release of the diary excerpts. In other words, Greene would have to determine whether the need for the excerpts in the trial must override any claim of executive privilege. The Bush administration followed by issuing its own claim of executive privilege over Reagan's diaries.

To further complicate the controversy, Judge Greene separately ordered Reagan to provide videotaped testimony in the Poindexter trial. He gave the former president until 9 February 1990 to decide whether to assert executive privilege and refuse to testify. On that date, Reagan agreed to provide the videotaped testimony. That same day, the Department of Justice waived its claim of executive privilege so that Reagan could present his testimony. Nonetheless, Judge Greene agreed to allow Reagan's attorneys and Bush administration lawyers to accompany the former president and advise him when to refuse to answer questions on the grounds of executive privilege. Reagan's attorneys stated that the former president would defer to President Bush "with respect to issues of executive privilege concerning national security or foreign affairs that may arise during the taking of the videotaped testimony."[62]

Reagan provided eight hours of videotaped testimony on 16 and 17 February 1990. Because he could not recall key events, information, and even some names related to the Iran-contra affair, he did not provide any significant new information about the controversy.

On 21 March 1990, Judge Greene ruled in favor of the Reagan and Bush administration's claims of executive privilege over the diary excerpts. Greene had again privately reviewed the diary entries and determined that they offered "no new insights" into the Iran-contra affair and, consequently, that the claims of executive privilege outweighed Poindexter's demand for access to the diary entries. Greene determined that "the claims of executive privilege filed on behalf of the former president and of the incumbent president are sufficient under the facts presented here to defeat the defendant's demand." Furthermore, Poindexter's "showing of need for the diary excerpts and their indispensibility for the achievement of justice in this case is meager." He explained that Poindexter's case may have been stronger if Reagan had refused to provide videotaped testimony. Greene made it clear that he had overturned his earlier decision to compel release of the diary entries because of the assertions of executive privilege. He determined that "courts must exercise both deference and restraint when asked to issue coercive orders against a president's person or papers."[63]

Executive privilege prevailed in this controversy. Significantly, it was Judge Greene, not Reagan's attorneys or the Bush administration, who forced the issue of executive privilege. Reagan's attorneys avoided using the phrase *executive privilege* in their formal response to Greene's deadline for asserting such authority as the basis for withholding the diary entries. The Bush administration initially tried to get around the issue of executive privilege, but that tactic failed. When compelled to do so, Reagan's attorneys and the Bush administration claimed executive privilege.

The Persian Gulf War, 1990–1991

The Persian Gulf War raised many controversies over access to information. As with any military operation, certain restrictions had to be placed on information about troop movements, campaign strategy, weapons capabilities, and so forth. The most controversial techniques for restricting military information were the journalist "pool system" and the "security review" process.

In brief, the pool system established specific rules governing how many journalists could cover events on the front lines, where the journalists could travel, and whom they could interview. Specifically, the U.S. military allowed selected journalists to travel to the front lines in groups of six or more persons to cover the war. The journalists had to travel with military escorts, who then supervised the reporters' conversations with the troops. When the pool of reporters returned from what some likened to a guided tour, all news stories and footage had to be submitted for a security review.[64] The U.S. military established this latter requirement to ensure that news reports did not disclose secret or sensitive information that could damage the war effort. The approved pool reports would then be shared among the press corps members stationed in Saudi Arabia. The Bush administration did not use executive privilege as a basis for restricting press access to military information. Instead, it justified its many restrictions on the basis of national security concerns.

An executive privilege dispute did arise concerning congressional access to information on U.S.–Persian Gulf policy. On 3 January 1991, Barbara Boxer (D-Calif.) introduced in the House a privileged resolution of inquiry, House Resolution 19, seeking specific information about Operation Desert Shield: the likelihood of a wider regional conflict in the Middle East, assessments of Iraqi military capabilities, projections of effects on international oil supplies, assessments of U.S. vulnerabilities to terrorist attacks, information about U.S. efforts to seek support for Operation Desert Shield from other governments, memoranda of meetings between U.S. officials and foreign leaders, analyses of budgetary options for the military operation, and analyses of postwar options for Iraq. The resolution called for the administration to provide all this information within ten days.[65]

On 23 January 1991, the counsel to the president, C. Boyden Gray, responded as follows:

> The resolution requests extremely sensitive information that, if disclosed, could cause grave damage to the national security at this time of crisis in the Persian Gulf region.
>
> [The requested information concerns] some of our nation's most sensitive national security secrets, including war plans. Even indirect knowledge of those secrets, especially our war plans, would be of obvious use to Iraq in countering steps that the president has ordered, and may yet order, in accordance with H.J. Res. 77. It would be unconscionable to expose U.S. and coalition military personnel in the Persian Gulf region to the risks associated with disclosure of this kind of information.

Because of the extraordinary sensitivity of such information, the courts have long recognized that the Constitution permits the president to protect such information from disclosure under the national security component of the executive privilege doctrine. This component of executive privilege also insulates from disclosure information relating to diplomatic discussions with foreign governments.

Moreover, insofar as documents requested by H. Res. 19 reflect predecisional discussions, advice, recommendations, and budgetary or other analyses, they are also protected from disclosure by the deliberative process component of executive privilege.

In short, we believe that enactment of H. Res. 19 would be contrary to the national interest, and that it would be unconstitutional.[66]

On 7 February 1991, chairman of the House Committee on Foreign Affairs, Dante B. Fascell (D-Fla.), and chairman of the House Committee on Armed Services, Les Aspin (D-Wis.), wrote to President Bush requesting "a more responsive answer than the initial reply by Mr. Gray." The letter further requested that the information be presented in "timely fashion" so that Congress could fulfill its oversight responsibilities.[67]

The White House dropped the use of executive privilege and substantially accommodated Congress's request for information. On 20 February 1991, National Security Adviser Brent Scowcroft responded to the Fascell-Aspin letter by providing summary information from the White House, Department of Defense, and Department of State. He also explained that CIA information relevant to the areas of inquiry would be provided separately in classified form. The White House presented the information in less detailed form than requested, but it dropped the use of executive privilege in response to congressional protest. Congress received much of the desired information and did not dispute the administration's final response that some details could not be provided, given the time constraints.[68] Widespread public support for Bush's military action also made Congress's efforts to compel the release of detailed information about the allied war effort politically difficult, to say the least. Consequently, the Bush administration was able to protect the information it did not want to release without formally exercising executive privilege, and without encouraging a constitutional conflict.

Department of Education and College Accreditation Standards, 1991

In 1991, the Department of Education was subjected to a good deal of criticism for challenging the use of cultural diversity standards in college accreditation decisions.[69] Specifically, on 11 April 1991, Secretary of Education Lamar Alexander challenged the Middle States Association of Colleges and Schools' practice of considering the extent of faculty, staff, and student diversity in deciding whether to grant accreditation. The Subcommittee on Human Resources and Intergovernmental Relations of the House Committee on Government Operations soon began an investigation into Alexander's controversial action. On 17 April 1991, the subcommittee, chaired by Ted Weiss (D-N.Y.), requested Department of Education documents pertaining to Alexander's challenge.

Although the department furnished many of the requested documents, it refused to supply others. On 7 May 1991, the department's general counsel, Edward Stringer, wrote to Weiss that certain documents had to be withheld from Congress. Stringer claimed the "attorney-client privilege" and "deliberative process privilege" as reasons for withholding the documents.[70]

The subcommittee rejected these claims of privilege. Staff members of the subcommittee and of the Department of Education met on 13 May 1991 to try to resolve the dispute. No agreement could be reached, and Stringer wrote another letter to Weiss to inform the chairman that the Department of Justice's Office of Legal Counsel had advised the Department of Education to claim executive privilege over the documents.[71]

The next day, the subcommittee rejected this use of executive privilege and voted six to three, along party lines, to issue a subpoena for the disputed documents. The Department of Education chose not to fight the subpoena, withdrew its claim of executive privilege, and turned over to Congress all the disputed documents.

President Bush never got personally involved in this controversy. Despite administration policy—carried over from the Reagan years—that executive privilege could be invoked only by the president or with his personal approval, the Department of Justice's Office of Legal Counsel advised the Department of Education to claim executive privilege. As the general counsel and the deputy general counsel to the clerk of the House wrote to Weiss:

> What was novel about this claim of privilege was the frankness with which the Office of Legal Counsel admitted that it was claiming executive privilege. The Justice Department's willingness to apply the term "executive privilege" to the decisional documents of a department, and to documents for which attorney-client privilege was attempted to be asserted, contrasts with other occasions when, for tactical reasons, the Justice Department has [devised] attempts at the withholding of similar records without admitting that it is really invoking executive privilege.[72]

The Department of Education had initially used other justifications for withholding the documents before eventually claiming the constitutional doctrine. The trouble was, without presidential approval, the department had no legitimate grounds on which to assert executive privilege. President Bush obviously did not believe that the disputed documents were so important that he was willing to risk a constitutional conflict over executive privilege. Congress proved its ability to compel the production of disputed documents through vigorous use of its authority to investigate and to subpoena evidence.

McDonnell Douglas A-12 Navy Aircraft Program, August–September 1991

In this controversy, President Bush asserted executive privilege, and that assertion went unchallenged by Congress.[73] On 1 August 1991, the Subcommittee on Legislation and National Security of the House Committee on Government Operations unanimously voted to subpoena Secretary of Defense Richard Cheney for a document regarding cost overruns on the McDonnell Douglas A-12 navy aircraft program, which had been terminated in January 1991. The subcommittee, chaired by John Conyers (D-Mich.), gave Cheney until 9 August 1991 to either turn over the requested information or respond to the subpoena.

On 8 August 1991, President Bush signed a memorandum to Cheney instructing the secretary of defense to claim executive privilege and not to comply with the subpoena. The president instructed Cheney as follows:

> It is my decision that you should not release this document. Compelled release to Congress of documents containing confidential communications among senior Department officials would inhibit the candor necessary to the effectiveness of the deliberative process by which the Department makes decisions and recommendations concerning national defense, including recommendations to me as Commander-in-Chief. In my judgment, the release of the memorandum would be contrary to the national interest because it would discourage the candor that is essential to the Department's decision-making process. Therefore, I am compelled to assert executive privilege with respect to this memorandum and to instruct you not to release it to the subcommittee.[74]

What is interesting about this case is that although governmental appropriations—not national security concerns—were at issue, the Conyers committee chose not to challenge Bush's claim of executive privilege. Bush prevailed for a number of reasons. First, the White House successfully lobbied the minority party members of the Conyers committee to back the president after the assertion of executive privilege. Second, Conyers determined that, with a committee divided along partisan lines, there would be little support on Capitol Hill for a contempt citation against Cheney. Third, there would have been little support for a contempt citation in any case, because Cheney, a former House member, was still very popular in Congress.

Congress could claim only one small achievement in this battle over executive branch information. That is, as a consequence of the Conyers committee's action, the president personally claimed executive privilege and established a precedent for the view that executive privilege can be claimed or approved only by the president himself and not by any other member of the executive branch of government.

The Quayle Council and the Food and Drug Administration, 1991–1992

In September 1991, the Human Resources and Intergovernmental Relations Subcommittee of the House Committee on Government Operations began an investigation into Food and Drug Administration (FDA) dealings with the Quayle Council on Competitiveness.[75] In brief, the Quayle Council had recommended a series of reforms of the FDA's drug approval process, and the FDA had accepted the recommendations, some of which were controversial.

The investigating subcommittee ran into difficulty gaining access to documents pertaining to the Quayle Council's work on FDA procedures. The FDA refused to provide certain documents that concerned "deliberative communications within the Council or otherwise reveal its deliberations."[76] On 13 November 1991, the subcommittee voted to subpoena the withheld documents and informed FDA Commissioner David Kessler that only the president could claim executive privilege over those materials. The subcommittee informed Kessler that he would be voted in contempt of Congress on 22 November 1991 if he did not deliver the disputed documents.

After several days of negotiation between the subcommittee and the White House counsel and the FDA, the White House decided against asserting executive privilege and agreed to release all the disputed documents. The Bush administration gave in to pressure from the subcommittee just one day before Kessler was to be held in contempt of Congress.[77]

Unlike in the Rocky Flats controversy (discussed next), in this case, the Bush administration weighed the relative risks associated with full disclosure and with nondisclosure and chose not to assert executive privilege. Congress succeeded again in forcing the issue of executive privilege from the cabinet level to the White House.

Rocky Flats Nuclear Weapons Plant, 1992

In September 1992, the Subcommittee on Investigations and Oversight of the House Committee on Science, Space, and Technology began seeking testimony from individuals with knowledge of a five-year-long FBI investigation into environmental crimes committed by Rockwell International at its Rocky Flats nuclear weapons plant in Golden, Colorado.[78] Although ten criminal violations of environmental law had been acknowledged in the Rockwell plea bargain with the government, no individual culpability had been assigned. The subcommittee, chaired by Howard Wolpe (D-Mich.), subsequently became interested in examining the plea bargain.

The Department of Justice instructed certain individuals who had been called to testify before the Wolpe committee not to divulge various kinds of information pertaining to the government's Rocky Flats investigations. For example, the department instructed an FBI agent who had investigated Rocky Flats which information to withhold. A department lawyer accompanied the man during the congressional inquiry to be sure that privileged information would not be compromised. The department similarly instructed the U.S. district attorney for Colorado, who refused to cooperate with the congressional inquiry.

Wolpe responded by sending a letter to President Bush requesting that the president either personally assert executive privilege or direct the witnesses to testify.[79] The president never responded to the request, and there was no presidential approval of the use of executive privilege in this case. White House counsel C. Boyden Gray wrote to Wolpe to clarify that the White House had no intention of claiming executive privilege and that the Department of Justice and the investigating committee should work out their differences.[80]

Without presidential support for a claim of executive privilege, the Department of Justice could not withstand further pressure from Congress for candid testimony. The Wolpe committee threatened to hold the U.S. district attorney for Colorado in contempt of Congress unless certain conditions were met—most importantly, rescinding the "gag rule" over witnesses.[81] The Department of Justice agreed to all the Wolpe committee's demands and waived all privileged information claims.[82]

What is noteworthy about this case is that the Department of Justice made executive privilege claims on behalf of the administration—without White House approval—and then backed down when the president would not support those claims. Congress used its powers of inquiry and subpoena to full effect in this case to get the information it needed to carry out its investigative functions. Unlike in the A-12 navy aircraft case, the president did not become personally involved, making it easier for Congress to prevail.

Overseas Arrests Controversy, 1989–1992

One of the most innovative secrecy devices of the Bush administration was the Department of Justice's "secret opinions policy."[83] Under that policy, the department could refuse to show Congress legal memorandum opinions from the Office of Legal Counsel (OLC). The secret opinions policy itself was controversial because Congress traditionally had not been denied access to OLC decision memoranda. During the Bush years, one such memorandum was especially controversial.

In 1989, the OLC issued an opinion entitled "Authority of the FBI to Override Customary or Other International Law in the Course of Extraterritorial Law Enforcement Activities." In brief, the memorandum—which overruled a 1980 Carter administration Department of Justice opinion—determined that the FBI could apprehend fugitives abroad without the permission of the host country. News of the memorandum resulted in congressional questions regarding the possible lack of statutory authority for such a policy and conflicts with international law.

Again, the administration made no claim of executive privilege when it refused to divulge the memorandum to Congress. Instead, it relied on the newly created "secret opinions policy." Congress refused to accept this basis as legitimate, and the Judiciary Committee voted to subpoena the memorandum. But the issue became more sensitive after the January 1990 arrest of former Panamanian leader Manuel Antonio Noriega, and the Department of Justice claimed that disclosure of the memorandum could harm the government's case against the former dictator. The department also maintained that the attorney-client privilege would be violated by release of the memorandum, and in the future, federal agencies would be hesitant to rely on the department for confidential legal advice.

In the end, both sides "won." A Supreme Court decision upheld the practice of apprehending fugitive criminals in foreign territories. Furthermore, the Department of Justice and the House Committee on the Judiciary agreed to an arrangement whereby committee members could review, but not copy, department documents pertaining to the memorandum, as well as the memorandum itself. The committee declared itself victorious, and the Bush administration, unable to keep the information from Congress, leaked the full memorandum to the *Washington Post*.

INSLAW Documents Controversy, 1991–1992

One government secrecy controversy that remains unresolved concerns a congressional investigation into allegations that during the Reagan administration, Department of Justice officials conspired to force the INSLAW computer company into bankruptcy and then have INSLAW's leading software product bought by another company.[84] When a subcommittee of the House Committee on the Judiciary sought documents regarding the INSLAW controversy, the Bush administration initially refused to release the documents, citing the "attorney-client privilege." The Bush White House never formally asserted executive privilege over these documents, although it did consider that option.[85] Instead, after a subcommittee subpoena of the disputed documents and a vote of the full committee to do the same, the Department of Justice chose to partially comply with the congressional demands. The department turned over the vast majority of requested materials but refused to turn over every document relevant to the congressional inquiry.

The Department of Justice position is that, in ongoing proceedings in which members of the department are involved, certain materials must be protected by the traditional attorney-client relationship. Therefore, even though Congress has the power of inquiry, the prerogative of the attorney-client relationship during ongoing proceedings must override that power. Furthermore, Congress's power of inquiry is more compelling when a dispute involves legislation than when it concerns the ongoing operations of another branch of government.

There has been no formal resolution to this interbranch dispute. The Bush administration never fully complied with the congressional subpoenas and declared numerous requested documents "missing." Consequently, the Bush administration partially succeeded in withholding information from Congress without any presidential assertion of executive privilege, and Congress partially succeeded in gaining access to disputed executive branch documents. More recently, the Clinton administration Justice Department reviewed INSLAW documents in order to edit and remove materials pertaining to national security.

Executive Privilege in the Bush Administration

The Bush administration demonstrated that it may be easier to withhold information in the post-Watergate environment by not asserting executive privilege and instead claiming other justifications for withholding information. Bush did not avoid executive privilege altogether, however. He personally instructed the use of executive privilege in one information dispute with Congress (the A-12 navy aircraft controversy) and reluctantly claimed executive privilege to protect his predecessor's diaries from a court subpoena.

More often than not, Bush avoided using executive privilege. On a number of occasions, when lower-level officials claimed executive privilege, Bush chose not to personally approve the use of that doctrine and instead accommodated Congress's demands (e.g., Persian Gulf War document request, Quayle Council controversy, Rocky Flats dispute, overseas arrests memorandum controversy, INSLAW investigation).

In general, during the Bush years, Congress achieved at least a partial victory—and sometimes a complete victory—when it challenged administration exercise of secrecy policies. But Congress did not, and could not, challenge every such exercise. Although Congress achieved its goal of having the controversial overseas arrests memorandum made public, it was able to do so only after learning unexpectedly of the existence of such a policy memorandum. The Department of Justice's "secret opinions policy" shielded vast amounts of information from congressional and public scrutiny. Consequently, the administration lost some information battles with Congress, but it won the information war by employing innovative and far-reaching secrecy devices.

When it comes to executive privilege, the post-Watergate presidents have had to operate in the shadow of Richard M. Nixon. The abuse of executive privilege in the Nixon White House made the confident exercise of that power very difficult for subsequent administrations. An examination of post-Watergate executive privilege controversies, beginning with the Ford presidency and running through the George H. W. Bush presidency, reveals the following:

- Because of the taint of Watergate, those presidents were largely reluctant to exercise certain constitutional prerogatives, such as executive privilege.
- None of these presidents rejected the legitimacy of executive privilege. Every one considered executive privilege a legitimate presidential prerogative and exercised that power at one time or another.
- These administrations, Republican and Democrat alike, tried to find ways to achieve the benefits of executive privilege while avoiding, when possible, use of the phrase *executive privilege*.
- Because of Watergate, Congress became especially vigilant in its attempts to constrain presidential exercise of prerogative powers. Congress was less deferential to claims of executive privilege than it had been prior to Watergate.
- None of these administrations tried to take an aggressive posture toward executive privilege to reestablish the political viability of that doctrine. Each administration perceived the political costs of doing so to be too great.

The United States needs to return to a pre-Watergate understanding of the legitimacy of executive privilege in our constitutional order. This understanding is informed by the writings of the American founding fathers and refined by the lessons of the post-Watergate era. In brief, it was far better when the legitimacy of executive privilege was widely accepted and a certain trust was placed in elected officials to exercise their constitutional responsibilities and powers judiciously. It is unhealthy for the political system to have executive branch officials developing duplicitous schemes to withhold information without using executive privilege.

Reestablishing the legitimacy of executive privilege requires an administration willing to assert its rightful constitutional authority to withhold information under the appropriate circumstances. The courts have shown considerable deference to the president's right of executive privilege, even when striking down a particular use of that power as inappropriate. Presidents who behave appropriately have less to fear constitutionally than politically in using executive privilege.

6

BEYOND THE WATERGATE TAINT I: BILL CLINTON AND THE EFFORT TO RESTORE EXECUTIVE PRIVILEGE

Unlike his post-Watergate predecessors, President Bill Clinton was not reluctant to exercise executive privilege. He believed that executive privilege is a legitimate presidential power that has eroded over time and needed to be restored to its proper constitutional stature. Nonetheless, Clinton used executive privilege beyond the traditional boundaries of protecting national security needs, the candor of internal deliberations when disclosure would harm the public, and ongoing criminal investigations. Clinton tried to use executive privilege on several occasions to thwart investigations into allegations of corruption or illegality—exactly the type of circumstances for which executive privilege should never be used.

Despite these failings, the Clinton years reveal that the era of presidential reluctance to use executive privilege is over. Unlike his post-Watergate predecessors, rather than cloak or avoid this constitutional principle, Clinton openly used executive privilege on a number of occasions and thus reignited the national debate over this constitutional principle. Nonetheless, reestablishing the constitutional stature and political viability of executive privilege requires that presidents exercise it judiciously. The failure of President Clinton to do so was a lost opportunity.

BILL CLINTON, 1993–2001

Like most modern presidents, Bill Clinton campaigned with promises of openness in his administration, but after he took office, he immediately began to try to control the flow of information from the executive branch. On numerous occasions, Clinton expressed displeasure at both the tactics of the media and leaks from the executive branch. His administration got off to a bad start with the media when aides declared the West Wing of the White House a journalists' "no-fly zone" and then proceeded to limit the flow of information. Most important, Clinton was mortified by what he perceived as overly broad and aggressive congressional and judicial investigations of his past financial dealings, his personnel and policy decisions, and his personal life.

In the summer of 1994, several years before the appointment of Kenneth Starr as independent counsel and before the public had ever heard of Monica Lewinsky, Clinton told reporters that he had read the first edition of this book and that he agreed with its generally sympathetic sentiment toward the legitimacy of executive privilege.[1] The president said that he took solace in reading about the problems he shared with his predecessors, one of which was how to maintain secrecy in an administration. Presidents do not just casually mention their reading preferences to the press; they do so to convey some purpose. Clinton clearly was comfortable revealing that he was thinking about revitalizing executive privilege long before the scandal that nearly brought down his presidency. In 1994, Clinton's White House counsel also issued a formal memorandum on the administration's procedures regarding the use of executive privilege. The memorandum clarified Clinton's approach to executive privilege, but it also caused problems for the president later on, when his actions did not dovetail with the procedures.

Clinton's Executive Privilege Policy

For more than the first year of the Clinton presidency, the administration operated under the guidelines of the 1982 Reagan memorandum on executive privilege. In 1994, Special Counsel to the President Lloyd Cutler issued a memorandum clarifying the administration's procedures for handling executive privilege claims. The memorandum stated: "The policy of this Administration is to comply with congressional requests for information to the fullest extent consistent with the constitutional and statutory obligations of the Executive Branch. . . . [E]xecutive privilege will be asserted only after careful review demonstrates that assertion of the privilege is necessary to protect Executive Branch prerogatives." Furthermore, "Executive privilege belongs to the President, not individual departments or agencies." The stated procedures for handling executive privilege disputes were consistent with the formal procedures of Clinton's predecessors. Yet in light of later events, one sentence from the Cutler memorandum stands out: "In circumstances involving communications relating to investigations of personal wrongdoing by government officials, it is our practice not to assert executive privilege, either in judicial proceedings or in congressional investigations and hearings."[2]

As described in this memorandum, the Clinton administration adopted the broad view that all White House communications are presumptively privileged. Furthermore, the administration position was that Congress has a less valid claim to executive branch information when conducting oversight than when conducting legislation.[3] This distinction lacks credibility,

yet several administrations have resorted to it to resist congressional oversight and investigations.

The Clinton administration also refused to release to congressional investigators any documents that the White House deemed "subject to a claim of
executive privilege." In other words, on numerous occasions, the White
House withheld documents under the principle of executive privilege without formally invoking that power. Consequently, the real extent of Clinton's
use of executive privilege has been masked by White House claims that many
uses of that power did not count because no one formally invoked it. Even
though Clinton articulated the view that he wished to revive the constitutional stature of executive privilege, and even though he formally invoked that
power numerous times, he also followed the long-standing presidential practice—going all the way back to Eisenhower—of sometimes refusing to provide information to Congress without formally claiming executive privilege.

Clinton's Exercise of Executive Privilege

President Clinton exercised executive privilege more aggressively than any
president since Nixon, and he used executive privilege more often than any
president since Eisenhower. Disputes over executive privilege were at the
core of some of the key controversies during the Clinton era, and one such
controversy almost ended his presidency.

Travel Office Firings, 1993–1996

In May 1993, the Clinton administration fired seven employees of the
White House Travel Office and set off a storm of protest when these individuals were replaced by staff who were personally loyal to the president and
the first lady. The administration alleged that the firings were the result of
mismanagement of the Travel Office and had nothing to do with any desire
to reward personal loyalists with government jobs. Critics of the administration alleged that the White House attempted to pressure the Internal Revenue Service and the Federal Bureau of Investigation (FBI) to investigate the
former Travel Office employees in order to cover up the real motive for their
firing. In June 1993, William Clinger, Jr., the ranking minority member of
the House Committee on Government Operations, called for a congressional investigation. The Justice Department commenced an investigation,
and the president promised his full cooperation. Nonetheless, in September
1994, the chief of the department's Office of Public Integrity wrote a memorandum stating that the White House was being uncooperative by failing

to produce all documents germane to the investigation.[4] The White House similarly resisted investigative efforts by the FBI and the General Accounting Office (GAO). The continuing controversy—which involved claims of executive privilege, lost White House documents, misplaced documents that may have reappeared in altered form, and ultimately charges of corruption—became known in the media as "Travelgate."

In January 1995, with the GOP takeover of the House of Representatives, Clinger became the chair of the House Committee on Government Reform and Oversight and announced his intention to fully investigate Travelgate. The committee submitted document requests to the White House in June and September 1995. By early 1996, the committee was unsatisfied with the White House response and subpoenaed all documents related to the Travel Office firings. Although the White House produced a large number of documents in response to committee subpoenas (some 40,000 pages), Clinton claimed executive privilege over 3,000 pages of documents related to the firings. White House counsel John M. (Jack) Quinn conveyed this claim of executive privilege in a letter to Clinger on 9 May 1996.[5] That letter followed a sequence of correspondences and phone discussions between the committee and Quinn, with each side alleging that the other was acting in bad faith.[6] Quinn was most blunt in accusing the committee of engaging in a "desperate political act" that "trivializes" the legislative power of investigation and "debases the integrity of the entire House."[7] In his 9 May 1996 letter, Quinn defined three broad categories of documents that the White House refused to disclose under the principle of executive privilege: documents pertaining to an independent counsel investigation, those "created in connection with Congressional hearing concerning the Travel Office matter," and documents that concerned confidential White House legal advice.

Clinger correctly protested that the White House had trivialized the principle of executive privilege by asserting it in regard to a controversy that did not affect either the national security or even the public interest in some demonstrable way. Indeed, he said that the whole matter was not worthy of a "constitutional confrontation," and he was right.[8] The committee report correctly repudiated the three categories of documents protected by executive privilege as entirely too broad. The report stated, "This vague, broad and non-descriptive category of withheld documents, if accepted by the committee, would be tantamount to accepting a type of broad, undifferentiated claim of executive privilege which was rejected by the court in *U.S. v. Nixon.*"[9] The committee voted to hold Quinn and two former White House aides in contempt of Congress. President Clinton requested from Attorney General Janet Reno an opinion on his claim of executive privilege, and she affirmed the refusal to produce the documents as a legitimate use of executive privilege. Reno maintained that the Department of Justice had reviewed the disputed documents and concluded that they "fall within the scope of executive privilege"; releasing the documents would have a "chilling" effect on investigations and would undermine the president's constitutional authority by destroying the confidentiality of internal deliberations.[10]

As the contempt of Congress resolution went to the full House, the White House divulged about one-third of the remaining disputed documents. These documents revealed nothing of a serious national security nature nor anything that could be deemed necessary to keep confidential in order to protect the public. Some of the documents, though, were an enormous embarrassment to the White House, lending credibility to the charge that the use of executive privilege in this case had been an attempt to cover up damaging information. In particular, some of the documents confirmed an effort by the White House to have the FBI investigate the former head of the Travel Office, and it was later learned that there were similar efforts to investigate former Reagan and Bush administration employees. At this point, bipartisan pressure on the White House to give up its claim of executive privilege over the remaining documents grew significantly.

The White House avoided a full House vote of contempt by agreeing to an accommodation with the committee whereby all remaining documents would be made available to committee members and staff through a review process. The procedure allowed only note taking, not photocopying, from documents under review, except in the case of FBI-related files, which could be photocopied.

This case followed a pattern similar to that in many uses of executive privilege by Clinton's predecessors: Congress sought access, the White House delayed and eventually claimed executive privilege when Congress would not give up, Congress issued subpoenas and threatened to hold White House officials (current and former, in this case) in contempt, the White House avoided a full House vote on contempt by caving in to Congress's demands, and a review of the documents revealed that there was no substantive reason for claiming executive privilege in the first place and ultimately dragging out the investigation. Indeed, in this case, some of the disputed documents included those involving discussions between the first lady and the White House staff and White House talking points for Democratic House committee members—materials not traditionally covered by executive privilege.[11]

William Kennedy Notes, 1993–1995

In 1993, news reports surfaced regarding the possible involvement of the president and first lady in an illegal land deal in Arkansas years earlier. These reports led to a series of congressional and independent counsel investigations of what became known in the media as the Whitewater scandal or "Whitewatergate." The Clintons' private attorney, Robert Barnett, withdrew from representing the president and first lady in the case and was ultimately replaced on 4 November 1993 by David Kendall. The next day, Kendall met with other lawyers who had been working on aspects of the Whitewater controversy, which was being investigated by the Resolution Trust Corporation and the Small Business Administration at the time. Attending the 5 November 1993 meeting with Kendall were a number of private attorneys for the Clintons, White House aide Bruce Lindsay (also an attorney), and attorneys with the White House Counsel's Office. The purported purpose was to inform Kendall about the various existing legal work on Whitewater. One of the White House attorneys, William Kennedy, took notes at the meeting, which took place at the office of Williams & Connolly, Kendall's law firm.

Nearly two years later, the Senate created a special committee to investigate the Whitewater controversy. In November 1995, the committee voted to subpoena Kennedy's notes, but the White House claimed that the notes were protected by the attorney-client privilege because private attorneys had been present and had given advice at the meeting. A White House memorandum defending the decision to resist the subpoena stated that "the Committee is attempting for the first time to invade the confidentiality of the attorney-client relationship between the President and his private counsel."[12] This assertion was highly controversial, because no president had ever claimed the attorney-client privilege in the case of a congressional inquiry, and Congress does not recognize that privilege as valid in the context of such an inquiry; nor have the courts ever recognized such a privilege as valid in the case of a congressional investigation.

It is puzzling that the White House chose to raise a common-law privilege rather than a constitutionally based power such as executive privilege. Perhaps a claim of executive privilege would have lacked credibility in this circumstance, but at least there would have been some precedent for it. Instead, the White House took the unprecedented tack of claiming that a meeting that involved White House counsel attorneys and concerned official governmental business was protected by the attorney-client privilege because private attorneys of the Clintons had also been present. If allowed to stand, such a position would mean that any time a president wanted to conceal official information from Congress, all he had to do was invite a private lawyer and hold the meeting at that lawyer's private office.

The White House reached an accommodation with the Office of Independent Counsel (OIC) that allowed the production of the Kennedy notes as long as the OIC agreed that the White House had not thereby waived any privileges, either common law or constitutional. This agreement pertained only to the OIC and did not support such an arrangement between the White House and Congress. The special Senate committee agreed in part to this arrangement, and White House counsel Jack Quinn requested that the House of Representatives agree to it as well.[13] House Speaker Newt Gingrich (R-Ga.) correctly rejected that request on the principle that the House could not agree not to waive a presidential privilege that does not exist—in this case, the attorney-client privilege to refuse a congressional request for information.[14] Also investigating Whitewater was the House Banking Committee. The committee chair James Leach (R-Iowa) had sent Gingrich a lengthy analysis of why the House must reject the White House request. The Speaker included in his letter to Quinn that analysis, along with one by the Congressional Research Service in support of the House position.[15]

The White House ultimately produced the notes for the Senate Whitewater Committee and the OIC, yet it claimed a victory for presidential prerogatives by ensuring that release of the notes did not undermine any privileges. Because the controversy was settled by an accommodation, no court ever got to decide the issue of whether the notes deserved the status of being privileged. It is highly unlikely that any court would have done so.

Mike Espy Investigation, 1994

An independent counsel investigated Clinton's first secretary of agriculture, Mike Espy, due to charges that Espy had accepted illegal gratuities from lobbyists who worked on behalf of clients with an interest in Department of Agriculture regulations. Clinton established a separate investigation of Espy through the White House Counsel Office. The purpose of the first investigation was to determine whether Espy was guilty of accepting illegal gifts. The purpose of the latter investigation was to recommend to the president whether any disciplinary action toward Espy was appropriate. Because Espy resigned his post and reimbursed those who had provided the questionable gifts, the White House counsel investigation recommended no disciplinary action.

Independent counsel Donald Smaltz sought access to all materials relating to the separate White House Counsel Office investigation of Espy. The grand jury then subpoenaed all such materials, setting up a constitutional clash. The president claimed executive privilege and deliberative process privilege—which is now considered a form of executive privilege—over eighty-four of the subpoenaed documents. Significantly, the president himself had not seen many of these documents. Thus, the Federal Circuit Court of the District of Columbia had to address a number of significant constitutional issues in what became known as the Espy case.[16] These issues included

the scope of executive privilege, whether the privilege applies to communications among White House staff when the president himself has not seen
those communications, and what is required for an independent counsel to
overcome a claim of privilege.

The Espy case stands as one of the key executive privilege decisions. The
court distinguished between a "presidential communications privilege" and
the "deliberative process privilege," which, according to the court decision,
are executive privileges that exist to protect confidential executive branch deliberations. The former belongs to the president and includes deliberations
between the president and White House staff or other executive branch officials, as well as deliberations among presidential advisers who are directly
involved in presidential decision making. Thus, the president himself need
not be a party to deliberations covered by the presidential communications
privilege. This privilege is rooted in the system of separated powers and is
difficult to overcome. An independent counsel would have to make a substantial showing that "the subpoenaed materials likely contain important
evidence" and that "the evidence is not available with due diligence elsewhere."[17] Although the court allowed for the possibility that a presidential
communications privilege could apply to deliberations in which the president was not a direct participant, it limited this power to decision-making
advice pertaining to the president's independent powers under Article II.
Thus, "The presidential communications privilege should never serve as a
means of shielding information regarding governmental operations that do
not call ultimately for direct decision making by the President."[18]

The deliberative process privilege, by contrast, is a common-law privilege
that belongs to executive branch officials more generally but is much more easily overcome by a showing of a need for information. Indeed, this latter privilege "disappears altogether when there is any reason to believe government
misconduct has occurred."[19] In this case, "the public interest in honest, effective government" overrides any claim of a need to withhold information.[20]

In the Espy case, the court used the Nixon case standard as the basis for determining whether Clinton could claim executive privilege over the materials
subpoenaed by the grand jury. The court adopted the Nixon case balancing
test and weighed the president's general need for confidentiality against the
public interest in disclosure. As in the Nixon case, the court reasoned that the
public interest was supported by a judicial role in furthering an investigation
of possible wrongdoing in public office. In weighing the need for information, two questions must be asked. First, is the information directly relevant?
Second, is the information available from another source? The court ultimately determined that the balance tipped in favor of the independent counsel's need for information in a criminal investigation. The White House,

according to the court, was withholding materials that were directly relevant to the investigation and could not reasonably be obtained elsewhere.

The court thus upheld the principle of executive privilege while striking down this particular use of it as improper. The court went to considerable lengths to substantiate the constitutional necessity of executive privilege and emphasized the presidential need for confidential deliberations. The Espy decision bears a general resemblance to the line of reasoning the Supreme Court used in the Nixon case, but this court provided a much more precise definition of the scope of executive privilege. In one important respect, the decision appears to expand executive privilege significantly by allowing presidents to assert that power over communications that do not directly involve the president himself. Yet the court also went out of its way to narrow the scope of that power by saying that such communications are privileged only when they pertain to independent powers that the president possesses under Article II.

This latter distinction is important, because a casual reading of the decision might lead some to conclude that all kinds of executive branch deliberations are covered by the presidential communications privilege. Indeed, in one instance, the Clinton White House attempted to shield deliberative materials from Congress by claiming that the Espy case broadly covered the Article II power to ensure that the laws are faithfully executed. In that case, a congressional committee tried to get access to deliberative materials pertaining to the president's controversial 1996 decision to use his presumed authority under the Antiquities Act of 1906 to declare 1.7 million acres of land in Utah a national monument. The committee objected that the Espy decision did not pertain to presidential authority granted by statute. In the face of a planned congressional contempt vote, the White House produced all the disputed documents, thus ending that debate over the actual scope of the presidential communications privilege.[21]

The Espy decision has had an important influence on the development of executive privilege law. The court's standards in that case have been applied to other executive privilege controversies as well. Importantly, the court made it clear that, despite some executive branch claims to the contrary, presidential communications are not "presumptively privileged."

Hudson, Wisconsin, Casino, 1995–1997

The first executive privilege case to arise after the establishment of the Espy standards pertained to a congressional investigation of whether the White House had improperly influenced a Department of Interior (DOI) decision to deny an application for a reservation gaming facility.[22] In late 1994, three Indian tribes applied for the right to assume ownership of fifty-five acres of land in Hudson, Wisconsin, for the purpose of establishing a casino. The regional and area offices of the Bureau of Indian Affairs supported the application. Formal approval by the DOI appeared inevitable, as it was common practice for the department to assent to applications supported by the local area office. To the surprise of many, in July 1995, the DOI rejected the application.

Several Native American tribes with nearby casinos had opposed the application, and they hired a lobbyist to try to defeat the application. Their lead lobbyist, Patrick O'Connor, was a former fund-raiser for the 1988 presidential campaign of DOI Secretary Bruce Babbit. During a meeting with the president, O'Connor used the opportunity to raise the issue, and he also contacted the Democratic National Committee (DNC), White House staff, members of the DOI, and members of Congress on behalf of his clients. Despite warnings that White House involvement in the decision process of an executive agency was illegal, there was evidence that certain White House staff members had become involved. The president himself had not only spoken with O'Connor but also written a note to Chief of Staff Leon Panetta asking, "What's the deal on the Wisconsin tribe Indian dispute?"[23] There was also evidence that some DNC staff may have been improperly involved in the casino application decision process. The most serious allegation was that Babbit and the White House had been involved in a scheme in which campaign contributions from the rival Native American tribes were made in exchange for rejection of the Hudson casino application.

Due to the seriousness of the allegations of political bribes and of the White House and DNC exerting political pressure on the decision-making process of an independent agency, the Committee on Government Reform and Oversight investigated the matter, leading to yet another executive privilege dispute with the Clinton White House. In the course of the investigation, the White House sought to withhold a number of documents, including the above-mentioned note from the president to Panetta. In mid-October 1997, committee staff met with White House Counsel Office staff to collectively review documents pertaining to the casino controversy. Although the White House considered some of the requested documents "subject to privilege," the Counsel Office agreed to allow the committee to review those materials, with the understanding that this was not a waiver of the right to claim privilege.[24] A White House privilege log provided to the committee identified ten documents that were considered "subject to executive privilege," "subject to attorney client communication privilege," or "subject to attorney work product privilege."[25]

On 4 November 1997, committee chair Dan Burton (R-Ind.) wrote to White House counsel Charles Ruff that committee reviews of the documents "do not suggest that they are the type of documents over which executive privilege historically has been asserted." Burton noted the common criteria for asserting executive privilege derived from the Reagan memorandum—for example, the existence of "compelling circumstances" such as national security. He pointed out that Clinton's claims of privilege in this case fell far short of the prevailing standards, and he requested that the president himself make a specific claim of privilege.[26] The following day, Burton and Ruff met to discuss the matter, and Burton agreed not to immediately make public a number of the disputed documents. On 6 and 7 November 1997, the committee held hearings on the casino application controversy but did not release the documents. On 18 November 1997, Burton wrote again to Ruff to inform the White House counsel that the committee attorneys had conducted a review of the documents and were "not able to discern any basis for a claim of privilege."[27]

On 25 November 1997, the committee's chief counsel, Richard D. Bennett, met with attorneys from the White House Counsel Office to further discuss the privilege dispute. The president's attorneys asserted that some of the disputed documents were "presumptively privileged" and that the burden was on the committee to make a substantial showing of need for the materials. They maintained that some other documents were protected by the common-law deliberative process privilege. Bennett followed up with a letter the next day detailing why he and the committee believed that the use of privilege in this case was unwarranted. Citing the Espy case, Bennett argued that because the casino application dispute did not involve direct presidential decision making, a claim of executive privilege had no basis. Indeed, the authority to grant or deny a casino application resides with the secretary of interior alone and, by definition, cannot be a matter of direct presidential decision making. Also, because of evidence of possible governmental wrongdoing, the basis for a claim of any common-law privilege disappeared.[28]

Applying the standards of the Reagan memorandum, the Espy case, and even the Clinton administration's own formal procedures for executive privilege, the committee's stand on these documents was unarguable. Lacking a compelling need for secrecy, and lacking any direct presidential involvement—the only presidential involvement in this case would have been illegal, and an even stronger rationale for a full investigation—there was no legal basis for privilege. Given the Clinton standard that executive privilege should not apply with regard to allegations of governmental wrongdoing, the case against the use of secrecy was especially strong. Furthermore, the White House's creative device of calling various documents "subject to privilege" rather than actually invoking privilege violated the long-standing procedure that presidents themselves must claim privilege to withhold documents.

The White House persisted in its tack, and the committee responded that it planned to use the documents listed in the privilege log in an open session.[29] To further substantiate its position that the documents were not entitled to privileged status, the committee commissioned a Congressional Research Service (CRS) study on the legal dispute, giving CRS staff access to the disputed documents. After examining the documents, the CRS concurred that none of them was entitled to privileged status. Indeed, the CRS report stated that the documents involved matters of political consideration and that the only possible harm resulting from their public release would be to the political standing of the White House. The report detailed that the various documents contained political discussions or dealt with legal issues but did not contain legal advice, and it affirmed that the White House could not claim a right to withhold information from a congressional committee by asserting common-law privileges. Further, because the documents concerned matters of possible governmental wrongdoing, there could be no legally sustainable basis for privilege.[30]

The Clinton White House stuck to its claim of privilege and argued that the committee had never shown a need for the materials that would justify overriding the maintenance of secrecy. The White House view was that because the documents did not contain proof of government misconduct, they were not essential to the committee's investigation.[31] This argument is unsupportable, because it effectively suggests that a committee investigation of possible wrongdoing is limited to reviewing only those documents that the accused parties might themselves consider incriminating. The committee replied that lacking a "convincing legal argument," the matter was "closed," and the documents would be used in open hearings.[32] In early 1998, the committee held hearings on the controversy and used the disputed documents. The White House's final stand was that, in a strict sense, privilege had never been waived, and the committee acted in bad faith by making public documents that the administration had originally provided under a confidentiality arrangement.

White House Antidrug Memorandum, 1996

In April 1995, FBI Director Louis J. Freeh and Drug Enforcement Administration chief Thomas A. Constantine wrote a memorandum to the president that was highly critical of the Clinton administration's battle against drug abuse in the United States. The focus of the memorandum was strong criticism of the fragmented nature of the antidrug effort, with various federal agencies and the White House drug control office all involved in overlapping and often conflicting activities. The memorandum suggested that there be some form of consolidation of the national antidrug effort, preferably under the leadership of the Justice Department. The memorandum also contained some language that could be interpreted as critical of the president himself, including the assertion that the antidrug effort lacked "any true leadership."

The existence of the Freeh-Constantine memorandum did not become public knowledge until June 1996, in the midst of Clinton's reelection campaign. Some Republicans, including presidential nominee Robert J. Dole, demanded that the Clinton administration produce the memorandum. Clearly, many in the GOP believed that they had something to gain by releasing a memorandum that was critical of the president's leadership in the "drug war."

The battle over public release of the memorandum went beyond partisan politics when members of Congress demanded that it be released for the purposes of an investigation. On 17 September 1996, the House Subcommittee on National Security, International Affairs, and Criminal Justice of the Committee on Government Reform and Oversight, chaired by William H. Zeliff, Jr. (R-N.H.), requested the memorandum. The counsel to the president, Jack Quinn, replied ten days later that the memorandum could not be released to Congress because it involved confidential internal deliberations. The White House offered instead to have the Department of Justice provide the subcommittee with a briefing about the memorandum. Clinger, chairman of the full Government Reform and Oversight Committee, replied that same day by issuing a subpoena for the document.

In response, the president requested an opinion from the attorney general whether a claim of executive privilege would be valid in this case. Reno replied that the memorandum "clearly falls within the scope of executive privilege" because it was a confidential communication to the president. Reno maintained that Congress did not have a strong interest in receiving the memorandum because the subcommittee had an "oversight interest" rather than a legislative one. Once again, she cited as authority the 1981 memorandum from Attorney General William French Smith to President Reagan, where this invalid distinction between legislative interests as opposed to oversight was first articulated.

On 1 October 1996, Quinn wrote to Zeliff that Clinton was formally invoking executive privilege over the Freeh-Constantine memorandum. Quinn emphasized the president's strong interest in confidential deliberations regarding law enforcement matters and the chilling effect of allowing disclosure of such confidences.[33]

Detailed press disclosures of the contents of the memorandum took the steam out of Congress's efforts to challenge Clinton's claim of executive privilege. The Zeliff subcommittee dropped the matter once Congress went into recess in October. It could have chosen instead to pursue the matter, especially given the fact that the White House had raised it to the level of an executive privilege claim and had articulated some questionable principles for its exercise. The subcommittee could have held recess hearings and even issued a criminal contempt citation if the White House continued to refuse to cooperate. Instead, it chose to let the matter drop.

Opponents of GOP efforts to get access to the memorandum charged that the obvious political interest involved was the true motivation for any inquiry. Even if it is true that the Republicans were motivated in part by partisanship and a desire to embarrass the president in an election year, that does not justify the assertion of executive privilege. In the absence of some real threat to the national security or the public interest, Congress's request for information must override executive privilege, unless it can be proved that Congress's actions were outside the scope of any legitimate investigation. Clinton never made a case that releasing the information would somehow cause a public harm, and he never proved that Congress lacked any legitimate basis for the investigation. In this case, the president's claim of executive privilege was able to stand because Congress gave up.

U.S.-Haiti Policy, 1996

Another case of failure of congressional follow-through concerned Clinton's assertion of executive privilege over White House documents pertaining to U.S. foreign policy in Haiti. In 1995–1996, the House Committee on International Relations, headed by Benjamin A. Gilman (R-N.Y.), investigated whether officials of Haiti's U.S.-installed regime were using death squads to kill political opponents and whether the Clinton administration had been concealing information about the political killings. Over the period of this long investigation, the committee requested approximately 1,000 White House documents germane to U.S.-Haiti policy.

After the White House resisted congressional attempts to get access to certain documents, Gilman tried to reach an accommodation whereby the White House counsel would brief committee staff on the documents, which included the confidential deliberations of the president and vice president. Under this arrangement, committee staff also would be allowed to read portions of the other withheld documents.[34] Quinn met with Gilman to discuss a compromise whereby committee staff, Gilman, and the senior minority party member of the committee would receive a briefing but would not be allowed access to any of the disputed documents. Gilman rejected the offer, and on 19 September 1996, the committee voted to subpoena the documents. Gilman accused the White House of engaging in delay tactics so that by the end of the congressional session, there would be no time left for a substantive, meaningful briefing.[35]

Clinton requested the attorney general's opinion whether he could issue a valid claim of executive privilege over the U.S.-Haiti documents. Reno replied on 20 September 1996 that, based on a Justice Department review of the documents, a claim of executive privilege was indeed appropriate in this case. Reno elaborated a detailed legal justification for the use of executive privilege, going so far as to argue that "the conduct of foreign affairs is an exclusive prerogative of the executive branch." She cited the "sole organ" doctrine and the controversial *U.S. v. Curtis-Wright* (1936) case as validation for this view. She also cited a 1969 memorandum by then assistant attorney general William Rehnquist in which he claimed that the president has the inherent right to withhold foreign policy information from Congress. Further, Reno wrote, "there is substantial question as to the extent of Congress' authority to conduct oversight of the executive branch's conduct of foreign affairs or its deliberations relating thereto." Reno once again maintained that Congress's interest in getting access to executive branch information to conduct oversight is less compelling than its need for such information in cases of legislation. She also stated the less controversial positions that the president has the right to confidential deliberations with his staff and that the conduct of diplomatic relations requires that the president be able to communicate in secret with foreign leaders.[36]

Three days later, Quinn wrote to Gilman to inform the committee that the president had invoked executive privilege over forty-seven documents pertaining to U.S.-Haiti policy. The president was willing to provide the committee with four of the documents it had requested, based on Reno's advice that those four were not covered by executive privilege. Quinn wrote: "The 47 documents over which the President has invoked executive privilege implicate his ability to conduct the nation's foreign affairs. . . . The President has determined that disclosure of these documents to the Congress would inhibit the candid discussion that he must have with foreign leaders in the conduct of the nation's foreign affairs and would interfere with the deliberative and analytic processes within the White House that are essential to the formulation of our foreign policy."[37]

The House International Relations Committee held hearings on the matter on 27 and 28 September 1996. Gilman and many members of the committee were highly critical of the president's use of executive privilege in the case, and Gilman went so far as to allege a presidential abuse of power and a "cover-up." Yet despite the heated rhetoric, Gilman and the committee ultimately did not pursue the matter and effectively allowed Clinton's use of executive privilege to stand.

A few facets of this controversy are striking. First, the two sides in the dispute came remarkably close to an accommodation that would have given the

House access to much more material than it ultimately received and would have avoided an executive privilege claim. Gilman wanted a briefing of committee staff and partial access to certain documents; the White House proposed instead to brief staff, Gilman, and the senior minority party member and not to allow partial access to the documents. Rather than try to resolve these differences, Gilman pursued a subpoena, and the president claimed executive privilege. Second, after raising the stakes of the battle so high, Gilman did not pursue a contempt resolution against Quinn. In the past, Congress has had great success in getting access to disputed materials by issuing contempt citations. Gilman pushed the matter to the level of a fundamental separation of powers conflict and then dropped it.

Because the committee failed to follow through, the disputed documents remain unavailable for inspection, making it impossible to judge whether the charges of presidential corruption and cover-up have any validity. Lacking such details, it appears that this case may have been Clinton's most valid claim of executive privilege, as the committee had specifically pushed for memoranda from the national security adviser to the president, as well as other potentially sensitive documents. Reno's memorandum defending executive privilege in this case made some highly dubious arguments, especially the claim that the president has unilateral authority over all U.S. foreign policy. That a congressional committee would raise the stakes of an information dispute to the level of an executive privilege claim and then back down in the face of the dubious legal principles articulated by Reno is nothing short of astonishing. Nonetheless, despite the fecklessness of the committee and some strained legal arguments for the use of executive privilege in this case, it appears that use of the privilege was valid. It is possible that the use of the privilege could have been justified on the more narrow grounds of protecting confidential deliberations that have a direct bearing on foreign policy development and national security.

Campaign Finance Abuses, 1997–2001

During the 1996 presidential campaign, there were reports of illegal foreign contributions to the DNC. Even more seriously, there were reports that senior White House officials, possibly including the president and vice president, were part of a large illegal fund-raising scheme in which DNC contributors were treated to special perks such as flights on *Air Force One,* attendance at White House coffees, and overnight stays in the Lincoln Bedroom, among others. FBI Director Freeh recommended that Attorney General Reno establish an independent counsel to investigate the matter.

Beginning in October 1996, the House Committee on Government Reform and Oversight, chaired by William F. Clinger in the 104th Congress, and then by Dan Burton in the 105th Congress, investigated the scandal. Clinger sent numerous requests to the president for documents and other materials germane to the investigation, which the White House resisted. Beginning in January 1997, Burton also issued a number of such requests for information. Burton met with the new White House counsel Charles Ruff in February, and Ruff declared the president's intention to turn over all requested documents and not to assert executive privilege. By 4 March, however, the documents had not been produced, so the committee issued a subpoena and gave the White House twenty days to respond. In April, after a period of White House–congressional wrangling over the appropriate protocols for viewing certain documents, the White House still had not responded to the subpoena. In late April, the committee issued six new subpoenas focusing on the records of individuals who were alleged to have had leading roles in the campaign finance scandal.

Ruff wrote to Burton on 30 April 1997 that the two sides were not very far apart in resolving the document dispute. Ruff asserted the White House desire to withhold certain documents that were "attorney-client and/or attorney work product materials" prepared by the Counsel Office staff. "Even with respect to those few documents as to which we assert a claim of privilege, our proposal would require us to identify those documents and would leave the Committee free to seek their production," Ruff added.[38] Ruff produced some documents a few days later, and Burton responded that the White House still had not produced all the key documents, and he reminded Ruff of the February pledge not to assert privilege. Burton insisted that the White House either produce the documents or make a formal claim of executive privilege.[39] On 9 May 1997, Burton again wrote to Ruff, demanding that either the White House comply with the subpoenas or the president formally claim executive privilege, even though Burton protested that the documents pertained to a criminal investigation and did not fall within the traditional definition of executive privilege. Burton also called Ruff to testify before the committee on 15 May 1997 "to explain why you should not be held in contempt of Congress."[40]

On 14 May 1997, the White House sent a log of forty documents that were "subject to executive privilege."[41] As the committee report correctly stated, even though this was not a signed claim of privilege by the president himself, this action "was effectively a claim of executive privilege."[42] The distinction was meaningless, as the effect was to hold back materials under the principle of executive privilege. As is so often the case, the threat of a contempt of Congress vote moved the process forward. Ruff met with Burton on 16 May 1997, and the two began to work out an agreement to allow the committee to see more of the disputed documents. Yet still more wrangling over documents was in the works, because the committee requested access to additional documents. After more negotiations, the committee eventually achieved access to the materials it sought, including the forty documents that were "subject to executive privilege."

The two sides entered into a "non-waiver agreement" in June 1997, whereby the committee achieved full access to the documents with the understanding that the White House's acceptance of that arrangement did not constitute a waiver of its right to claim privilege over those or any similar materials.[43] Just to be sure that Congress was not giving up its rights under the agreement, Burton wrote to Ruff that the White House did not possess an attorney-client privilege in the case of congressional investigations, and "accordingly, the Congress would not assert the President has waived a privilege which it does not necessarily recognize exists."[44] Upon reviewing the materials, the committee concluded that none was an appropriate source of an executive privilege claim.[45]

That did not end the dispute over executive privilege. In a September 1997 deposition before Congress, deputy White House counsel Bruce Lindsay refused to answer certain questions because of the possibility that he might discuss matters covered by executive privilege. During the deposition, Lindsay used his cell phone to call Ruff for advice on handling the questions. After concluding the call, Lindsay told the committee that "Mr. Ruff informs me—he says that these sorts of conversations give rise to serious executive privilege concerns; that at this time I should not respond, and that he will be happy to discuss it with you after the deposition."[46] Burton later correctly protested that the committee's questions did not delve at all into matters traditionally covered by executive privilege; rather, they concerned a discussion between Lindsay and the president about an earlier personal conversation Clinton had had with one of the individuals implicated in the fund-raising scandal.[47] Once again, the White House resorted to the "subject to privilege" standard when Ruff replied that Lindsay had not formally claimed executive privilege in the deposition.[48] The committee report noted that "the White House made a distinction without a difference, as Lindsay refused to answer the question."[49]

On another front, the committee sought access to a confidential memorandum from Freeh to Reno in which Freeh recommended the appointment of an independent counsel to investigate the fund-raising scandal. Reno refused to disclose the memorandum, saying that to do so would compromise the confidentiality of Department of Justice decision making. Reno and Freeh jointly wrote to Burton that the memorandum contained confidential advice regarding an ongoing Department of Justice investigation and that it would be inappropriate to divulge it to Congress. The committee persisted and issued a subpoena for the Freeh memorandum, but Reno refused to comply. Significantly, officials at the Department of Justice made a clear distinction between allowing congressional access to department memoranda concerning closed investigations and closing off such access in the cases of ongoing investigations.

In early 2001, President George W. Bush expressed his desire to put an end to the various Clinton scandal investigations. The Department of Justice declared its investigation of the 1996 campaign finance scandal closed. Burton, still chair of the committee, expressed his displeasure and his intention to keep the congressional investigation alive. Burton requested access to documents pertaining to Freeh's recommendation that there should have been an independent counsel appointed to investigate the scandal. Ironically, the Department of Justice, at the urging of President Bush, refused to cooperate. Bush declared executive privilege and initiated a constitutional conflict with Congress (discussed in detail later).

Lewinsky Scandal, 1998–1999

On 19 December 1998, the House of Representatives approved two articles of impeachment against President Clinton for having committed perjury and obstruction of justice during the so-called Lewinsky scandal. On 12 February 1999, the U.S. Senate voted not to remove Clinton from office. Clinton thus suffered the disgrace of being the second U.S. president to be impeached by the House, though the severity of that disgrace was somewhat mitigated by the lack of even a simple majority in the Senate for either of the articles of impeachment.

In brief, during his deposition in Paula Jones's sexual harassment lawsuit against him, President Clinton denied that he had had an affair with a twenty-one-year-old intern named Monica Lewinsky. News reports of the possible affair caused a firestorm, and leading presidential observers maintained that if the president had lied in a deposition, his presidency would not survive the scandal. Evidence later revealed that the president had indeed lied in his deposition and had therefore committed perjury. Further, credible evidence emerged that established presidential acts of obstruction of justice. Eventually, however, it became clear that predictions of the Clinton presidency's inevitable demise were baseless. Regardless of the legal evidence against the president, public opinion was strongly opposed to the president's impeachment and possible removal from office, and the nation's elected representatives could not easily ignore such public sentiment.

The investigation of the president's possible wrongdoing was conducted by the OIC under the leadership of Kenneth Starr. (Since its creation to investigate the president and first lady's involvement in Whitewater, the OIC had moved on to investigate a string of other matters.) During the investigation, Starr and his team received possibly incriminating information about the president's sex life that was germane to the Jones sexual harassment suit; this information directly contradicted Clinton's own deposition. Starr brought this information to Reno, who authorized the OIC to expand the scope of its investigation. Starr's investigation culminated in a published report months later that made a forceful case that the president had acted illegally and violated his oath of office. These charges ultimately led to Clinton's impeachment in the House.

The Clinton administration made extensive and improper use of executive privilege during the Lewinsky scandal in an effort to thwart the OIC investigation. Although the president's attorneys offered some valid arguments in defense of executive privilege, these arguments ultimately failed because the debate with the OIC was not over the basic legitimacy of that power but over its application in the context of a presidential sex scandal.

One of the original proposed articles of impeachment against Clinton concerned abuse of powers—in particular, excessive and unwarranted use of executive privilege.[50] Many of the advocates of Clinton's impeachment argued reasonably that the use of executive privilege to conceal wrongdoing and to frustrate and thwart legitimate inquiries by the OIC constituted an abuse of presidential powers. However, the executive privilege language was not in the article eventually voted out by the House Judiciary Committee (and later rejected by the full House). The authors of this article of impeachment may have been persuaded by arguments that a president should not be punished for defending himself by using the legitimate powers at his disposal. They also believed that the two remaining articles of impeachment were their strongest.

The confusion over whether to proceed with the charge of abuse of executive privilege indicates that, for many, the proper exercise of this constitutional prerogative remains unclear. During much of 1998, Clinton's lawyers argued that the president has a broad-based right to assert executive privilege, and to deny that claim was nothing less than to strip away the legal protection for confidential White House deliberations. The OIC countered that the Clinton scandal involved personal rather than official governmental matters; therefore, the White House's various claims of executive privilege could not stand. Each side cited substantial constitutional law, scholarly opinion, and historic precedent in defense of its case.[51]

Judge Norma Holloway Johnson of the U.S. District Court for the District of Columbia ultimately sided with the OIC. She did so not because she believed that Clinton's arguments in defense of executive privilege were weak but because Starr made a compelling showing of the need for access to the information shielded by executive privilege. Judge Johnson applied the classic constitutional balancing test, similar to that used in *U.S. v. Nixon* and in the Espy case: in a criminal investigation, the need for evidence outweighs any presidential claim to secrecy.[52]

Judge Johnson's decision resolved the immediate controversy but did little to clearly fix the proper parameters of executive privilege. As a consequence, the OIC declared victory because it had achieved access to testimony crucial to its investigation, and the White House declared victory because Johnson had upheld the principle of executive privilege. Despite eventually dropping this claim of executive privilege, the White House later asserted additional claims as the investigation moved forward.

It is hard to imagine a more dubious use of executive privilege than to conceal Clinton's actions in the Lewinsky scandal. National security was obviously not at issue, although White House counsel tried to argue that by harming "the president's ability to 'influence' the public," the investigation undermined his ability to lead foreign policy.[53] The White House's case for executive privilege ultimately hinged on the claim that the president had the right to protect the privacy of internal deliberations.

Indeed, presidents are entitled to seek and receive candid, confidential advice. Executive privilege extends to presidential advisers because they must be able to deliberate and discuss policy options without fearing public disclosure of their every utterance. Without that protection, the candor and quality of presidential advice would clearly suffer. But the Clinton administration maintained that the court's opinion in the Espy case justified *any* claim of privilege regarding records or recollections of discussions between the president and his aides, between and among aides, and even between the first lady and an aide. As a general principle, it is correct that such discussions can be covered by the privilege.[54] The key issue here was whether these White House discussions had anything to do with official governmental business, as opposed to being merely deliberations over how to handle political strategy during a scandal.

To prevail, Clinton needed to make a compelling argument that the public interest would somehow suffer from the release of information about White House discussions of the Lewinsky investigation. Not only did he fail to do this; for months, he even refused to answer the basic question whether he had formally invoked the privilege.

Judge Johnson ultimately ruled against Clinton's use of executive privilege in the Lewinsky investigation. Although much of her reasoning gave credibility to some debatable White House arguments, she correctly determined that the balancing test weighed in favor of the independent counsel's need for access to information crucial to a criminal investigation.[55] The White House dropped its flawed claim of executive privilege following her ruling.

White House counsel Charles Ruff nevertheless declared victory because the judge had upheld the legitimacy of executive privilege and therefore preserved this presidential power for future use. This assertion simply lacks credibility. It is hard to believe that the president used executive privilege so aggressively during the Lewinsky scandal because he was motivated by a desire to protect a constitutional principle for his successors. It is difficult to imagine that a president who wished to protect this constitutional principle would do so during a sex scandal rather than a military operation or some other crisis with national security implications. The evidence suggests that Clinton used executive privilege merely to frustrate and delay the Starr investigation.

Even after losing in court, the White House made additional claims of the privilege. For example, in August 1998, a White House attorney and deputy White House counsel claimed executive privilege in testimony before the grand jury. Clinton told the grand jury that he merely wanted to protect the constitutional principle and did not want to challenge the independent counsel's victory; yet several days later, the president challenged one unfavorable court ruling and directed another aide to assert executive privilege.[56]

Clinton's success in frustrating and delaying the Starr investigation through numerous claims of executive privilege and the use of other legal devices helped save his presidency. The many delays allowed the administration to build a case before the public that the drawn-out and expensive OIC investigation was all Starr's fault. In the end, there were no real "winners." The president may have saved his administration, but his actions certainly were not vindicated. By his actions, Clinton, like Nixon before him, damaged the credibility of the principle of executive privilege.

FALN Pardons, 1999

On 11 August 1999, President Clinton offered clemency to sixteen members of the Puerto Rican nationalist group know as the FALN—the Spanish acronym for Fuerzas Armadas de Liberacion Nacional (Armed Forces of National Liberation). The presidential pardons were controversial for a number of reasons. Most prominently, critics alleged that the president had failed to follow the proper procedures for issuing the pardons. Second, Clinton had pardoned individuals who were terrorists and considered dangerous by the U.S. government. Third, some alleged that Clinton's motives for the pardons were political, not legal or even compassionate. First Lady Hillary Rodham

Clinton was a candidate for the U.S. Senate in New York, and some suggested that the president's pardons were an attempt to help his wife win the support of voters of Puerto Rican descent.

Dan Burton (R-Ind.), chairman of the House Committee on Government Reform, requested White House and Justice Department documents pertaining to the pardon decision, as well as testimony of key administration officials involved in the decision process. Clinton refused, and on 16 September 1999, Burton's committee issued subpoenas for documents and testimony from White House counsel Beth Nolan. Reno wrote to the president that Nolan could not be compelled to testify, and White House deputy counsel Cheryl Mills wrote to Burton that "the president's authority to grant clemency is not subject to legislative oversight."[57] The White House Counsel Office offered to supply the committee with over 11,000 pages of documents pertaining to the pardons—for example, letters to the White House urging the pardons—but it refused to supply any documents that concerned "the president's internal, deliberative process."[58] Clinton rejected the subpoenas and claimed executive privilege.

The president's actions ignited a firestorm of protest. GOP critics said that Clinton was trying to influence the votes of New York State's 1.3 million citizens of Puerto Rican descent, and many Republicans charged that executive privilege was being used once again to protect the president from embarrassment. In addition, back in 1996, the Justice Department had formally recommended that the president not issue clemency to the terrorists because they still posed a real threat. That the president did not follow standard procedures for issuing pardons led some to charge that the pardons themselves were illegitimate. But leaving aside the issue of whether the terrorists deserved pardons, the fact is that the president had the authority to do what he did. The president derives his authority to pardon from the Constitution. Although there are Department of Justice regulations that presidents generally follow in issuing pardons, there is no requirement that they do so in every case.

Twice in the modern era, presidents have previously issued pardons without any Department of Justice input: President Gerald Ford's pardon of Richard Nixon, and President George H. W. Bush's pardons in December 1992 of several Iran-contra figures. These two cases and the Clinton pardons for the terrorists have something important in common: each case was hugely controversial, lending credibility to suspicions that the president understood that the decision to pardon was so politically volatile that it had to be made without any involvement by other governmental officials. One important difference is that in the Clinton case the Department of Justice had reviewed the merits of the appeals for clemency and advised against issuing the pardons. Three years after that recommendation, Clinton went ahead and acted on his own. Clinton may have looked bad in ignoring the recommendation of his own Department of Justice, but he had the right to do so. The clemency rules in the Department of Justice are merely advisory in nature when it comes to the president's actions.

In asserting executive privilege, the president fueled accusations that he was trying to cover up an embarrassment to his administration rather than protect a constitutional principle. However, the president had claimed executive privilege over documents that pertained to confidential deliberations and legal advice over the issuing of pardons. And given that the pardon power is absolute, it was more difficult to make the argument that Congress had a compelling need for the documents and testimony. Congress had no authority to challenge the pardons, unless it could prove that Clinton had exchanged pardons for bribes. Nonetheless, because Clinton had asserted privilege over documents pertaining to the 1996 Justice Department recommendation against issuing the pardons, Congress's desire to know the nature of that advice and why he ultimately rejected it was to be expected.

Some members of Congress also protested that this was an inappropriate use of executive privilege because it did not involve national security or some other compelling circumstance that required secrecy. Indeed, given the traditional standards for asserting executive privilege—protecting national security or maintaining secrecy when it is in the public's interest to do so—it is difficult to make a case for executive privilege in this case. Nonetheless, without access to these documents currently, it is not possible to make a firm determination whether the president was concealing embarrassing information, given the Justice Department's 1996 recommendation, or whether divulging legal advice on the pardons would have jeopardized the lives or safety of individuals who had provided information to the government about the terrorists. If it was the latter, a good argument could be made that executive privilege was in the public interest, to the extent that secrecy protected certain individuals who had stepped forward to provide information necessary to the pardon review process.

Executive Privilege in the Clinton Administration

In attempting to revive executive privilege, Clinton faltered more than he succeeded. At this writing, the record on some of his uses of executive privilege remains unavailable. Nonetheless, a great deal of information about his claims of executive privilege became available while he was in office, most notably during the Lewinsky scandal. At present, the record reveals an administration that largely resorted to executive privilege in a Nixon-like fashion to conceal politically embarrassing or incriminating information from the public.

Clinton's legacy on executive privilege appears to be similar to Nixon's, in that both contributed to the negative connotation of the words *executive privilege*. In the wake of the Lewinsky scandal, it appeared that, as far as executive privilege was concerned, the post-Clinton years could look very much like the early post-Watergate years: a time during which presidents limited or concealed their use of executive privilege to avoid the inevitable public rebukes. Yet the George W. Bush presidency revealed no such reluctance; in fact, Bush, too, tried to revitalize executive privilege, and in an even more aggressive fashion than did his predecessor. Bush's actions on executive privilege were a part of a broader administration strategy to expand the reach of various executive powers.

7

BEYOND THE WATERGATE TAINT II:
GEORGE W. BUSH, BARACK OBAMA, AND THE GROWING
DISCORD OVER EXECUTIVE PRIVILEGE

Mark J. Rozell and Mitchel A. Sollenberger

President George W. Bush engaged in a number of highly contentious battles over executive privilege. Bush's efforts to aggressively use and expand executive privilege dovetailed with his administration's very expansive view of presidential powers. Many attributed Bush's aggressive use of his powers to the tragedy of 11 September 2001 and to the subsequent War on Terror.[1] Advocates of Bush's broad exercises of authority maintained that his actions were driven by necessity. Nonetheless, it is also clear that Bush's efforts to enlarge the powers of the presidency predated 11 September 2001, that he came to office with an agenda to regain what he considered lost or declining powers of the presidency.

Vice President Richard Cheney made public utterances early in the first term that the Bush administration would be dedicated to restoring the balance of powers in the system of separated powers to ensure that the president was able to fully exercise his rightful authority. In early 2002, Cheney went so far as to suggest that the modern era has been characterized by legislative encroachments on presidential powers combined with presidential acquiescence in the face of such congressional power-grabs.[2]

Thus, the debate over Bush's use of executive privilege can best be waged in the context of the president's own view of executive powers. Given this context it is not at all surprising that Bush aggressively defended and expanded executive privilege, even going so far as trying to goad Congress into fights that would end up in court. Whether Congress was controlled by Republicans or by Democrats, Bush adopted an approach that put aside conciliation and compromise in favor of pushing battles to the brink in order to win favorable outcomes for the executive branch. This strategy did little to reestablish the stature of executive privilege, and it very likely did further harm to the future standing of this principle.

This chapter describes in detail and analyzes the major executive privilege controversies during the George W. Bush presidency. These incidents range from the White House refusal to disclose decades-old Department of Justice (DOJ) material to information that led to the firing of several U.S. attorneys. Although there were a number of lesser battles and threats of executive privilege, the controversies addressed here offer a comprehensive overview of the Bush administration's uses of this power during its two terms. The chapter also examines the early decisions of the Barack Obama administration that have significance to the evolution of the debate over executive privilege.

Department of Justice Documents and
Congressional Oversight

President Bush made his first formal claim of executive privilege on 12 December 2001. This claim was in response to a congressional subpoena for prosecutorial records from the DOJ. The House Government Reform Committee, then chaired by Representative Dan Burton (R-Ind.), was investigating two separate matters that concerned Department of Justice decision making. First, the committee was examining the decision by former attorney general Janet Reno, who refused to appoint an independent counsel to investigate allegations of campaign finance abuses in the 1996 Clinton-Gore campaign. Second, the committee was examining allegations of FBI corruption in its Boston office handling of organized crime in the 1960s and 1970s. The committee made it clear that it was not requesting Department of Justice documents or other materials pertaining to any ongoing criminal investigations.

At the core of this battle was a dispute over whether an administration could withhold any and all documents that involve prosecutorial matters, even if those matters are officially closed. Burton and other members of the committee were upset that the Bush administration was trying to expand the scope of its authority to withhold information from Congress by refusing documents from terminated Department of Justice investigations. They were also troubled with the Bush Justice Department decision to declare that the unfinished investigation of the 1996 campaign finance controversy would be closed. Burton and his colleagues clearly believed that former attorney general Reno had hampered legitimate investigations and that Bush's desire to have certain Clinton-era controversies ended had the effect of denying full public disclosure of governmental misconduct. Burton penned a strongly worded letter to Attorney General John Ashcroft protesting the administration's "inflexible adherence to the position" that all deliberative materials from the Department of Justice be routinely withheld from Congress. Burton pointed out that the administration had not made a valid claim of executive privilege and therefore had no right to withhold the documents requested by his committee.[3]

White House counsel Alberto R. Gonzales recommended that the president would need to assert executive privilege in response to any congressional subpoena for the documents or if Ashcroft appeared before the committee. The committee subpoenaed the documents and called Ashcroft to appear at a hearing on 13 September 2001. Because of the terrorist attacks two days before the scheduled hearing, Ashcroft's appearance was delayed. A new hearing was then scheduled for 13 December 2001. Bush instructed Ashcroft not to comply with the congressional request for any deliberative documents from the Department of Justice. "Disclosure to Congress," the president remarked, "of confidential advice to the attorney general regarding the appointment of a special counsel and confidential recommendations to Department of Justice officials regarding whether to bring criminal charges would inhibit the candor necessary to the effectiveness of the deliberative processes by which the Department makes prosecutorial decisions." Bush concluded that because he believed that "congressional access to these documents would be contrary to the national interest, I have decided to assert executive privilege with respect to the documents and to instruct [the attorney general] not to release them or otherwise make them available to the Committee."[4] Far from being an initial offer that would bring compromise between the branches the president's order led to a clash with Burton over the administration's refusal to cooperate with the legislative investigations.

At the hearing (Ashcroft was not present), Burton fumed, "This is not a monarchy. . . . The legislative branch has oversight responsibility to make sure there is no corruption in the executive branch."[5] In place of Ashcroft, the Department of Justice Criminal Division Chief of Staff issued the administration's statement before the committee. The statement claimed that revealing information about DOJ investigations would have a "chilling effect" on department deliberations in the future. Nonetheless, during the hearing the witness, Michael Horowitz, allowed that although the administration had adopted the policy that Congress should never receive access to deliberative documents, in the future the DOJ could conduct a case-by-case analysis of the validity of congressional requests for such documents.[6] This statement indicated for the first time that there was some flexibility on the administration's part with regard to the principle of withholding deliberative materials.

The DOJ followed with a letter to Burton that emphasized the president's assertion of executive privilege over the subpoenaed documents and expressed a desire to reach some accommodation. Assistant Attorney General Daniel Bryant announced the unwillingness of the DOJ to release certain memoranda that pertained to former attorney general Reno's decision not to appoint a special counsel to investigate allegations of campaign improprieties in the 1996 Clinton-Gore campaign. Regarding the investigation of allegations of FBI corruption, he expressed at some length the DOJ's willingness to "work together" with the committee to provide "additional information without compromising the principles maintained by the executive branch."[7] Burton responded that the offer of accommodation was meaningless because ultimately the administration remained unwilling to allow the committee to review the most crucial documents for the purposes of an investigation.[8] White House Counsel Gonzales followed with the assurance that the administration did not have a "bright-line policy" of withholding all deliberative documents from Congress. Yet Gonzales proceeded to assert that "the Executive Branch has traditionally protected those highly sensitive deliberative documents against public and congressional disclosure," a characterization that Burton strongly rejected.[9]

It is truly puzzling that President Bush took his first official executive privilege stand over materials concerning closed DOJ investigations. The administration acknowledged that it was necessary to regain the lost ground of executive privilege after the years of Clinton scandals and misuses of that power. Yet it chose to do so in a circumstance in which there appeared little justification for the exercise of that power. Certainly there were no national security implications, or a public interest at stake, and the claim of privilege did not even fall into the category of protecting the integrity of an ongoing criminal investigation.

The dispute between the branches became especially heated when news stories reported that the FBI had abused its authority when it investigated organized crime in the 1960s and 1970s. There was credible evidence that the FBI had caused the wrongful imprisonment of at least one person while it protected a government witness who committed multiple murders even while he was in protection. Burton demanded access to ten key DOJ documents in order to investigate the allegations of wrongful conduct by the FBI. The documents that Burton requested were on average twenty-two years old.[10] The administration refused to turn over these documents and Burton threatened to take this controversy to the courts.

Burton had the unanimous support of the committee, as evidenced by a 6 February 2002, hearing at which all the members, Republican and Democrat alike, joined in lambasting the administration's actions and declared their intention to carry the fight for the documents as far as necessary.[11] The complete unanimity of the committee was remarkable, especially given that the administration—during a period of war and with extraordinary high levels of public approval—had made direct appeals for support to GOP members of the committee on the eve of the hearing. At the beginning of the hearing several GOP members openly declared their disdain for this tactic and said that, regardless of party affiliation or a president's popularity, they were ready to defend Congress's prerogatives. Some members used colorful language to describe their anger at the administration's refusal to cooperate with the committee.

The administration witness at the hearing, Daniel Bryant, an assistant attorney general in the Office of Legislative Affairs of the Department of Justice, asserted the position that all prosecutorial documents are "presumptively privileged" and never available for congressional inspection. This claim ran counter to a long history of congressional access to DOJ prosecutorial documents, especially in cases of closed investigations where the need for secrecy has disappeared.[12] It also appeared to contradict earlier administration policy clarifications that there was no blanket policy of withholding such materials from Congress. Bryant stated that the administration was willing to give an oral presentation about the general contents of the disputed documents to members of the committee, but not to allow the members to actually see the documents. This offer only brought more comments of disdain from committee members.

On 1 March 2002, the two sides reached an accommodation in which the committee would be permitted to openly view six of the ten disputed documents. The agreement allowed both sides to declare victory. The committee claimed that it had won the right to access the most important documents that were necessary for its investigation of the Boston FBI office scandal. The administration took the view that it had allowed access only to a narrow category of documents—in this case, those that concerned an indicted FBI agent were considered necessary to Congress's oversight function. The administration continued to insist that it did not have to give Congress access to deliberative documents. Ultimately, the committee accepted this agreement because of a lack of a consensus that members should instead continue to push for all ten documents.

The also administration prevailed in withholding three key documents pertaining to former attorney general Reno's decision not to appoint a special counsel to investigate campaign finance abuses by the 1996 Clinton-Gore campaign. The inability of the committee to achieve a total victory reflected the unwillingness of certain Democratic members to push for these three documents.

The resolution of this controversy was somewhat reminiscent of many former executive privilege battles, especially ones during the Reagan years. In each of those battles the administration staked out a strong stand on executive privilege and signaled a refusal to compromise; Congress persisted and used its authority to pressure the administration to turn over the disputed materials; the administration ultimately relented on either all the documents, or at least the key ones; both sides walked away and declared victory.

In this case, though, the committee achieved only a partial victory. Furthermore, that the administration held the line on certain categories of documents signaled the likelihood of additional disputes between the branches during the Bush presidency.

The Presidential Records Act of 1978
and Executive Order 13223

The next effort by the Bush administration to invoke executive privilege stemmed from the Presidential Records Act, which Congress passed in 1978 to establish procedures for the public release of the papers of presidential administrations. Initially the act allowed for the public release of presidential papers twelve years after an administration had left office. The principle being furthered by the law was that these presidential records ultimately belong to the public and should be made available for inspection within a reasonable period of time. Section 2206 of the act gave responsibility for implementing this principle to the National Archives and Records Administration (NARA). The act retained the public disclosure exemptions of the Freedom of Information Act (FOIA) that stated certain materials involving national security or state secrets could be withheld from public view for longer than the twelve years period.

The only major change from 1978 until the Bush administration occurred on 18 January 1989, when President Ronald Reagan issued Executive Order 12267, which expanded certain implementation regulations of NARA. The executive order identified three areas in which records could be withheld: national security, law enforcement, and the deliberative process privilege of the executive branch (Section 1g). In addition, it gave a sitting president primary authority to assert privilege over the records of a former president. Furthermore, although the executive order recognized that a former president has the right to claim executive privilege over his administration's papers, the Archivist of the United States did not have to abide by his claim. The incumbent president could override the Archivist with his own assertion of executive privilege, but that had to occur within a period of thirty days after the decision of the Archivist. After that period, absent a formal claim of executive privilege, the documents were to be automatically released.

On 1 November 2001, President Bush issued Executive Order 13223 to override portions of Reagan's 1989 order and to vastly expand the scope of privileges available to current and former presidents. Bush's executive order dropped the law enforcement category and added two others: the presidential communications privilege and the attorney-client or attorney work product privileges. In addition, former presidents had the power to assert executive privilege over their own papers, even if the incumbent president disagrees. The executive order also gave Bush the power to assert executive privilege over a past administration's papers, even if the former president disagreed. The Bush standard therefore allowed any claim of privilege over old documents by an incumbent or past president to stand.[13] Furthermore, the order required anyone seeking to overcome constitutionally based privileges to have a "demonstrated, specific need" for presidential records (Section 2c). The Presidential Records Act of 1978 did not contain such a high obstacle for those seeking access to presidential documents to overcome. Thus, under Bush's executive order, the presumption was always in favor of secrecy, whereas previously the general presumption was in favor of openness.

President Bush's action set off challenges by public advocacy groups, academic professional organizations, press groups, and some members of Congress. All were concerned that his executive order vastly expanded the scope of governmental secrecy in a way that was damaging to democratic institutions. Several groups, including the American Historical Association, the Organization of American Historians, and Public Citizen, initiated a lawsuit to have it overturned. Congress held hearings that were highly critical of the change.[14] A federal district court on 1 October 2007, struck down the provision of the Bush EO that had allowed a former president indefinitely to withhold the release of records from his administration.[15] The Bush administration did not contest this ruling. Once the Democratic Party seized control of Congress in 2007, there were additional hearings and challenges to Bush's EO. And in 2009, President Barack Obama reversed the Bush EO altogether.

It is clear that Bush's executive order improperly trenched on an Act of Congress and attempted to expand executive privilege far beyond the traditional standards for the exercise of that power. A number of problems with the executive order stand out.

First, presidential papers are of such importance to our governing system and to the American public that they should be handled by statute, not executive order. Presidential papers are ultimately public documents that are part of our national records and are paid for by public funds. These materials should not be treated merely as private papers that any president or former president can order hidden from congressional and public view. Ultimately they provide detail on and insight into important events in our nation's history. They should not and must not be forgotten.

Second, there is precedent for allowing an ex-president to assert executive privilege.[16] Yet the standard for allowing such a claim is very high, and executive privilege cannot stand merely because an ex-president has some personal or political interest in preserving secrecy. A former president's interest in maintaining confidentiality begins to erode substantially from the day he leaves office and it continues to erode even further over time. Bush's executive order did not acknowledge any such limitation on a former president's interest in confidentiality.

Third, the executive order made it far too easy for executive privilege claims by former presidents to stand and almost impossible for those challenging them to get information in a timely and useful way. The legal constraints could have effectively delayed requests for information for years as these matters were fought out in the courts. These obstacles alone likely would have settled the issue in favor of former presidents because many with an interest in access to information would have concluded that they do not have the ability or the resources to stake a viable challenge. The burden shifts then from those who must justify withholding information to those who have made a claim for access to information.

Fourth, executive privilege may actually have been frivolous in this case because there were already other secrecy protections in place for national security purposes. For instance, sensitive Central Intelligence Agency information is not only protected by certain exemptions in the FOIA but also by other statutes that shield "intelligence sources and methods" from disclose.[17] What the Bush administration tried to do was expand executive privilege substantially to cover what existing statutes and regulations already protected. Furthermore, a general interest in confidentiality is not enough to sustain a claim of executive privilege over old documents that may go back as far as twenty years.[18] Ultimately, President Obama did the right thing in reversing this ill-conceived executive order.

The Energy Task Force Controversy

The Bush administration was especially aggressive in its efforts to defend and expand what it considers constitutionally based presidential prerogatives. The 11 September 2001 terrorist attacks against the United States certainly provided a powerful context for the administration to enlarge executive power. Indeed, as noted above, Vice President Cheney had said that the administration was committed to reversing the modern trend that he perceived of legislative encroachments on executive powers combined with weak presidential responses to those encroachments.[19] Cheney, with the backing of President Bush, would lead an effort to protect, and even enhance, executive powers in a controversy over internal discussions of national energy policy development.

In this case, on 29 January 2001, President Bush announced the creation of the National Energy Policy Development Group (NEPDG), better known as the energy task force.[20] The group's purpose was to develop "a national energy policy designed to help the private sector, and government at all levels, promote dependable, affordable, and environmentally sound production and distribution of energy for the future."[21] Bush appointed various federal officials to the task force with Vice President Cheney as chairman.[22] The task force held a total of ten sessions between January and May of 2001,[23] with group members and staff conducting numerous supplemental meetings "to collect individual views" for future energy policy decision making.[24] These meetings included "nonfederal energy stakeholders, principally petroleum, coal, nuclear, natural gas, and electricity industry representatives and lobbyists" and, to "a more limited degree . . . academic experts, policy organizations, environmental advocacy groups, and private citizens."[25] The task force issued its final report on 16 May 2001[26] and formally disbanded on 30 September 2001.[27]

The Bush administration resisted efforts by members of Congress and outside interest groups to reveal information about the task force meetings. This struggle developed into a full-blown legal controversy and ultimately a Supreme Court decision that addressed broader issues pertaining to presidential secrecy, protecting internal deliberations in an administration, and separation of powers.

Congress and the Energy Task Force

Challenges to task force secrecy began with a 19 April 2001 letter from Democratic Representatives John Dingell (D-Mich.) and Henry Waxman (D-Calif.). They wrote the task force's executive director, Andrew Lundquist, and requested that he answer "a series of questions relating to the participants, the purpose, the outcome, and the role of federal employees at these meetings" and that he send "copies of all documents and records produced or received by the task force" under the Federal Advisory Committee Act (FACA),[28] which mandates that executive branch advisory committees adhere to various openness requirements such as making available to the public their minutes, records, reports, and other documents.[29] That same day, Dingell and Waxman wrote the General Accounting Office[30] and encouraged Comptroller General David Walker to investigate the operations of the energy task force. These congressional requests were due in large part to press reports that the task force had been meeting in secret with representatives of various groups that had a direct interest in the development of the nation's energy policy.

After two weeks, David Addington responded to the 19 April letter. However, he refused to divulge significant information germane to the request and noted that "the FACA does not apply to" the task force because section 3(2) of the act exempts "any committee that is composed wholly of" federal employees.[31] Addington's letter sparked an angry reply from Dingell and Waxman. Again, the congressmen stated that the energy task force was in violation of FACA—not only through its actions of failing to fully answer their questions, but also by refusing to hand over all relevant documents.[32] Meanwhile, as a result of Dingell and Waxman's 19 April letter, the GAO requested detailed information including "copies of documents and phone records" concerning the task force. On 16 May, Addington replied that the GAO needed to state where the agency's power to investigate originated because it may very well "intend to intrude into the heart of Executive deliberations," which "the law protects to ensure the candor in Executive deliberations necessary to effective government."[33]

On 22 May, Representatives Dingell and Waxman wrote another strongly worded letter to Addington, stating: "We are dismayed by your lack of full cooperation with GAO." Turning to the assertion that "the law protects" the task force from congressional oversight, the congressmen asserted that they were "not aware of any . . . law [of executive protection] which is applicable to Congressional investigations." Furthermore, they questioned the idea of invoking executive privilege, stating that only "the President himself" could claim such a right and if he had done such, to send a note of clarification on the subject.[34] Three days later, Addington replied with an admonishment for the congressmen: "The letter of May 22, 2001, confirms that it is the GAO, and not the House of Representatives, whose power is intended to be exercised by the conduct of the proposed inquiry, and thus it appears that the letter of May 16th to the General Counsel of the GAO *was addressed to the proper party*."[35]

As requested, GAO's General Counsel Anthony Gamboa answered Addington's 16 May letter with the assertion that the agency did have the authority to investigate the energy task force. "Under 31 U.S.C. §717," Gamboa declared, the "GAO is required to evaluate a program or activity when requested by a congressional committee of jurisdiction." That request came from Representatives Dingell and Waxman with their 19 April letter. In addition, Gamboa said that 31 U.S.C. §712 and 31 U.S.C. §716(a), respectively, gave the GAO the power to review matters involving "public money" and the "broad statutory right of access to" all energy task force records.[36]

In a rejoinder, Addington raised the concern that §717 did not truly apply to the task force. That section only gave the GAO the power over "a program or activity," not "the Vice President and the other officers of the United States." Addington asserted that the GAO has no authority over constitutional officers in the executive branch. Without a doubt, the GAO's power should be "narrowly circumscribed" and it has "limited" ability to investigate. Furthermore, as ranking minority members, Dingell and Waxman "do not constitute a 'request' from 'a committee of Congress with jurisdiction over the program or activity.'"[37] Only a majority of a committee of Congress can issue such a request, which was something that had not yet been done. However, Addington did state that the GAO has the narrow authority to investigate the use of public money. Therefore, he assured Gamboa that the Vice President would send all documents related to the costs incurred by the task force.[38]

The GAO's response was to send two letters; the first asserted its right to investigate all matters related to the task force and the second demanded a detailed list of documents concerning organizational makeup and energy policy deliberations.[39] On 2 August these letters compelled Vice President Cheney to inform Congress that the Comptroller General had "exceed[ed] his lawful authority" under §716.[40] Cheney further claimed that the GAO lacked the authority to seek access to task force information regarding policy development because the organization only has the power to review the results of programs. In turn, the GAO issued a statement in which it refuted Cheney's interpretations of the scope of its authority and continued to request information relating to the task force.[41]

Dingell and Waxman, taking into consideration Addington's 7 June remarks concerning the GAO's power to investigate only when requested by a congressional committee, sent a general letter of Congress to Cheney in which they expressed their dismay at his refusal to cooperate with the GAO.[42] The last substantial action before the 11 September terrorist attacks came from a GAO statement that professed the need for more candid information from the vice president's office. As the Comptroller General Walker stated, "This is a very serious matter with significant implications for GAO, the Congress, and the American people." Walker's remarks ended with a warning of "possible litigation."[43] However, shortly after 11 September the GAO curtailed its threat to sue: "Given our current national focus on combating terrorism and enhancing homeland security, this matter is not a current priority. We will determine whether and when we should proceed to court on this matter in due course."[44]

By early December, Waxman again requested information about the task force. "In light of Enron's financial collapse," he ordered that Cheney's office "release information about secret contacts . . . with [the] Enron Corporation." Waxman now had an issue that could galvanize the public. Indeed, he warned the Bush administration that its actions created "an appearance of impropriety."[45] Waxman had tied the task force to the Enron collapse and thus made the claims of secrecy and cover-up much more convincing.

On 3 January 2002, Addington announced that although the energy task force met with Enron representatives on numerous occasions, these officials "did not communicate information about its financial position in any of the meetings with the Vice President or with the National Energy Policy Development Group's support staff." Addington's letter listed the number and dates of these meetings,[46] but in an 8 January reply, Waxman again asserted his dissatisfaction with the information given. Although he commended Cheney "for revealing the information disclosed," he wrote that the 3 January letter failed to provide any of the "important details about these meetings." Waxman listed a number of needed facts: one, "the subjects discussed at the meetings"; two, "any requests for changes in federal policies made by Enron executives at the meetings"; three, "copies of any documents presented or discussed at the meetings"; and four, "the names of persons attending the meetings."[47] Cheney's office did not respond. As such, Waxman sent two additional letters on 16 and 25 of January concerning disclosure of matters relating to Enron.[48]

In the meantime, Comptroller General Walker announced that he would decide within a month "whether to file suit regarding GAO's access to NEPDG records."[49] Despite this statement various members of both the Senate and House began to pressure the GAO to move forward with its lawsuit. On 22 January, Senators Joseph Lieberman (D-Conn.), Ernest Hollings (D-SC), Carl Levin (D-Mich.), and Byron Dorgan (D-ND) sent a letter of support to the GAO in its investigation of the task force.[50] Two days later, Dingell and Waxman requested that the GAO legally challenge the task force's refusals to hand over all energy policy information.[51]

In response to all of these maneuverings, Vice President Cheney declared on 27 January that the administration was steadfast in its refusal to provide even some of the most basic information about the meetings because of an important principle involved: doing so would contribute to a further withering of traditional presidential prerogatives. In a news interview, Cheney made the following extraordinary statement: "In 34 years [in Washington], I have repeatedly seen an erosion of the powers and the ability of the president of the United States to do his job. We saw it in the War Powers Act. We saw it in the Budget Anti-Impoundment Act. We've seen it in cases like this before, where it's demanded that presidents cough up and compromise on important principles."[52]

On January 30, the GAO had finalized its decision to "take the steps necessary to file suit in United States District Court." Walker defended the GAO's statutory authority to access the energy task force's records and refuted Cheney's defense for withholding information. Furthermore, Walker stated that if the Bush administration wanted to stop the GAO it could at anytime through the president's power "under GAO's statutory access authority . . . to preclude judicial enforcement of GAO's access rights" or an assertion of executive privilege. Yet the administration did neither. As such, Walker stated the GAO would bring the matter to the courts "to enforce our access rights against a federal official."[53]

On 22 February, Walker filed suit against the Vice President,[54] stating that GAO's "repeated attempts to reach a reasonable accommodation on this matter have not been successful."[55] In the U.S. District Court for the District of Columbia, Judge John Bates ruled against Walker, dismissed the suit, and rejected the organization's standing claims.[56] The GAO decided not to attempt an appeal because doing so would require significant time and resources, and because other private litigants were already pursuing the same information through other lawsuits.[57] In its final report, the agency stated that the vice president's "unwillingness to provide NEPDG records and other related information precluded us from fully achieving our objectives in accordance with generally accepted government auditing standards and substantially limited our ability to answer" Congress.[58]

The efforts of some members of Congress and the GAO to gain access to various energy task force documents were thus unsuccessful. The Bush administration used three primary justifications to prevent disclosure. First, FACA did not apply to the task force because it consisted only of federal employees and thus was exempted from disclosure requirements. Second, the GAO had no authority to investigate the executive branch other than when dealing with public money. Finally, Democratic congressmen could not hold the White House accountable because, as minority members of Congress, they lacked the power to make a committee request for information.

Judicial Watch and the Sierra Club Join Forces

The only recourse—apart from Congress starting a full investigation—was for private litigants to pursue the disclosure of information against the administration. Judicial Watch, Inc., and the Sierra Club soon filed separate suits, later consolidated, against the energy task force.[59] The two groups alleged that the task force gave significant roles to private individuals, which resulted in a FACA violation.[60] They sought the release of documents relating to task force meetings to determine the extent of the allegedly illegal nature of the group. In July 2002, U.S. district court of D.C. Judge Emmet G. Sullivan granted the groups' request for discovery.[61] In so doing he held that the terms of FACA create "substantive requirements to which the government must adhere." The court went on to reason that if the facts of the complaints were true, the government then would be in violation of "the public access provisions of [FACA]."[62] Sullivan did not address the administration's separation of powers argument, which asserted that the application of FACA in this circumstance "interferes with the President's constitutionally protected ability to receive confidential advice from his advisors, even when those advisors include private individuals."[63] The court merely noted that a resolution to this question was "premature."

The administration immediately requested a motion for a stay of the proceedings and argued that "requiring [the White House] to review documents responsive to plaintiffs' discovery requests, disclose those for which no viable claim of [executive] privilege exists, and assert any applicable privileges with respect to specific documents, impermissibly interferes with 'core Article II' functions and imposes an unconstitutional burden on the Executive Branch."[64] The U.S. district court of D.C. rejected this argument and held that the White House responds "to discovery requests on a regular basis, asserting executive privilege with respect to specific requests for particular items when necessary."[65] The court determined that the administration was seeking a new constitutional right of immunity against disclosures under FACA. The result would be "to relieve" the President of his "responsibility" of even asserting executive privilege. The stay was therefore denied.[66]

Rather than comply with the discovery order, Cheney filed an interlocutory appeal in which he asked for review of the complex and serious constitutional issues raised. The U.S. district court of D.C. dismissed the appeal and held that it did not disregard the "defendants' constitutional challenges"; rather, "it is out of concern for the seriousness of this issue" that it decided discovery was appropriate.[67] The administration then asked the D.C. circuit (appeals) court to issue a writ of mandamus to require the district court to stop the discovery process and argued that the broad inquiry would violate the principle of separation of powers.[68] The appeals court declined and determined that "so long as the separation of powers conflict that petitioners anticipate remains hypothetical, we have no authority to exercise the extraordinary remedy of mandamus."[69] Any alleged harm, the court concluded, would be mitigated through a "narrow, carefully focused discovery" process.[70]

The Supreme Court Takes Up the Case

On 15 December 2003, the Supreme Court granted certiorari to decide whether the discovery was constitutional and if the appeals court had the power to stop it.[71] In the Bush administration's brief to the Court, the central component of its argument was a separation of powers claim, which hinged on the president's "specific constitutional authority under both the Opinion and Recommendations Clauses[64] to request the opinions of department heads and to propose such legislation as the President may deem necessary."[73] Turning to the issue of executive privilege, the White House argued that such a claim was limited and would not protect the president from all discovery requests. The fact was that "the President's constitutional interests in being able to obtain confidential advice regarding his constitutionally assigned responsibilities is [*sic*] not coextensive with, nor fully protected by the possibility of invoking, Executive privilege."[74]

The administration next asserted that "Congress does not have the power to inhibit, confine, or control the process though which the President formulates the legislative measures he proposes or the administration actions he orders."[75] As such FACA violates separation of powers concerns[76] because Congress cannot "validly regulate the process by which the President gathers advice and information to formulate his policies and recommendations, and it has no greater legislative authority to empower private individuals to intrude into that process."[77] The end result was that a separation of powers claim, not just the use of executive privilege, prevents both Congress and private citizens from intruding upon executive branch deliberations.[78]

During oral argument U.S. Solicitor General Ted Olson specifically addressed the concern of why the president had not made an executive privilege claim: "The act of forcing the President to invoke executive privilege every time someone files a lawsuit . . . means that FACA would be used in every case to file a lawsuit to challenge the President and the Vice President's ability to . . . obtain opinions."[79] Olson also remarked that executive privilege might not cover "every scrap of paper,"[80] whereas an assertion of a separation of powers violation would guarantee protection from disclosure. Finally, Olson argued that using executive privilege would place too big of an administrative burden on the White House by requiring "the President and the Vice President to spend time with documents" searching for what is and is not privileged.[81] What the administration sought was blanket protection from any discovery request—which was something executive privilege could not provide.

In its opinion the Supreme Court vacated the judgment of the appeals court, and remanded the case for rehearing.[82] Speaking for the Court, Justice Anthony Kennedy sided with the administration's argument that separation of powers considerations were of paramount concern. Citing *U.S. v. Nixon* he declared that the lower courts must "give recognition to the paramount necessity of protecting the Executive Branch from vexatious litigation that might distract it from the energetic performance of its constitutional duties."[83] These concerns are even greater when considering civil litigation, the Court held. Rejecting the appeals court's claim that *Nixon* stood as an absolute barrier against discovery protection, Kennedy asserted that the need for information in civil cases "does not share the urgency or significance of" a criminal subpoena request.[84] The failure to disclose information in a civil case, he reasoned, "does not hamper another branch's ability to perform its 'essential functions' in quite the same way."[85] Addressing the application of FACA to the White House, Kennedy argued even if the Court declared that the act "embodies important congressional objectives, the only consequence from respondents' inability to obtain the discovery they seek is that it would be more difficult for private complainants to vindicate Congress policy objectives under FACA."[86]

After it declared that the "Executive Branch, at its highest level" needs judicial help "to protect its constitutional prerogatives,"[87] the Court turned to the issue of executive privilege. Here Kennedy held that "the breadth of the discovery requests in this case compared to the narrow subpoena orders in *United States* v *Nixon*, our precedent provides no support for the proposition that the Executive Branch 'shall bear the burden' of invoking executive privilege with sufficient specificity and of making particularized objections."[88] The fact is that contrary to what the lower courts determined, "*Nixon* does not leave them the sole option of inviting the Executive Branch to invoke executive privilege while remaining otherwise powerless to modify a party's overly broad discovery requests." Using executive privilege, Kennedy declared, "is an extraordinary assertion of power 'not to be lightly invoked.'"[89] Once invoked, the judicial branch "is forced into the difficult task of balancing the need for information in a judicial proceeding and the Executive's Article II prerogatives. This inquiry places courts in the awkward position of evaluating the Executive's claims of confidentiality and autonomy, and pushes to the fore difficult questions of separation of powers and checks and balances."[90] Kennedy therefore ordered the appeals court to give due consideration to "the weighty separation-of-powers objections" when reconsidering the appeal and addressing the discovery issue.[91]

The Significance of the Supreme Court's Action

As one commentator said of *Cheney*, even "a dense reader could not possibly miss the Court's point."[92] Not only had many of the lower courts' arguments been refuted, but the high court had handed to the administration a significant victory. The Supreme Court appears to have bought into the administration's assertion that forcing disclosure would have a negative impact on the president's ability to carry out his responsibilities under Article II of the Constitution. As such, the decision established a rather high standard of judicial deference to executive authority.

Acting on the Supreme Court's clarifications the appeals court had no other choice but to rule for Cheney and issue a writ of mandamus ordering the district court to dismiss Judicial Watch and the Sierra Club's complaints.[93] Circuit Judge A. Raymond Randolph wrote that FACA must be interpreted "strictly" in light of the "severe" separation of powers concerns. He therefore reasoned that Congress could not have intended FACA coverage to include presidential advisory committees (which are normally exempt from FACA if composed of federal employees) when private citizens merely participate in "meetings or activities."[94] "The outsider," Randolph stated, "might make an important presentation, he might be persuasive, the information he provides might affect the committee's judgment. But having neither a vote nor a veto over the advice the committee renders to the President, he is no more a member of the committee than the aides who accompany Congressmen or cabinet officers to committee meetings."[95] Randolph concluded that "separation-of-powers concerns strongly support this interpretation of FACA." Therefore, in "making decisions on personnel and policy, and in formulating legislative proposals, the President must be free to seek confidential information from many sources, both inside the government and outside."[96]

The appeals court's decision largely bypassed the constitutional concerns when it focused on the statutory issue of whether FACA even applied to the energy task force. However, in so doing the court greatly enhanced the administration's ability to block the disclosure of information. Narrowing the committee membership standard to only those who have a vote or veto allows for the executive branch to involve any number of private citizens or groups without worrying about openness or accountability as long as they are not given ultimate decision-making authority. This understanding, as Michael J. Mongan reports in his review of the act, is misguided. In fact, Mongan notes that "the legislative history—not to mention the text—of FACA reveals no congressional intent to cabin the definition of 'member' so narrowly."[97] In effect the intent of Congress appears to have been misconstrued.

The Supreme Court's opinion strengthened the Bush White House's argument that it had the right to withhold from the public and Congress information dealing with public policy discussions with private parties. No doubt the Court was correct that one should be mindful of the vexing constitutional issues at stake. However, there are also important tradeoffs between transparency and secrecy that must be considered and resolved. The disclosure of information has long been held as one of the primary ways to combat fraud and abuse in government. As Supreme Court Justice Louis Brandeis once stated: "Publicity is justly commended as a remedy for social and industrial diseases. Sunlight is said to be the best of disinfectants; electric light the most efficient policeman."[98] On the other hand, there needs to be some level of confidentiality at the executive level where a president has the ability to discuss public policy matters in confidence. Such conflicts thus involve a balancing test to determine, under the circumstances, which branch's interests are more compelling.

The problem with the judiciary's answer to this controversy is that it provided far too much protection to the executive branch at the cost of openness and accountability. The solution, in essence, offset the balance of power between the president and Congress. What the courts ended up endorsing was an immunity from disclose for the White House that precludes any type of nuanced approach that could recognize tradeoffs and political accommodations that seek to balance the interests of the two branches. These decisions merely gave a license for presidents so disposed to maintain a shroud of secrecy at the expense of accountability, which is so essential to our republican form of government.

Nonetheless, some leading thinkers on executive power differ and, like Cheney, perceive the former Bush administration's efforts as a corrective against the modern trend of supposedly weak presidential responses to legislative encroachments. They see the judicial resolution as, in essence, restoring the balance. Unitary executive scholar and advocate John Yoo asserts that the Bush administration indeed had been "energetic" in its efforts to protect and expand executive powers. For example, he maintains that the president:

> has re-classified national security information made public in earlier administrations and declined, citing executive privilege, to disclose information to Congress or the courts about its energy policy task force. The White House has [also] declared that the Constitution allows the president to sidestep laws that invade his executive authority. That is why Mr. Bush has issued hundreds of signing statements—more than any previous president—reserving his right not to enforce unconstitutional laws.[99]

According to Yoo, these actions were not only perfectly justifiable on administrative and policy-making grounds, but they were constitutionally mandated as well. As for the energy task force controversy, he said that the Bush White House was correct in defending its executive branch prerogatives. In addition, he noted the Supreme Court's ruling was the natural conclusion when one looks at the facts of the case. "I would think," Yoo insisted, "that this is the kind of case where you would want the government to get that kind of protection."[100]

In retrospect, could this controversy over access to documents have been handled differently? The whole episode was potentially avoidable in the first place. The Bush administration came to office under some suspicion by its critics for the president's and vice president's various ties to the oil industry. Thus, as scholar Louis Fisher suggested, it was politically foolish for the administration to so heavily consult industry advocates in the task force meetings without including sufficient countervailing voices from environmental, consumer protection, and labor groups. Had the administration done so, it could have easily replied to any request for information about the task force meetings by revealing that it had invited a balanced group of interested parties and therefore avoided the political fallout from the accusations of a cover-up.[101] Nonetheless, despite the political shortcomings of the administration's actions, it is possible that some in the Bush White House, especially the vice president, actually wanted a constitutional battle because they believed that they could win and that a victory would further the cause of reestablishing presidential prerogatives.

In all likelihood there would have been a resolution more favorable to those seeking access had Congress acted more forcefully and not relied on the GAO or outside groups to file lawsuits. Congress did not exhaust all of its constitutional mechanisms for getting access to the information that it had wanted and thus became the architect of its own ultimate defeat at the hands of the judicial branch. But what if Congress instead had held more hearings, issued subpoenas for documents and testimony, and threatened contempt citations against the administration if it failed to cooperate? Such an approach worked during the 2001–2002 period when the House Government Reform Committee headed by Rep. Dan Burton (R-Ind.) had demanded access to DOJ documents and eventually prevailed. The GOP-led committee indeed had challenged the Bush administration in a number of separation of powers disputes, and Burton had made it clear that a part of his job in that capacity was to protect the institutional prerogatives of Congress against what he saw as an administration engaging in frequent power-grabs against the legislature. Yet, in the case of the energy task force controversy, Republican voices against the administration were largely quiet or nonexistent. The White House prevailed ultimately as a consequence of legislative inaction.

The outcome was all the more regrettable because the implicit claim of executive privilege by the administration in this case was not very strong. At the outset, the requests for information about the energy task force were overly broad. The initial GAO request, for example, demanded "records" in the forms of e-mails, voice mails, drawings, plans, checks and cancelled checks, bank statements, ledgers, books, diaries, logs, video recordings, telexes, notes, invoices, and drafts.

Over time the GAO narrowed its request merely to factual information such as the names of persons who attended meetings and the costs of those meetings, but not deliberative information. That was reasonable, although because of the initial broad request Cheney may have dug in because he believed he would ultimately be dragged into a multistep process of the GAO seeking more and more information over time. He may also have been concerned that the releasing of the names of those who met with the task force would result in their being called to testify before Congress. Nonetheless, once the GAO narrowed its request to factual-based and not deliberative information, the administration's claim to a compelling need for secrecy weakened considerably. It is a bit surprising, therefore, that the Supreme Court gave so much deference to the administration's positions on secrecy and separation of powers.

The lesson for Congress is that it should not rely on outside interests or an arm of the legislative branch (the GAO in this case) to take up a challenge against executive power. Congress has the institutional means to confront the executive branch, although it does not always have the will to do so. There are numerous instances of Congress gaining access to executive branch information by using its constitutionally based powers to challenge administrations. Indeed, when Congress has acted in this fashion, it has prevailed far more often against the executive than it has failed to achieve access. Only Congress is best positioned to protect its own powers and prerogatives.

Presidential Pardons and the Expansion of Executive Branch Secrecy

President Bush attempted to put his own unitary stamp on the presidential power of secrecy in 2002 when he directed his administration to refuse to release documents related to former president Bill Clinton's last-minute pardons. Although Bush never made a formal claim of executive privilege, he did use the codified version of the presidential communications privilege exemption found in the FOIA to block access to the pardon files.[102] This incident parallels closely with the energy task force controversy involving Vice President Cheney. Although again there was not a formal claim of executive privilege, in protecting the administration from having to release requested information regarding the energy task force hearings, Bush directed the vice president to invoke many of the traditional bases of a formal privilege claim. In both of these cases, the failure to utter the words "executive privilege" did not matter because the administration advanced the same principle with different language.

The problem of withholding these pardon documents was that they were in the possession of the Justice Department's pardon office and they had never been seen by the president or any White House official. The question came down to whether the FOIA privilege exemption could be expanded to include documents that had never been directly associated with the president. The administration seemed to say it could. A Justice Department official remarked that "The pardon power is exclusively granted to the president" and any "information, any advice and any memos would be part of the deliberative process. We want to preserve the integrity of that process."[103] This understanding of what can be classified as privileged reaches beyond the traditional executive privilege areas of presidential communications and deliberative process. It was a more expansive position from what previous administrations had claimed in that it provided protection to all executive branch officials regardless of their association to the president or to the White House more generally.

In 2003 U.S. district court of D.C. judge Gladys Kessler accepted the Bush administration's argument noting that the presidential communications privilege claimed in Exemption 5 of FOIA "must be viewed in its broader, historical context, allowing presidential advisors to provide the President with the fullest and most candid information and advice regarding decisions to be made in many sensitive areas, including the granting or denial of pardon requests."[104] In light of this rather expansive reading of the presidential communications privilege, the case was appealed to the D.C. circuit court.

At the circuit court level, writing for the majority, Judge Judith Rogers noted the importance of striking "a balance between the twin values of transparency and accountability of the executive branch on the one hand, and on the other hand, protection of the confidentiality of Presidential decisionmaking and the President's ability to obtain candid, informed advice."[105] Rogers acknowledged that Congress had placed great emphasis on disclosure in FOIA requests. With that in mind, she declared that the presidential communications privilege only applies to documents "solicited and received" by the president or "his immediate White House advisers who have 'broad and significant responsibility for investigating the advice to be given the President.'"[106] Limiting the definition of executive privilege, the court said, recognized certain "principles underlying the presidential communications privilege" and conceded "the dangers of expanding it too far."[107]

More specifically, Rogers believed that an "extension of the privilege to internal Justice Department documents that never make their way to the Office of the President on the basis that the documents were created for the sole purpose of advising the President on a non-delegable duty is unprecedented and unwarranted."[108] She warned that "a bright-line expanding the privilege could have the effect of inviting use of the presidential privilege to shield communications on which the President has no intention of relying in exercising his pardon duties, for the sole purpose of raising the burden for those who seek their disclosure."[109]

The D.C. circuit court correctly balanced the competing needs for candor in presidential-level discussions and the goal of openness in government that Congress had intended when it established the FOIA provisions. All too often presidents try to modify legislative enactments not through the process of amending existing laws but by announcing a presidential right and expanding power without any constitutional, legal, or historical justification. In this case, the Justice Department tried to expand the definition of presidential communications privilege to reach down into all levels of the executive branch. If such a characterization held, then any action by a department or agency would be given a much higher level of protection from disclosure. In a sense what the Justice Department wanted in this case was to make all departments and agencies an extension of the presidency and receive the benefits of constitutional protection of the office of the president. Extending presidential power and control into all levels of government is inherently dangerous. The circuit court was correct to reject this position and the ruling was a clear defeat for President Bush.

The U.S. Attorneys Firings

President Bush's early efforts to expand executive privilege set off firestorms of protests. Yet criticism from Congress and from outside interests did not dampen his commitment to protecting and expanding presidential secrecy. Thus, in 2007 Bush fueled more firestorms when he made multiple claims of executive privilege to conceal White House documents and to prevent presidential aides from testifying before Congress about the controversial decision to force the resignations of a number of U.S. attorneys.

The controversy over the forced resignations or "firings" of the U.S. attorneys highlighted an enduring issue in debates over executive privilege: that is, whether some legislative or judicial "line-drawing" would help in the future to resolve such battles. Although it is tempting to constrain the future use of executive privilege, we see things differently. That is, this controversy showcased the necessity of leaving the definition of executive privilege broad enough to allow for a process of give-and-take between the branches, even if it meant an occasional game of brinksmanship that locked the opposing sides in a protracted battle. The theory of separated powers envisions the inevitability of occasional conflicts between the branches, which is far preferable to resorting to narrow legalisms that would constrain the flexibility built into the system.

The Process of Appointing U.S. Attorneys

U.S. attorneys function as chief prosecutors for violations of federal criminal and civil law and act as defense counsel on behalf of the United States in civil actions brought against the government in districts for which they are appointed.[110] There are currently ninety-three U.S. attorneys serving in the ninety-four federal judicial districts (one U.S. attorney is appointed to serve the Guam and the Northern Mariana Islands districts). Congress has given the responsibility of appointing U.S. attorneys to the president with the advice and consent of the Senate.[111]

Although presidents have the authority to nominate whomever they choose, the custom of senatorial courtesy has produced a system where the decision has been transferred to the home-state senator of the president's political party. If there are no friendly senators in the state then the responsibility usually falls on the senior House member, state governor, or party chairman to recommend a candidate. However, even minority party members of the Senate are often consulted about appointment changes in the federal judicial districts within their states.

There have been two recent changes to the method of appointing U.S. attorneys that directly relate to the controversy in question. On 9 March 2006, Congress passed the reauthorization of the USA PATRIOT Act which, among other things, modified the way interim U.S. attorney appointments were managed. Prior to this law, the attorney general could make interim appointments for no more than 120 days. Once the appointment term expired the district court could appoint a U.S. attorney until the president and Senate filled the vacancy.[112] However, the PATRIOT Act eliminated the time limit giving the attorney general the authority to fill a vacancy indefinitely.[113] Those changes lasted from 9 March 2006 to 14 June 2007, when President Bush signed into law the Preserving United States Attorney Independence Act of 2007.[114]

The Plan to Replace the U.S. Attorneys

After Bush's reelection in 2004, the White House began to consider removing U.S. attorneys and appointing new ones.[115] On 3 February 2005, Alberto Gonzales replaced John Ashcroft as attorney general. Less than a month after taking office Gonzales signed a confidential memorandum that reorganized the process for hiring and firing U.S. attorneys and other political appointees. He gave the primary vetting responsibility to his chief of staff, D. Kyle Sampson, and to the deputy director of the Executive Office for U.S. Attorneys, Monica M. Goodling. During this time Goodling, Sampson, and John Nowacki prepared a list of U.S. attorneys to be dismissed,[116] which Sampson sent to the White House.[117]

Not until January 2006 did the process to replace U.S. attorneys heat up again. At that time Sampson recommended to White House Counsel Harriet Miers that the Department of Justice and the White House work together to determine which U.S. attorneys to replace. Sampson thought that a "limited number of U.S. attorneys could be targeted for removal and replacement, mitigating the shock to the system that would result from an across the board firing." He also provided a list of candidates to be removed.[118] The next month Goodling sent an e-mail with an attached spreadsheet that listed all U.S. attorneys that included information, among other things, on their political activities and whether or not they were members of the conservative Federalist Society.[119]

By September, Sampson urged a plan to not only dismiss various U.S. attorneys, but to do so by using the newly passed interim appointment law. He wrote that by avoiding Senate confirmation, "we can give far less deference to home state senators and thereby get 1.) our preferred person appointed and 2.) do it far faster and more efficiently at less political costs to the White House."[120]

On 15 November 2006, Sampson sent his dismissal plan to the White House for approval. A final meeting with Justice Department officials to discuss the U.S. attorney matter occurred on November 27 with Gonzales; Deputy Attorney General Paul J. McNulty; Sampson; Goodling; Assistant Attorney General for Legislative Affairs William Moschella; and then director of the Executive Office of U.S. Attorneys (EOUSA) Michael A. Battle attending.[121] A week later the White House gave its final approval. On 7 December the Justice Department phoned seven U.S. attorneys informing them of their removal.[122] Although the formal list of dismissals only included these seven, the Justice Department had removed several other individuals during the previous two years.[123]

Congress Responds, a Scandal Brews

Initially Congress barely reacted, but then after a number of news reports several members questioned the administration's actions. On 9 January 2007, Senators Patrick Leahy (D-VT) and Dianne Feinstein (D-Calif.) wrote to Gonzales and expressed their concerns. They requested that he refrain from "moving forward with" the changes and to "provide information regarding all instances in which you have exercised the authority to appoint an interim United States Attorney." The senators also asked for all "information on whether any efforts have been made to ask or encourage the former or current U.S. Attorneys to resign their position."[124] Two days later Senators Leahy, Feinstein, and Mark Pryor (D-Ark.) introduced legislation to prevent Gonzales from circumventing the Senate's advice and consent authority.[125]

An 18 January Senate Judiciary Committee hearing was the first time Congress formally questioned the attorney general about this matter. Gonzales, in a rather heated exchange with Feinstein, responded to several questions related to the controversy. Gonzales said he did not deny that the Justice Department had asked the U.S. attorneys to resign, but that such a request was part of a performance evaluation. "I think I would never ever make a change in a U.S. Attorney position for political reasons or if it would in any way jeopardize an ongoing serious investigation. I just would not do it."[126]

Not satisfied with such answers, the committee held additional hearings. In opening the 6 February hearing Senator Charles Schumer (D-NY) intoned: "I am committed to getting to the bottom of [this matter]. If we do not get the documentary information that we seek, I will consider moving to subpoena that material, including performance evaluations and other documents."[127] He added: "What happened here does not sound like an orderly and natural replacement of underperforming prosecutors; it sounds more like a purge. . . . it appears more reminiscent of a different sort of Saturday Night Massacre."[128]

Deputy Attorney General McNulty testified that the Justice Department had removed the U.S. attorneys for reasons of job performance, not political considerations. He added that the "indisputable fact is that United States attorneys serve at the pleasure of the president. They come and they go for lots of reasons."[129] When pressed to explain the removals of the U.S. attorneys in question, McNulty was evasive and said that he would not "discuss specific issues regarding people" because that would be "unfair to individuals to have a discussion like that in this setting in a public way."[130] Senator Arlen Specter replied that the committee routinely investigates personal aspects of people's lives during confirmation hearings.

Gonzales tried to diffuse the scandal with an op-ed column in the *Washington Post* in which he repeated that the reasons for the firings were "related to policy, priorities and management" and were not for political retaliation. He ended: "Like me, U.S. attorneys are political appointees, and we all serve at the pleasure of the president. If U.S. attorneys are not executing their responsibilities in a manner that furthers the management and policy goals of departmental leadership, it is appropriate that they be replaced."[131]

Gonzales's chief of staff Sampson resigned on 12 March 2007, saying "information given Congress that minimized White House involvement in the firings was the result of [Gonzales's] failure to tell key Justice Department officials about the extent of his communications with administration officials about the plan."[132] His replacement, Chuck Rosenberg, proceeded to ask the Justice Department's Inspector General to investigate whether the career prosecutor appointments had been politicized.[133]

Bush and Congress Dig In

On 20 March 2007, President Bush called the announcement and subsequent explanation of the U.S. attorney changes "confusing and, in some cases, incomplete. Neither the Attorney General nor I approve of how these explanations were handled. We're determined to correct the problem."[134] Bush announced the implementation of several steps to show the administration's "willingness to work with the Congress." These included allowing the attorney general and some of his staff to testify; permitting "relevant committee members, on a bipartisan basis, to interview key members of my staff to ascertain relevant facts"; and disclosing "all White House documents and e-mails involving direct communications with the Justice Department or any other outside person, including Members of Congress and their staff, related to this issue."[135] Bush maintained that he was offering a "reasonable solution" and concluded that he would "not go along with a partisan fishing expedition aimed at honorable public servants."[136] The proposal did not permit White House officials to testify about the U.S. attorney controversy. Asked by a reporter if he was willing to "go to the mat" and "take this to court," Bush replied "Absolutely."[137]

Thus, what Bush had characterized as a good-faith compromise was instead an open defiance of Congress's requests for certain relevant documents and for meaningful testimony. And he effectively dared Congress to take him to court.

On March 21, the House Judiciary Committee approved subpoenas for White House Counsel Karl Rove, Sampson, Miers, Deputy White House Counsel William Kelley, and Special Assistant to the President in the Office of Public Affairs J. Scott Jennings.[138] On March 22, the Senate Judiciary Committee approved subpoenas for Rove, Miers, and Kelley. However, Republican Senator Arlen Specter (Pa.) realized that "If we have the confrontation, we're not going to get this information for a very long time."[139] Neither committee actually issued any subpoenas at this point, as Congress wanted to give the president time to respond.

At a Justice Department press conference Gonzales said he had no prior knowledge of the process: "Mr. Sampson was charged with directing the process to ascertain who were weak performers, where we could do better in districts around the country. That is a responsibility that he had during the transition." He added, "I never saw documents. We never had a discussion about where things stood. What I knew was that there was ongoing effort that was led by Mr. Sampson, vetted through the Department of Justice, to ascertain where we could make improvements in U.S. attorney performances around the country."[140] Yet at the 29 March Senate Judiciary Committee hearing Sampson responded that "I don't think the attorney general's statement that he was not involved in any discussions of U.S. attorney removals was accurate. . . . I remember discussing with him this process of asking certain U.S. attorneys to resign."[141]

On 10 April, the House Judiciary Committee served the first subpoena for documents ordering that Gonzales turn over all information relating to the removals of U.S. attorneys. "We have been patient in allowing the [Justice] department to work through its concerns regarding the sensitive nature of some of these materials," Rep. John Conyers Jr. (D-Mich.), the panel's chairman, wrote Gonzales in a letter that accompanied the subpoena. "Unfortunately, the department has not indicated any meaningful willingness to find a way to meet our legitimate needs."[142] Two weeks later the committee passed a resolution that authorized House lawyers to apply for a court order granting Goodling immunity in exchange for her testimony. The U.S. district court of D.C. granted that immunity. In May the Senate Judiciary Committee subpoenaed Gonzales and demanded that he turn over all the relevant e-mails.[143] In June the Senate and House judiciary committees issued subpoenas to Miers and the former deputy assistant to the president and director of political affairs, Sara Taylor.

President Bush Invokes Executive Privilege

On 27 June 2007, Solicitor General and Acting Attorney General Paul Clement notified the president that it was his "considered legal judgment that you may assert executive privilege over the subpoenaed documents and testimony." Clement believed that these related to "internal White House communications about the possible dismissal and replacement of U.S. Attorneys" and thus such information falls "squarely within the scope of executive privilege." He reasoned that one "of the underlying purposes of the privilege is to promote sound decisionmaking by ensuring that senior Government officials and their advisers speak frankly and candidly during the decisionmaking process." Clement claimed that the deliberations in question "relate to the potential exercise by the President of an authority [nomination and removal] assigned to him alone." He declared Congress's oversight interest "sharply reduced by the thousands of documents and dozens of hours of interviews and testimony already provided to the Committees by the Department of Justice as part of its extraordinary effort at accommodation."[144]

The next day White House Counsel Fred Fielding wrote to Conyers and Leahy that Bush was claiming executive privilege and thus "the White House will not be making any production in response to [the] subpoenas for documents." Fielding said that "the President attempted to chart a course of cooperation. It was his intent that Congress receives information in a manner that accommodated Presidential prerogatives." He added that over "8,500 pages" of Justice Department documents had been released and numerous department personnel "have testified in public hearings." The president, he said, was willing to go further to allow White House staffers to testify and to produce additional communications between the White House and Justice Department. This offer "took care to protect fundamental interests of the Presidency and the constitutional principle of separation of powers." Fielding maintained that the president would be constrained in his ability to "receive candid and unfettered advice" if White House advisers were constantly afraid of being compelled to testify or to release documents to Congress.[145]

On 9 July Fielding again wrote Conyers and Leahy and this time asserted executive privilege regarding the testimony of Miers and Taylor. He claimed that the White House had acted "to protect a fundamental interest of the presidency" by not revealing internal decision-making processes.[146] Two days after this latest executive privilege claim, the Senate Judiciary Committee held another oversight hearing and Taylor testified, although she refused to answer questions that she considered protected by the privilege. Miers refused to testify and agreed to follow Bush's request not to appear before the committee.

House and Senate Judiciary Committees Vote for Contempt

On 25 July 2007, the House Judiciary Committee voted 22–17 to cite Miers and White House Chief of Staff Joshua Bolten for contempt of Congress.[147] Conyers said that this measure was taken "not only to gain an accurate picture of the facts surrounding the U.S. attorneys controversy, but to protect our constitutional prerogatives as a co-equal branch of government."[148] A Justice Department official said that contempt charges would not be enforced because "the House or Senate would have to ask the United States attorney for the District of Columbia to convene a grand jury with the aim of indicting Ms. Miers and Mr. Bolten."[149]

The following day Leahy issued subpoenas for Rove and Jennings to appear before the Senate Judiciary Committee at a 2 August hearing.[150] In addition, Schumer and other Democratic senators called for the appointment of a special prosecutor to determine if Gonzales "misled Congress or perjured himself" during his 24 July testimony before the Senate Judiciary Committee.[151]

On 1 August Bush invoked executive privilege for a third time in this controversy within a month, this time to prevent Rove from testifying.[152] Leahy protested that someone "who is now refusing to comply with Senate subpoenas, spoke publicly in speeches about these firings when the scandal first broke, but is suddenly unable to talk it about when he is under oath?"[153] Two weeks later, in a letter to Bush, Leahy expressed his frustration at the lack of cooperation from the White House and the "political corruption of law enforcement" in the scandal. Leahy ended with the warning that "the stonewalling leaves me and the Senate Judiciary Committee with few options other than considering citations for contempt of Congress against those who have refused to provide relevant testimony and documents to the Congress."[154]

On 16 August Leahy requested that the Justice Department Inspector General Glenn A. Fine "investigate and evaluate potential misleading, evasive, or dishonest testimony by Attorney General Alberto Gonzales before the Senate Judiciary Committee on July 24, 2007."[155] A few weeks later Fine said that there were ongoing investigations of questionable testimony that was provided by Gonzales.[156] Under fire, Gonzales resigned his post and Bush nominated former circuit court judge Michael B. Mukasey to serve as attorney general. Then in December the Senate Judiciary Committee voted to hold Bolten and Rove in contempt of Congress. The White House remained defiant; as Press Secretary Dana M. Perino said, "the constitutional prerogative of the president would make it a futile effort for Congress to refer contempt citations to U.S. attorneys."[157] Leahy fumed: "White House stonewalling is unilateralism at its worst, and it thwarts accountability. Executive privilege should not be invoked to prevent investigations into wrongdoing."[158] Nonetheless, the legislative session ended and Senate Majority Leader Harry Reid (D-NV) declared that the chamber would not take up the issue again until 2008.[159]

In early 2008 the House of Representatives voted 223–32 to issue contempt citations against Miers and Bolten.[160] The administration refused to enforce the contempt charges and the House quickly filed a lawsuit in the U.S. district court of D.C. The House requested that the court declare that Miers was not immune from testifying before a congressional committee and also sought the disclosure of documents withheld by Bolten.[161]

A central focus of this suit was the claim of absolute immunity that Principal Deputy Assistant Attorney General Stephen Bradbury articulated in his Office of Legal Counsel (OLC) July 10 memorandum. He declared that "Since at least the 1940s, Administrations of both political parties have taken the position that 'the President and his immediate advisers are absolutely immune from testimonial compulsion by a Congressional committee,'" which "'may not be overborne by competing congressional interests.'" Bradbury added the rationale that the "separation of powers principle" not only makes the president himself immune to testimony, but it also applies "to senior presidential advisers." Bradbury even broadened the absolute immunity claim to include former presidential aides such as Miers when Congress seeks "testimony about official matters that occurred during their time" in office.[162]

Yet it is inaccurate to claim that absolute immunity has a long history of protecting White House officials from compelled congressional testimony. Not even a claim of executive privilege has been successfully used to block executive branch advisers from appearing before Congress. As the House Judiciary Committee noted: "White House aides, in the past, have appeared before congressional committees in overwhelming numbers—both voluntarily and pursuant to subpoenas. Since World War II, close presidential advisers—including former Counsels and Special Assistants—have appeared before congressional committees to offer their testimony on more than *seventy* occasions."[163] In addition, the argument that absolute immunity protects White House officials from testifying in cases of wrongdoing is misguided in light of the fact that executive privilege does not provide such protection. No theory of executive autonomy protects against corruption or wrongdoing. The D.C. circuit court has recognized the duty to shed light on "government misconduct" and that privilege claims do not overwhelm the vital need to ensure the existence of honest and effective government.[164]

On 31 July 2008, the U.S. district court of D.C. rejected the administration's position that current or former presidential aides have absolute immunity. Indeed, in a single sentence, Judge John D. Bates eviscerated the administration's argument: "The Executive's current claim of absolute immunity from compelled congressional process for senior presidential aides is without any support in the case law."[165]

Later on in his opinion Bates made clear the novelty of Bush's broad interpretation of his powers: the executive branch "cannot identify a single judicial opinion that recognizes absolute immunity for senior presidential advisors in this or any other context. That simple yet critical fact bears repeating: the asserted absolute immunity claim here is entirely unsupported by existing case law."[166]

Citing the Supreme Court decision of *United States v. Bryan,* Bates stated that "compliance with a congressional subpoena is a legal requirement." He then discussed the importance of *Harlow v. Fitzgerald,* where White House staffers argued that they had an absolute immunity against civil damages claims arising from their official duties. Bates said that the *Harlow* Court "rejected that position" and declared that there was "no reason to extend greater protection to senior aides based solely on their proximity to the President."[167] The "'alter ego' immunity that the Executive requests here due to Ms. Miers's and Mr. Bolten's close proximity to and association with the President has been explicitly and definitively rejected, and there is no basis for reaching a different conclusion here."[168]

Bates next addressed the argument that compelled congressional testimony has a chilling effect on the executive branch. He noted that "the historical record" argues against this understanding and added that "senior advisors to the President have often testified before Congress subject to various subpoenas dating back to 1973." Thus, "it would hardly be unprecedented for Ms. Miers to appear before Congress to testify and assert executive privilege where appropriate."[169] The simple fact, as Bates pointed out, is that even the president himself "may not be absolutely immune from compulsory process."[170] Indeed, Congress does not lack authority to investigate the executive branch. "Congress's power of inquiry," Bates described, "is as broad as its power to legislate and lies at the very heart of Congress's constitutional role," which means that "the subpoena power in this case is no less legitimate or important than was the grand jury's in *United States v. Nixon.*"[171]

Bates found no legal rationale at all to support a claim of presidential autonomy. He argued that "it is certainly the case that if the President is entitled only to a presumptive privilege, his close advisors cannot hold the superior card of absolute immunity."[172] Even if the president possessed a limited autonomy, it "cannot mean that the Executive's actions are totally insulated from scrutiny by Congress"; Bates reasoned that "would eviscerate Congress's historical oversight function."[173] He then noted that the executive branch's interest in absolute immunity really is about independence from congressional and judicial checks. Such a "proposition is untenable and cannot be justified by appeals to Presidential autonomy."[174]

Bates's decision was a resounding repudiation of the theory that the president and his advisers could act without regard to Congress or the judiciary. On 26 August Bates dismissed a White House request to delay testimony by Miers and the House Judiciary Committee reacted by scheduling a hearing.

Nonetheless, the D.C. circuit court granted the Bush administration's appeal of Bates's decision and issued a temporary stay in the case. However, the court decided not to grant an expedited briefing and oral argument schedule, which meant that the controversy was left to Bush's successor, Barack Obama, to resolve. In its *per curium* opinion, the court noted that this dispute "is of potentially great significance for the balance of power between the Legislative and Executive Branches." The court suggested that the case would become moot because the subpoenas issued by the House Judiciary Committee would expire at the end of Congress, therefore giving "the new President and the new House an opportunity to express their views on the merits of the lawsuit."[175] Nonetheless, in early March 2009, the new administration helped broker an agreement between the House Judiciary Committee and former Bush White House staffers that largely sidestepped the executive privilege questions. As such the impact of Bush's absolute immunity claim remains unresolved.

Summary and Analysis

This controversy reveals the primary weakness in the procedures that Congress relies on when issuing a contempt citation. Enforcement traditionally comes from the executive branch. When Congress cites an executive official for contempt a U.S. attorney is the one who enforces it. However, when the Justice Department has already taken a position on the constitutionality of the administration's action (as was the case here), any action might be slow in coming, if at all.

Administrations rarely push such a confrontation so far. For example, in 1998 the Clinton Justice Department eventually compromised with a Republican-controlled House committee after the committee had issued a contempt citation for Attorney General Janet Reno.[176] In at least one case, the executive branch did not initially see the need to cooperate with Congress and the judicial branch had to intervene. Under an order from President Reagan, EPA Administrator Anne Gorsuch refused to provide documents to a House committee. Only after a federal court urged compromise between the branches did the Justice Department agree to release the documents.[177]

After the Gorsuch incident the executive branch has guarded against future legislative incursions. In a 1984 opinion, the OLC stated that based on a separation of powers analysis, no U.S. attorney is required to enforce a contempt citation of Congress that is directed against an executive official who is carrying out the president's claim of executive privilege. However, the opinion did state that its conclusions were limited "to controversies similar to the one to which this memorandum expressly relates, and the general statements of legal principles should be applied in other contexts only after careful analysis."[178]

The Bush White House followed a similar path as in the Gorsuch case. Yet even if the Justice Department ever refuses to enforce contempt charges, Congress still possesses its own power to issue a warrant and detain individuals. This right was first employed in 1795 when the Speaker of the House ordered the Sergeant-at-Arms to arrest and detain two men accused of "bribery, libel, and failure to appear before committees." In 1800, the Senate asserted the same right when the editor of a Republican newspaper, William Duane, failed to appear before the Senate. During this episode the Senate debated its inherent power at some length. As Richard E. Levy explained: "The argument in favor of such a power rested on the inherent authority of public bodies 'to do all acts necessary to keep themselves in a condition to discharge the trusts confided in them.'" Levy explained that this "inherent authority was reflected in the historical practices of the British Parliament, state legislatures, and courts." Yet, the power could only be exercised "through enactment of necessary and proper laws pursuant to Article I."[179]

In 1821, the Supreme Court upheld this power in *Anderson v. Dunn*.[180] The Court concluded that if such authority was refused it would lead "to the total annihilation of the power of the House of Representatives to guard itself from contempts, and leaves it exposed to every indignity and interruption that rudeness, caprice, or even conspiracy, may meditate against it."[181] The principle underscored in *Anderson* is that Congress must possess certain powers necessary to protect the functioning of its own processes even if such implicit powers do not appear to be expressly legislative in nature.

Of course, Congress does not have to rely on any direct authority in this area to enforce its will. Rather, the legislative branch has a variety of constitutional-based powers at its disposal that it may use to pressure the executive branch to cooperate. The legislative power itself, control of the budget, the confirmation and treaty-approval powers, among others, are all at Congress's disposal should legislators want to challenge executive branch lack of cooperation or overreaching of authority. The usual problem for Congress is not a lack of authority, but a failure to exercise its existing powers.

Regrettably, President Bush was willing to push this controversy to the brink, perhaps in the hope of winning a judicial decision that would be a victory for his expansive definition of presidential powers. Yet if the issue ends up in court, both the president and Congress risk setting a precedent that creates unwarranted judicial parameters on the future exercise of executive privilege. Perhaps that is what Bush wanted because he thought that he would win. The trouble is that a precise legislative or judicial line-drawing on the use of executive privilege will inevitably constrain a future leader who needs secrecy—or free a future leader who should be constrained.

And there is no reason to suppose that another administration faced by strict limits on executive privilege will inevitably choose greater transparency. Future presidents will be as likely to sidestep the principle altogether and find other statutory or constitutional bases for secrecy. The worst outcome in this battle would be a bad precedent that undercuts the delicate balance of negotiations that has long characterized disputes over executive privilege.

In early 2009, the Obama administration disappointed many critics of Bush's actions by urging further negotiation and compromise rather than pushing Rove finally to testify.[182] Most disappointing, when asked whether Obama would support his predecessor's claim of executive privilege in this controversy, the White House counsel Gregory Craig stated: "The president is very sympathetic to those who want to find out what happened. But he is also mindful as president of the United States not to do anything that would undermine or weaken the institution of the presidency. So, for that reason, he is urging both sides of this to settle."[183] It is hard to imagine how Obama could weaken the institution of the presidency by doing away with a meritless claim of absolute immunity for current and former White House aides. At the time of this writing in mid-2009, negotiations continue over the nature of testimony that Rove eventually should provide before the House committee.

The EPA Case and Agency Level Privilege

Another example of President Bush's attempt to expand executive privilege occurred in a case involving his refusal to provide Environmental Protection Agency (EPA) documents to the House Oversight and Government Reform Committee. The information sought by the committee pertained to correspondence between the EPA and the Office of Information and Regulatory Affairs of the Office of Management and Budget (OIRA) in the agency's decision to deny the state of California the authorization to regulate the greenhouse gas emissions of motor vehicles.[184]

In a 20 June 2008, letter to Chairman Henry Waxman (D-Calif.), EPA Associate Administrator Christopher P. Bliley notified the committee that Bush claimed executive privilege on a number of documents which "identify communications or meetings between senior EPA staff and White House personnel, or otherwise evidence information solicited or received by senior White House advisors." Regretting that the committee still sought information after the release of thousands of pages of documents, Bliley noted that "the Committee's subpoenas infringe upon the Executive Branch's strong interest in protecting the confidentiality of communications with and/or information received or solicited by the President and his senior advisors."[185]

Waxman immediately responded: "Today the President has asserted executive privilege to prevent the Committee from learning why he and his staff overruled EPA. There are thousands of internal White House documents that would show whether the President and his staff acted lawfully. But the President has said they must be kept from Congress and the public." "This Committee," Waxman continued, "has a fundamental obligation to learn the truth about what actually happened on these critical health and environmental decisions. That is why we have been seeking documents in both cases that would provide important details about the President's role" in this matter. Waxman said he wanted to confer with his colleagues "about this new development and consider all our options before deciding how we should proceed."[186]

Attorney General Michael Mukasey supplied the legal arguments for Bush's executive privilege claim. Mukasey's analysis suffered from poor citations, bad reasoning, and irrelevant conclusions. His memorandum to the president focused on four primary assertions. First, Mukasey argued that the documents protected were drafted "for the purpose of assisting the President in making a decision" about the ozone regulation.[187] At several points Mukasey repeatedly asserted this very point as if it were factually accurate. Indeed, although a president's decision making can likely be protected under the presidential communications privilege, such a claim can only be made on a "quintessential and non-delegable Presidential power."[188] Congress directed the EPA administrator to assess whether "the State standards will be, in the aggregate, at least as protective of public health and welfare as applicable Federal standards."[189] Nothing in the law directs the EPA administrator to confer with the president or provides evidence that agency decision making would fall under the quintessential powers of the president.

Mukasey's second claim dealt with the deliberative process privilege and his statement that "communications that do *not* implicate presidential decisionmaking" are protected from disclosure. He cited as evidence multiple OLC memoranda, and he maintained that "based on this principle, the Justice Department under Administrations of both political parties has concluded repeatedly that the privilege may be invoked to protect Executive Branch deliberations against congressional subpoenas."[190]

Certainly executive privilege does expand outside of the president and his immediate advisors; however, the deliberative process privilege has a lower threshold of protection for the executive branch. It is misleading merely to note that executive branch officials are protected and then not acknowledge that there is a difference between presidential and agency- or department-level documents. For support of this assertion Mukasey referenced a number of OLC memoranda. Repeated citations of self-serving executive branch documents do not add up to a valid legal basis for privilege, no more so than, say, the House of Representatives defining its constitutional powers based on references to multiple internal congressional staff memoranda.

At first blush Mukasey's point about protecting certain executive branch deliberations may sound reasonable. However, he sidestepped the issue of whether a department or agency—not the president—can withhold information from Congress by just stating the EPA documents needed protection. Then he made repeated assertions, not by citing the Constitution, case law, or historical examples, but by noting that other executive branch officials have said it is so.

Next Mukasey noted that in order for Congress to overcome a claim of executive privilege it must show that "the subpoenaed documents are 'demonstrably critical to the responsible fulfillment of the Committee's functions.'" Based on this requirement he determined that the committee had not met that standard. "Given the overwhelming amount of material and information already provided to the Committee," Mukasey declared, "it is difficult to understand how the subpoenaed information serves any legitimate legislative need." He concluded that the executive branch's strong interest in protecting these documents outweighed the committee's need for disclosure.[191]

There are two overriding problems with Mukasey's point. First, merely because the executive branch discloses some or even many documents, that does not mean that the most important or relevant documents were provided. With that argument a future president—if wanting to hide information from Congress—would only have to release boxes after boxes of material that has nothing to do with the congressional investigation in order to meet the fallacy of this *non sequitur*. Second, the fact that the attorney general is the one who made this determination raises a question of bias. Mukasey is not a neutral decision maker and cannot through executive fiat say certain information should be withheld from Congress.

Finally, after summarizing various documents that he deemed would provide Congress with the same information Mukasey pointed out that during a 20 May 2008, hearing none of the committee members asked the OIRA administrator any questions related to the agency's role in the EPA decision,[192] the implication being that the committee did not do due diligence in seeking alternative sources for the same information. The problem with this argument is that it does not follow that just by not asking questions at one committee hearing Congress gives up its right to executive branch documents. That is not a valid legal standard by any definition for withholding information.

The overarching goal of Mukasey's legal reasoning was to protect not only presidential decision making from congressional disclosure but all executive branch information. Such an argument would guard communications that were not even connected to a presidential act. Although Congress has been delegating power to agencies since the latter part of the nineteenth century, that does not necessarily mean a president has the responsibility of direct supervision. There are incidences when the enabling legislation is sufficiently unclear as to create a practice where a head of an agency might consult with the president or his White House advisors. Unitary executive advocates argue this point while claiming that the president's duty to see that all "laws be faithfully executed" provides additional evidence for this understanding.

Neither of these arguments gives a president the power to counter the wishes of Congress or use congressionally created agencies and officials in an attempt to withhold information from the legislative branch. In this case, the Clean Air Act empowers the EPA Administrator to evaluate state motor vehicle standards.[193] In short, environmental regulations are not core presidential powers. The Supreme Court has weighed in on the question of congressional and presidential powers in this type of situation before. In *Kendall v. United States* the argument had been made that the president could direct and control the Postmaster General "with respect to the execution of the duty imposed upon him" by law. That belief was based on the obligation imposed on the president "to take care that the laws be faithfully executed." The Court declared that this "is a doctrine that cannot receive the sanction of this court. It would be vesting in the President a dispensing power which has no countenance for its support in any part of the Constitution, and is asserting a principle, which, if carried out in its results to all cases falling within it, would be clothing the President with a power entirely to control the legislation of Congress and paralyze the administration of justice."[194]

The Court's decision directly countered the unitary executive argument made in that case but, more important, it refuted the contention that the president has direct control and authority over the EPA Administrator in the current situation. There is an expectation of autonomy from presidential control if the congressional delegation of power is given solely to an agency official and it does not interfere with a constitutional power of the president. As the Supreme Court announced in *Kendall*: "To contend that the obligation imposed on the President to see the laws faithfully executed implies a power to forbid their execution is a novel construction of the Constitution, and entirely inadmissible."[195] In the case of executive privilege the president cannot force an agency official to withhold from Congress information that has no relationship to the president's core constitutional duties. Even if the decision making issue at hand were a delegation of presidential authority to the EPA—which it was not—a president cannot properly conceal such documents with a claim of privilege.

In May 2009, the Obama administration effectively ended the Bush policy approach when it announced that the federal government would impose new national tailpipe emissions standards. Further, on 30 June, the EPA officially reversed the Bush administration decision not to allow California to impose its own greenhouse gas emissions limits.[196]

Valerie Plame and Covering Up Claims of
Executive Branch Wrongdoing

In 2008, President Bush claimed executive privilege over a congressional request for an interview transcript with Vice President Cheney and several FBI reports on the leaking of the name of Valerie Plame, who had been a Central Intelligence Agency (CIA) operative. Bush claimed executive privilege over these documents right before the House Oversight and Government Reform Committee was scheduled to vote on a resolution citing Attorney General Mukasey in contempt of Congress. In a 15 July 2008 letter to Chairman Waxman the administration claimed the reports "deal directly with internal White House deliberative communications relating to foreign policy and national security decisions faced by the President and his advisers, communications that lie at the absolute core of executive privilege." Additionally, the congressional inquiry "raises a serious additional separation of powers concern relating to the integrity and effectiveness of future law enforcement investigations by the Department." Disclosing reports that contain voluntary interviews with the vice president and senior White House staff "would significantly impair the Department's ability to conduct future law enforcement investigations where such investigations would benefit from full and voluntary White House cooperation."[197]

The Bush administration had used many court-based and statutorily created categories of executive privilege to withhold information from Congress before. Walling off the executive branch by withholding information through another claim of unitary protection therefore was not unusual in the Bush presidency. Attorney General Mukasey once again announced the underlying justifications for an assertion of privilege in this case. In a letter to Bush, he said that a claim of privilege would not be about hiding an act of wrongdoing but rather protecting the separation of powers as well as the integrity of future Justice Department investigations of the White House. "I am greatly concerned about the chilling effect that compliance with the committee's subpoena would have on future White House deliberations and

White House cooperation with future Justice Department investigations," Mukasey wrote Bush. "I believe it is legally permissible for you to assert executive privilege with respect to the subpoenaed documents, and I respectfully request that you do so."[198]

Mukasey claimed that executive privilege "extends to all Executive Branch deliberations, even when the deliberations do not directly implicate presidential decisionmaking."[199] He noted that the information requested was protected by the presidential communications privilege, deliberative process privilege, and the law enforcement component of executive privilege. Moreover, the committee "has yet to identify any specific legislative need for the subpoenaed documents, relying instead on a generalized interest in evaluating the White House's involvement in the Plame matter as part of its review of White House procedures governing the handling of classified documents."[200]

For much of the letter Mukasey combines the different threshold standards together in a way that is often confusing and is, for the most part, bad reasoning based on faulty analysis. There is in fact a clear distinction between the president and the rest of the executive branch in terms of what can and cannot be protected from a congressional investigation. Arguing in rather befuddled language that there is no difference between the two seems disingenuous. In addition, repeating that Congress has not met the "demonstrably critical" need does not mean it is so. A deliberative process claim, which most of the documents in question fall under, cannot stand up to a showing of government misconduct or wrongdoing.[201] The unlawful release of a CIA agent's name clearly meets this threshold standard. It is also not accurate that the law enforcement privilege protects information from closed investigations.

What the Bush administration tried to do in this case was expand executive privilege to protect the attorney general from disclosing nonpresidential documents to a congressional committee. In its reply to Waxman the administration even declared that if the committee did not move ahead and cite Mukasey for contempt then the Justice Department was "prepared to continue the accommodation approach."[202] This offer bordered on a bribe to Congress and even if it was not illegal it was certainly unethical. Moreover there was clearly a conflict of interest on the part of Mukasey in giving executive privilege advice to President Bush on a contempt of Congress vote that applied directly to the attorney general. The resulting executive privilege claim protected Mukasey from having to respond to a contempt citation.

At its heart this executive privilege claim was an attempt to protect the release of an FBI interview by Vice President Cheney to a congressional committee. The information requested by Congress did not involve a discussion between the president and vice president that dealt with a core presidential power. Instead it was an interview of Cheney conducted by a government attorney and FBI agents in the Plame investigation that was not protected by grand jury secrecy requirements or with any expectations that the information given would remain sealed or not be disclosed to Congress at some point.[203] The refusal to release the interview and other information to Congress was therefore an attempt to expand executive privilege to provide greater protection of the vice president and executive branch. The evolution of case law on executive privilege, as well as its many precedents, does not provide support for such an expansive definition of this power. Congress has the authority to conduct its oversight duties over all areas of the executive branch including the president and vice president's offices. Nothing in the Constitution, case law, or interbranch practice counters that point.

At this writing in mid-2009, the Obama Justice Department has opposed the release of the Cheney interview transcript on the grounds that so doing would have a chilling effect on future White House officials when considering whether to cooperate with government prosecutors.[204] Yet again, proponents of government openness who had expected a different approach from the new administration were left disappointed.

Executive Privilege and the Bush Legacy

The Bush years fueled substantial national debate over executive branch secrecy and more generally over the efforts of the president to expand his powers. The president's very expansive definition of executive powers and efforts to effect his vision will constitute a key element of the Bush legacy for many years.

Although Bush perceived his actions as necessary to restore what he considers the proper balance in the system of separated powers, in the end his overly broad use of executive privilege, particularly in circumstances in which his claims were inherently flawed, more likely contributed to a further downgrading of the stature of this constitutional principle. Executive privilege already suffered a bad reputation due to the misuse of that power by presidents, most notably in the Watergate scandal and the Lewinsky investigation. To restore the good name of executive privilege truly requires its cautious exercise by presidents under circumstances that justify a clear need for secrecy. Yet Bush's executive privilege claims did not rise to the level of protecting some broad national interest.

In some controversies the president engaged in a kind of brinksmanship in his efforts to expand executive privilege, with mixed results in the courts at least. For example, Bush gave former presidents greater power by allowing them to block the release of information well after they left the White House. Yet a federal district court overruled that portion of the president's executive order. In the case of the energy task force he won a remarkable victory when the Supreme Court validated the administration's assertion that forcing disclosure would have a negative impact on the president's ability to carry out his responsibilities under Article II of the Constitution. The Court's decision established a rather high standard of judicial deference to executive authority and strengthened the White House's argument that it has the right to withhold from the public and Congress information dealing with public policy discussions with private parties.

Even in efforts where the administration was not successful it still pushed for greater executive power. The refusal to provide Justice Department documents that were on average twenty-two years old seemed like a puzzling case to assert executive privilege. However, by the administration pushing back against Congress it possibly set a precedent for future presidents to attempt to follow. Even though Burton's committee was able to gain access to a number of critical documents, it did not receive access to all of them. Although a weak claim, the administration still maintained it had won a victory for the institution of the presidency. Conceivably, future presidents can take the view in this case that access was granted to only a narrow category of documents, which did not include those of a deliberative nature.

The dangers of permitting the executive branch to piecemeal build a case for a more expansive view of executive privilege are many. Certainly executive privilege provides the president and his advisers an environment where they can be assured that their deliberations on sensitive issues will not be exposed. However, taken to the extreme, executive privilege can be used to hinder a fundamental principle of our government, which is the need for proper checks and balances. A closed executive branch prevents Congress from carrying out many of its essential functions. Far from protecting vital national security information in most of the Bush administration's executive privilege cases, the White House has prevented Congress from viewing documents and material that relate to key aspects of the interworkings of government. Ensuring that public officials are not corrupted and finding a workable national energy policy are not just the goals of the executive branch. These concerns should be primarily initiated by Congress, which has the legislative responsibilities of oversight and passing laws. Creating a closed-door policy where the executive branch alone decides these important issues removes Congress from the governing picture and does much to encumber our constitutional form of government.

In the case of the U.S. attorneys firings Congress has the responsibility to ensure that the offices and policies that it puts in place are functioning properly. Here the signs that the nation's chief prosecutors are being corrupted for political purposes and failing to carry out their duties in an unbiased fashion raises important concerns of fundamental fairness within the justice system. By not being forthcoming about this important issue and failing to fully disclose all details the administration hindered the duties of Congress to provide effective oversight over the internal operations of government. Although the controversy is still ongoing at the time of this writing, there is cause for concern that the Bush administration created a dangerous precedent. By not disclosing all documents, Congress and the public are forced to question not only the process of appointing U.S. attorneys but the officeholders as well. Many of these officials are loyal public servants who do their jobs properly. However, in light of this controversy, how does Congress or the public know that there were not additional cases of U.S. attorneys pressured by certain politicians to prosecute or not prosecute cases?

In addition, creating an environment in which secrecy and distrust are the norm runs the risk of government becoming an unchecked power. Executive privilege does not provide presidents the power to do whatever they want when they want, or to conceal information that might be politically embarrassing or disadvantageous in some other way. Instead our government is based on the premise of accountability of actions. Without knowing what the executive branch is doing, no one can be held accountable for their actions and possible wrongdoings.

It is perhaps too easy to blame the misuse or overreaching of power on presidents who seek to expand their authority and govern unilaterally whenever they think they can get away with it, or to complain about court decisions that have tended to provide too much protection to the executive branch at the cost of openness and responsibility. But ultimately, checking presidential excesses is the duty of the legislative branch. Here we find the overall record to be mixed. Congress generally has not vigorously defended its own prerogatives in this area and thus has enabled presidents to try to expand their powers because they believe quite simply that they can get away with it. Congressional acquiescence has also contributed to a judicial atmosphere of deference to the executive branch, as precedents for expanded presidential authority continue to mount.

Congress certainly has constitutional powers that it can use to constrain the exercise of executive privilege in those situations in which presidents overreach or try to expand their authority. However, the Constitution is not a self-enforcing document. Members of Congress must use their institutional resources to counter a president bent on expanding executive power. Clearly some of the cases discussed above are good examples of Congress doing just that. Burton's committee pushed hard and got much of what it had requested. When the Democrats took control of the legislative branch, there was some renewed interest in overturning the Bush executive order on presidential records. In the U.S. attorneys firings controversy, the Senate and House Judiciary committees made a strong push to compel testimony, with both chambers issuing contempt measures from the committees. These examples show what Congress potentially can do, if it has the determination to protect its own role in the system of separated powers.

The future for executive privilege remains murky. President Bush further diminished the stature of this constitutional principle. His successors may find that although Bush created some precedents for trying to expand this authority into new areas, it is likely that these leaders will also find themselves subject to protests of abuses of power in cases where they have legitimate needs for secrecy.

President Barack Obama: The New Transparency?

As he campaigned for the presidency in 2008, Barack Obama promised a new era of transparency in government and an end to the Bush-era secrecy practices. Not surprisingly, his election invited high expectations among advocates of government openness and, in his first months as president, there were some important victories and also considerable disappointments. On his first full day in office on 21 January 2009, Obama signed a "memorandum on transparency" to signal the immediacy of his policy shift away from the Bush years.[205]

Another one of Obama's first presidential acts, taken on that same day, was to reverse the Bush executive order that had revised the Presidential Records Act of 1978. Obama had thus quickly taken what many had seen as the first major step to signal that he intended to fulfill the promise of government openness. This action looked all the more telling because there was no loud public outcry for such immediate action on that issue and certainly the president could have easily sidestepped it and thus chosen to benefit from the additional secrecy protections that the Bush EO had provided presidents.[206]

Nonetheless, over the next several months Obama's record on government secrecy issues suggested that he was not inclined to depart from all of Bush's practices. The continuing controversy over whether former Bush White House officials could claim executive privilege to avoid congressional testimony created an unwanted complication for the new president. Indeed, there was considerable pressure on Obama to step forward and compel Karl Rove in particular to testify about the scandal involving the removal of U.S.

attorneys during the Bush administration.[207] Obama's initial reluctance to get directly involved seemed puzzling given his past promises of transparency, his easy reversal of the offending Bush EO, and the complete lack of merit to the claim that former White House aides possess absolute immunity to testimony. Here we had the former aide Rove claiming executive privilege, an Article II–based presidential power, with the backing of private citizen George W. Bush, as the sitting president took no action and his White House counsel even said that to do so might have the effect of undermining executive powers.

At this writing in mid-2009, a path has been cleared for Rove to eventually testify before Congress, and the Obama administration had played an active role in brokering a deal to make Rove's appearance on Capitol Hill more likely. Nonetheless, in staying out of the controversy himself, the president bypassed an opportunity to have declared a firm stand against the view that current and former White House aides possess a form of absolute immunity. In addition, the deal brokered created a bad precedent. Remarkably, the involved parties agreed that the testimony was not to be public and not even in person, but rather "transcribed depositions." Further, under this agreement the depositions were not to touch on discussions with the president, or any presidential decisions, or even discussions with any officials from the White House counsel's office, thus potentially sheltering those persons ultimately responsible for the U.S. attorneys firings scandal. And there was no clear specification of the scope and limits of executive privilege claims that could be made by those providing testimony.[208]

In June 2009 Obama disappointed many advocates of transparency when his administration refused multiple requests to view White House visitor logs. As happened in the Bush years, public interest groups and media organizations requested access to the logs in order to fully disclose the names of persons with whom the White House was consulting on policy development. In refusing these requests, Obama effectively adopted the approach of his predecessor, which had led to some of the most contentious political and legal battles over government secrecy during the previous administration. Like Bush, Obama relied on the argument that the daily visitor logs are presidential records and thus are not available for inspection.[209] Yet Obama reversed this posture when he later announced that the White House visitor logs would be made public after all. Unfortunately, the president decided only to release lengthy lists of names, with no mention of the purpose of White House visits or even differentiations between tourists and people consulted on policy development. This action enabled Obama to appear to be favoring openness while providing no substantively useful information.

Perhaps most discouraging of all has been the Obama Justice Department decision to side with the former Bush administration claim of executive privilege to prevent the release of the transcript of the Cheney interview with a special prosecutor who was examining the leak of Valerie Plame's identity as a CIA agent. The core of the Bush administration's position was that compelling the release of such information would make future vice presidents or even presidents reluctant to cooperate with criminal investigations for fear of disclosure. The Obama Justice Department agreed and even said in a court filing that one of the reasons for taking this position was that a future vice president indeed might not cooperate because of the fear "that it's going to get on the 'Daily Show,'" a popular late-night comedic cable television program.[210]

This argument, as well as the position of the Bush Justice Department, brought a strong rebuke from Judge Emmet G. Sullivan of the U.S. district court of D.C., who properly told the Obama Justice Department to provide him with a copy of Cheney's statement for review. Although at this writing the Obama Justice Department has cooperated with this request, the Assistant Attorney General Lanny Breuer stated in an affidavit in support of keeping the Cheney remarks secret that by compelling disclosure, "there is an increased likelihood that such officials could feel reluctant to participate."[211]

In other areas not directly pertaining to executive privilege the president has made several important government secrecy–related decisions that suggest how he might manage future executive privilege disputes. One of the earlier controversies centered on the release of numerous Department of Justice memoranda that provided the legal justification to detain and use certain techniques on terrorism suspects. As Obama said in a White House press statement, the release of the documents "is required by the rule of law." He acknowledged that "the United States must sometimes carry out intelligence operations and protect information that is classified for purposes of national security," yet in this case he believed "that exceptional circumstances surround these memos and require their release."[212]

Although Obama chose to release the OLC memoranda he ultimately decided against doing the same in the case of the detainee abuse photographs. After noting that the photos in question were not "particularly sensational" and that they were a part of an already closed military investigation where the people involved were held accountable, Obama declared "that the publication of these photos would not add any additional benefit to our understanding of what was carried out in the past by a small number of individuals. In fact, the most direct consequence of releasing them, I believe, would be to further inflame anti-American opinion and to put our troops in greater danger."[213]

In other areas of national security concern, Obama has largely adopted the

Bush administration's underlying rationale for protecting information. For example, the Obama Justice Department petitioned the Ninth Circuit Court to reconsider, *en banc,* its decision in *Mohamed, et al. v. Jeppesen Dataplan, et al.,* a case dealing with a challenge by five foreign nationals to the government's alleged actions of apprehending and taking them to foreign countries for interrogation by foreign and U.S. officials in what is called extraordinary rendition.[214] A federal district judge had earlier thrown out the case relying on the Bush administration's invocation of the state secrets privilege, which argues that certain national security information or programs are so sensitive and vital to the protection of the country that they cannot be disclosed to the public or courts. On appeal Obama's Justice Department adopted the same position and argued that the case should not go forward based on the claim that the extraordinary rendition program was protected under state secrets. A three-judge panel rejected that argument,[215] and the Obama administration decided to request an *en banc* review because "allowing this suit to proceed would pose an unacceptable risk to national security and that the reasoning employed by the panel would dramatically restructure government operations by permitting any district judge to override the executive branch's judgments in this highly sensitive realm."[216]

Civil libertarians were not happy with the decision. One American Civil Liberties Union lawyer fumed that "the Obama administration has now fully embraced the Bush administration's shameful effort to immunize torturers and their enablers from any legal consequences for their actions."[217] Curiously, Obama had remarked previously that the state secrets doctrine had been overused by past presidents and that his administration "must not protect information merely because it reveals the violation of a law or embarrassment to the government." However, in the same speech he said that the "principle is absolutely necessary in some circumstances to protect national security."[218] He went on to articulate some procedures his administration would adhere to when invoking state secrets:

> We will apply a stricter legal test to material that can be protected under the state secrets privilege. We will not assert the privilege in court without first following our own formal process, including review by a Justice Department committee and the personal approval of the Attorney General. And each year we will voluntarily report to Congress when we have invoked the privilege and why because, as I said before, there must be proper oversight over our actions.

Obama ended by noting that he would "deal with Congress and the courts as co-equal branches of government. I will tell the American people what I know and don't know, and when I release something publicly or keep something secret, I will tell you why."[219]

This statement is strange, especially in light of the Ninth Circuit rendition case where the administration asserted that the information in question was not only too sensitive for the public, but also for the courts. How does asserting state secrets respect the position of the judicial branch? In essence the administration claimed that the courts cannot be trusted to review sensitive material. In addition, creating internal procedures closed off to judicial, and perhaps congressional, review does not make the declaration of state secrets any more legal or constitutional. The personal approval of the attorney general or any other high-ranking executive official cannot replace the traditional checks and balances approach of judicial review or congressional oversight. And no president can resolve the inherent conflict of making a unilateral state secrets claim by saying that each year his administration will "voluntarily" notify Congress.

The first nearly half year of the Obama administration thus provides some telling evidence of the president's leanings on executive privilege and other government secrecy issues. As a candidate for president, Obama had promised a fundamental change from his predecessor's tendency toward excessive secrecy. But perhaps not surprising, and certainly not so to those who have followed such issues over the years and frequently ended up disappointed by past presidents, Obama's record to date is not consistent. He began his administration with some important actions that showcased his commitment to government transparency, but then in a number of disputes over executive privilege and other secrecy practices, his administration adopted positions similar to those of his predecessor. And unfortunately, Obama's administration has done so in response to some truly meritless claims, such as absolute immunity for current and former White House aides, or refusal to release statements for fear of mockery by late-night comedians. Thus, as with past presidents who had entered office with promises of a new era of openness, Obama to date has not been willing to make any substantial shift away from many of the secrecy practices of modern administrations, and he has even furthered some of the Bush-era policies that expanded executive branch secrecy.

CONCLUSION: RESOLVING THE DILEMMA

The dilemma of executive privilege is one of permitting governmental secrecy in a political system predicated on leadership accountability. On the
surface, the dilemma is a complex one to resolve: how can democratically
elected leaders be held accountable by the public when they are able to deliberate in secret or make secretive decisions?

Under certain circumstances, presidential exercise of executive privilege
is compatible with our constitutional system. But in recent years executive
privilege has fallen into disrepute because of various misuses and abuses of
that power. The modern pattern is one of executive branch recriminations
toward legislators and independent counsels for meddling where they do
not belong and counteraccusations that executive branch failure to divulge all information constitutes either criminal activity or an attempt to
conceal embarrassing information. Currently, there appears to be a lack of
recognition by the political branches of each other's legitimate powers and
interests in the area of governmental secrecy. To restore some sense of balance to the modern debate over executive privilege, the following must be
recognized.

First, when used under appropriate circumstances, executive privilege is a
legitimate constitutional power. The weight of the evidence refutes the assertion that executive privilege is a "constitutional myth." Consequently, presidential administrations should not be devising schemes to achieve the ends
of executive privilege while avoiding any mention of this constitutional
principle. Furthermore, Congress must recognize that the executive
branch—like the legislative and judicial branches—has a legitimate need to
deliberate in secret and that not every assertion of executive privilege is automatically a devious attempt to conceal wrongdoing.

Second, executive privilege is not an unlimited, unfettered presidential
power. Executive privilege should be exercised only rarely and for the most
compelling reasons. Congress has the right—and often the duty—to challenge presidential assertions of executive privilege when such assertions
clearly are not related to such legitimate needs as protecting national security
or the candor of internal deliberations. Merely proclaiming that certain materials have a bearing on national security or internal deliberations does not

automatically end the debate in the executive's favor. Presidents need to demonstrate more than just some vague interest in security or secrecy for an executive privilege claim to stand.

Third, there are no clear, precise constitutional boundaries that determine, a priori, whether any particular claim of executive privilege is legitimate. The resolution to the dilemma of executive privilege is found in the political ebb and flow of our separation of powers system. There is no need for any precise definition of the constitutional boundaries surrounding executive privilege. Such a power cannot be subject to precise definition, because it is impossible to determine in advance all the circumstances under which presidents may have to exercise that power. The separation of powers system provides the appropriate resolution to the dilemma of executive privilege and democratic accountability.

Resolving the Dilemma: The Separation of Powers

In response to a constitutional dilemma such as the one posed by executive privilege, it is often tempting to try to devise a remedy that would eliminate any potential future conflict. Raoul Berger believes that there is just one way to resolve this constitutional dilemma: eliminate the source of power from which the dilemma originates. In his view, "secrecy in the operations of government is an abomination."[1] Berger concludes that the case of the Nixon presidency proves his point. Under the Nixon presidency, Berger writes, "'confidentiality' was the vehicle for the cover-up of criminal acts and conspiracies by [Nixon's] aides, an instrument he repeatedly employed to the obstruction of justice."[2]

Berger's assessment of Nixon's exercise of executive privilege is unarguable, and one could easily add to the list of presidential misuses of executive privilege the more recent actions of the Bill Clinton and George W. Bush administrations. In fact, many critiques of executive privilege focus on the misuses and abuses of a few administrations. Such critics of executive privilege as Berger have argued that there must be completely open deliberations within the executive branch of government (a position rejected even by the "open" presidencies of Gerald Ford and Jimmy Carter). Berger is not alone in arguing that complete openness is the only means by which to ensure accountability in the executive branch.[3]

Underlying this argument against executive privilege is the view that Congress must always be the supreme branch of government due to the need for democratic accountability and the specific powers conferred on the legislative branch by Article I of the Constitution. Berger accepts no exceptions to that rule. He dismisses the existence of residual or prerogative powers for the president, even in foreign affairs and emergency situations.

James W. Ceaser argues that the belief that Congress must always be the supreme branch, even at the expense of tying the hands of the executive during times of emergency, "is based on a narrow and legalistic understanding of the Constitution and on a failure to recognize the real purpose for which the founders adopted the theory of separation of powers."[4] The failure to understand or to accept the founders' theory of the separation of powers has resulted in the quest for absolutes on the issue of executive privilege. Berger and others dogmatically opposed to executive privilege under any circumstance want to eliminate such a power because of past abuses and the real potential for future abuses. Yet this remedy elevates the exception—the abuse of power—to the status of rule, leading to the call for a broad, sweeping solution.

Many of former president Nixon's defenders elaborated the equally suspect argument that Congress and the public have no authority to limit and constrain the exercise of executive powers. The extreme statement of this view was Nixon's claim that any action undertaken by the president is legitimate. Nixon's attorneys submitted the argument that how executive privilege is exercised "is a matter of presidential judgment alone."[5] In *U.S. v. Sirica* (1973), Judge George MacKinnon expressed best of all the notion of an unlimited executive privilege: "In my opinion an absolute privilege exists for presidential communications. . . . [S]trict confidentiality is so essential to the deliberative process that it should not be jeopardized by any possibility of disclosure."[6]

President George W. Bush's administration more recently adopted the controversial stand that any time a prosecutorial matter was involved, Congress had no right to executive branch information. The administration even extended this principle to include closed investigations. The former president also took the position that he could assert executive privilege to prohibit any current or former White House aide from giving congressional testimony, even in the case of subpoenas to answer questions about possible wrongdoing by the administration. Bush's actions in part reflected an administration view that the past three decades have witnessed a substantial flow of power away from the executive branch and toward Congress. The Bush administration suggested a need to revitalize presidential powers in light of this perceived shifting of the balance between the branches, including the exercise of executive privilege.

Neither dogmatic view of executive privilege presents an accurate assessment of the separation of powers system. Neither provides a workable resolution to the dilemma of executive privilege. The separation of powers system as envisioned by the Framers provides the proper resolution to the inherent conflict between governmental secrecy and the right to know.

The alternative proposed by Berger and his followers—completely open executive branch deliberations—is worse than the danger they seek to eliminate. Any power once created can be abused. And because secrecy is occasionally vital to the proper functioning of the presidency, periodic attempts to abuse this power may be an unavoidable risk that must be accepted. To demand that presidents exercise their powers fully to advance an activist policy agenda, strictly conform to the letter of every legal and constitutional provision in the exercise of their powers, yet remain fully subordinate to the legislative authority in all areas is to expect nothing less than an ideal world—one in which the trustworthiness of chief executives is never at issue, the legal and constitutional provisions pertaining to the presidency are unmistakably clear and consistent and do not unduly constrain the exercise of presidential authority, and legislators are concerned only with high-minded matters of policy and the public good. As the founders understood so well, such a state of affairs never will exist, given the undeniable foibles of human beings. There are better ways to check the potential abuse of power than to eliminate the source of power altogether. The dilemma of executive privilege can be resolved by means other than eliminating that authority or effectively trying to do so through the use of onerous legalistic constraints.

The extreme presidentialist view—in which the chief executive exercises his authority unfettered by congressional constraints, Congress defers to executive fiat, and the only check on presidential power takes place on election day—also misunderstands the separation of powers. The resolution to the dilemma of executive privilege is not simply to allow the president to determine for himself the scope and limits of his own authority.

The Framers' theory of the separation of powers can resolve the dilemma of executive privilege and the right to know. Such an understanding begins with the writings of the most influential thinkers of modern constitutionalism: Locke and Montesquieu. Locke articulated a system of separated powers to limit the potential for governmental tyranny. As Louis W. Koenig has written, "John Locke would have been flabbergasted" by the Nixon assertion that any action undertaken by the president is legal.[7] Yet limited governmental power can never bow to the "fundamental law of nature," which counsels self-preservation. Therefore, Locke advocated a strong executive capable of acting with unity and "despatch," one with the "power to act with discretion, for the public good, without the prescription of the law, and sometimes against it."[8] Montesquieu similarly advocated a governmental system in which power checks power but that allows the executive to act independent of the direct popular will when necessary.

A proper understanding of the separation of powers is rooted in the founding period and the early years of the Republic. The founders recognized an implied constitutional prerogative of presidential secrecy—a power that they believed was necessary and proper. The leading founders either exercised or acknowledged the right of executive branch secrecy in the early years of the Republic. In devising our constitutional system, they sought to limit governmental powers to reduce the threat of tyranny. But this perceived need to limit power never implied either weak government or a subordinate executive branch. As political scientist L. Peter Schultz has written, "the separation of powers constitutes an attempt to solve one of the major problems of government, that of providing for both reasonable government and forceful government without sacrificing either."[9]

It is well recognized that the leading founders exercised considerable foresight in establishing a constitutional system capable of adapting to the needs of changing times. That foresight has been especially useful in the areas of national security and foreign policy, where claims of executive privilege are especially compelling. In writing Article II of the Constitution, the Framers did not constrain presidential power with constitutional exactitude.

Finally, a proper understanding of the separation of powers is founded on the notion that there are inherent limitations on the prerogative powers of the presidency. Both Congress and the judiciary, when given good reason to believe that a claim of privilege is being abused, have institutional mechanisms to compel the president to divulge information. The separation of powers system provides the vital mechanisms by which the other branches of government can challenge executive claims of privilege. The answer to the question of how executive privilege can properly be exercised and constrained is found in an examination of the roles of the other branches of government in ensuring that the executive branch does not abuse the right to withhold information.

The Role of Congress

One solution to the dilemma of executive privilege that is occasionally proposed is to establish a statutory definition of that power, specifying the circumstances under which executive privilege can be exercised.[10] Fortunately, no such legislative solution to the dilemma has been enacted. Any a priori solution is bound to fail, given the impossibility of determining all the circumstances under which executive privilege may be exercised in the future. As former attorney general Edward Levi explained, "the lesson of history is that the reasonableness of an assertion of confidentiality cannot be determined in advance on the basis of neat categories."[11]

Congress already has the institutional capability to challenge claims of executive privilege by means other than eliminating the right to withhold information or attaching statutory restrictions on the exercise of that power. For example, if members of Congress are not satisfied with the response to their demands for information, they have the option of retaliating by withholding support for the president's agenda or for his executive branch nominees. In one case during the Reagan years, members of the Senate Judiciary Committee threatened not to confirm the nomination of William Rehnquist as chief justice until the president dropped an executive privilege claim over documents from Rehnquist's tenure in the Justice Department during the Nixon administration. That action resulted in President Reagan acceding to the senators' demands. If information can be withheld only for the most compelling reasons, it is not unreasonable for Congress to try to force the president's hand by making him weigh the importance of withholding information against the importance of advancing a nomination or piece of legislation. Presumably, information being withheld for purposes of vital national security or constitutional concerns would take precedence over pending legislation or a presidential appointment. If not, then there appears to be little justification in the first place for withholding the information.

Congress possesses numerous other means by which to compel presidential compliance with requests for information. One of these is Congress's control over the governmental purse strings, a formidable power over the executive branch. Additionally, Congress has often been successful using the subpoena power and the contempt of Congress charge to compel the release of withheld information. It is not merely the exercise of these powers that matters, but the threat that Congress may resort to such measures.

In the extreme case, Congress also has the power of impeachment—the ultimate weapon with which to threaten the executive. Clearly, this congressional power cannot routinely be exercised as a means of compelling disclosure of information and is not going to constitute a real threat in commonplace information disputes. Nonetheless, in the case of a scandal of Watergate-like proportions, when all other remedies have failed, Congress can threaten to exercise its ultimate power over the president. In 1998, Congress considered an impeachment article against President Clinton for abuse of presidential powers, including executive privilege, but it ultimately dropped that particular article.

In the vast majority of cases—and history verifies this point—it can be expected that the president will comply with requests for information rather than withstand increased pressure from Congress. Presidential history is replete with examples of chief executives who tried to invoke privilege or threatened to do so, only to back down in the face of congressional challenges.

If certain members of Congress believe that the executive privilege power is too formidable, the answer resides not in crippling presidential authority but in exercising to full effect the vast array of powers already at Congress's disposal. Sotirios A. Barber contends that presidential preeminence in foreign policy making "cannot be explained by comparing the executive and legislative powers enumerated in the Constitution." Barber correctly explains that Congress possesses formidable powers but at times has failed to fully exercise them.[12] Three decades ago, Senator J. William Fulbright (D-Ark.) argued that Congress too often acquiesced to presidential authority in foreign affairs and charged his colleagues not to allow the chief executive to act unilaterally in foreign policy in a secretive fashion. "I conclude that when the president, for reasons with which we can all sympathize, does not invite us into his high-policy councils, it is our duty to infiltrate them as best we can."[13]

Louis Koenig refutes the oft-stated belief that the presidency has become imperial while Congress's powers have atrophied. Koenig cites the example of the Nixon presidency as proof that Congress both possesses and can exercise formidable powers when it wants to.

> The imperial presidency thesis excessively downgrades Congress and misstates the historical experience of the presidency. Time and again, Congress prevailed over Nixon. Congress ended his once secret war in Cambodia by cutting off its funds. His claims of massive powers to impound funds or abolish programs were rejected both by Congress and the courts. His modest program proposals were rejected by Congress more frequently than any other contemporary president. Ultimately, Nixon's certain impeachment by the House of Representatives drove him from the presidency. . . . [The presidency] contains substantial weaknesses of power which the imperial thesis obscures.[14]

The resolution of executive-legislative disagreements over withheld information need not occur through such combative techniques. Rooted in the separation of powers is the notion that the potential stalemate that results from executive branch refusal to release secretive information can be overcome by mutual accommodation and compromise. I disagree with the assessment of former attorney general William French Smith, who argued that there are inherent problems with entrusting members of Congress with sensitive information.[15]

In most interbranch battles over access to executive branch information, both sides are willing to engage in an accommodation process to satisfy the needs of each. Depending on the level of importance that Congress attaches to certain documents, it may be possible to satisfy members through a briefing by executive branch officials or a private showing of disputed documents, with the understanding that no copies are to be made and no notes taken. The accommodation process does not always work, however. In some cases, the executive branch simply refuses to consider a serious compromise and instead uses the process to further delay the production of materials or to make an appearance of accommodating Congress. In such cases, Congress has a duty to protect its prerogatives and use whatever authority it possesses to secure access to the disputed materials.

Although it is considered a controversial alternative today, the divulging of sensitive information to a few trusted and highly respected members of Congress has succeeded in the past. For example, during World War II, President Franklin Roosevelt frequently confided sensitive national security information to trusted members of Congress, and they respected the sanctity of that information. In certain extraordinary circumstances, the president can, in secret chambers, discuss a problem with a few members of Congress who are highly trusted within their own institution.[16]

The area of treaty negotiations is particularly complex because of the obvious need for confidential discussions, combined with the Senate's constitutional authority of "advice and consent." To publicly divulge negotiating positions before a diplomatic agreement has been reached may be highly imprudent. The flexibility of negotiating positions is compromised by such revelations, making it difficult, if not impossible, to achieve agreement between or among the parties. William Rehnquist has argued that the use of private discussions between the president and some members of Congress can satisfy both Congress's right to know and the needs of diplomatic negotiations.

> Frequently the problem of overly broad public dissemination of such negotiations can be solved by testimony in executive session, which informs the members of the committee of Congress without making the same information prematurely available throughout the world. The end is not secrecy as to the end product—the treaty—which of course should be exposed to the fullest public scrutiny, but only the confidentiality as to the negotiations which lead up to the treaty.[17]

A statutory resolution to the dilemma of executive privilege is not needed. Congress already possesses the constitutional means by which to challenge executive branch withholding of information. And Congress has had a good deal of success using its existing powers to compel disclosure of withheld information. In fact, Congress appears to have gained the upper hand in its disputes with the executive branch over information policy. When it comes to the issue of executive privilege, there is no convincing evidence for the view that the president is imperial, capable of doing whatever he wants.

The Role of the Courts

In the realms of foreign affairs and national security policy making, the courts generally have been deferential to the so-called political branches. The judiciary's role in the separation of powers scheme is not regarded as one of arbitrating conflicts between the political branches over foreign policy. On many occasions, the courts have recognized that the judicial branch may not be best suited to deciding complex matters of foreign affairs, national security, and intelligence policy.[18] Louis Fisher explains the usual judicial response to congressional attempts to challenge the president's national security decisions:

> Congress must be prepared, and willing, to exercise the ample powers within its arsenal. When it acquiesces to executive initiatives, the record clearly shows that legislative inaction will not be cured by judicial remedies. Four times during the Reagan administration, members of Congress filed suit in federal court to have President Reagan's military actions in El Salvador, Nicaragua, Grenada, and the Persian Gulf held unconstitutional and illegal. Four times the federal courts gave Congress the same message: if you fail to challenge the president, don't come to us. Justice Lewis Powell put it well in the treaty termination case of *Goldwater v. Carter* (1979): "If the Congress chooses not to confront the president, it is not our task to do so" [444 U.S. 996, 998]. Congress has the constitutional power. It needs also the institutional courage and constitutional understanding to share with the president the momentous decision to send U.S. forces into combat.[19]

This recognition of the limitations on the courts' role does not preclude the judiciary from arbitrating constitutional, rather than policy, disputes. As the Supreme Court affirmed in *U.S. v. Nixon,* the separation of powers does not guarantee "an absolute, unqualified presidential privilege of immunity from judicial process under all circumstances. The president's need for complete candor and objectivity from advisers calls for great deference from the courts. However, when the privilege depends solely on the broad, undifferentiated claim of public interest in the confidentiality of such conversations, a confrontation with other values arises."[20] The Court made it clear that when a claim of privilege is made to protect national security or foreign policy deliberations, that claim is often difficult for another branch to overcome in a balancing of constitutional powers.[21] But while upholding the "constitutionally based" nature of the privilege, the Court also made it clear that the privilege may, at times, have to defer to the constitutionally based powers of a coordinate branch of government. Although the Court did not specify the exact balance of power between the branches, it did affirm that the judicial branch has the authority to compel the production of information claimed to be privileged when such information is needed as evidence in a criminal case.

> We conclude that when the ground for asserting privilege as to subpoenaed materials sought for use in a criminal trial is based only on the generalized interest in confidentiality, it cannot prevail over the fundamental demands of due process of law in the fair administration of criminal justice. The generalized assertion of privilege must yield to the demonstrated, specific need for evidence in a pending criminal trial.[22]

Other court cases affirm that it is appropriate to apply a balancing test of competing interests when disputes arise over executive branch information policies.[23] In *U.S. v. Nixon,* the Supreme Court exhibited the capacity of the judiciary to act as a viable check on presidential abuses of executive privilege. The Espy case is another example of a court resolving a dispute over a claim of privilege by applying a sensible balancing test.

There also is considerable legal precedent for in camera review of sensitive information by the courts.[24] Rather than simply compelling disclosure of privileged information for open court review, it may be appropriate for the executive branch to satisfy the court in secret chambers of the necessity of nondisclosure. Alternatively, judges may prefer to rely on executive officials' affidavits about the sensitivity of certain documents rather than to read such materials themselves in chambers. The courts have repeatedly affirmed their right to decide whether the necessity of protecting sensitive information outweighs the need for evidence in criminal justice matters,[25] and little evidence exists to support the claim that the judiciary does not perform this duty carefully and prudently. As Chief Justice John Marshall asserted in the *U.S. v. Burr* (1807) decision, the president has the right to protect privileged information, but this right does not override the authority of the judiciary to review protected documents.

> The president, although subject to the general rules which apply to others, may have sufficient motives for declining to produce a particular paper, and those motives may be such as to restrain the court from enforcing its production. . . . I can readily conceive that the president might receive a letter which it would be improper to exhibit in public. . . . The occasion for demanding it ought, in such a case, to be very strong, and to be fully shown to the court before its production could be insisted on. . . . Such a letter, though it be a private one, seems to

partake of the character of an official paper, and to be such as ought not on light ground be forced into public view.[26]

The judiciary clearly plays a less active role than Congress in resolving executive privilege disputes. Institutional compromise between the political branches should most often resolve informational controversies. Constant judicial intervention in such controversies is neither practical nor desirable. Nonetheless, the courts must often get involved in conflicts in which they are a party and in disputes that the political branches cannot resolve without judicial intervention.

In recent years, the prospects for judicial resolution of privilege controversies seem to have increased, as the executive and legislative branches have engaged in more contentious battles over information. As long as the so-called political branches cannot reach accommodations, the courts may have to become involved, as happened in the Clinton years.

The dilemma of executive privilege cannot be resolved with constitutional exactitude. To try to do so would be to attempt to impose a solution that is antithetical to our constitutional culture. The dilemma can best be resolved on a case-by-case basis, through the normal ebb and flow of politics as envisioned by the Framers of our governing system. Exactitude cannot be achieved in a government that must accommodate ever-changing circumstances. The genius of the American constitutional system is its enormous capacity to maintain its legitimacy and stability by accommodating changing circumstances without sacrificing the fundamental values that underlie the system.

The search for constitutional absolutes—for example, that executive privilege is a myth, or that executive privilege is an unfettered prerogative—is misguided. Our constitutional system cannot guarantee how every information policy dispute in government will be resolved, nor should it. Two executive privilege claims that, on the surface, appear equally valid may be treated very differently in different circumstances (e.g., political composition of Congress, membership of a particular investigating committee, popularity of the president). In the George H. W. Bush administration, one presidential claim of executive privilege that had little to do with national security prevailed in part because of the popularity of a cabinet member (former congressman and Secretary of Defense Richard Cheney), who otherwise might have been held in contempt of Congress; also contributing to the executive victory was the lack of follow-through by the chair of the committee conducting the investigation. On numerous other occasions, Congress has prevailed over claims of privilege because of its vigorous challenges to those actions or because of the unwillingness of some presidents to resist congressional demands.

It is implausible that a strict, legalistic definition of executive privilege could determine in advance the appropriate resolution to each information dispute. Yet the negative connotation of executive privilege, due to the abuses of that power by presidents Nixon, Clinton, and more recently, George W. Bush, is problematic. Modern presidents who attempt to reestablish executive privilege naturally find their efforts heavily criticized because of suspicions that their administrations might have something to hide.

Through the normal political process of confrontation, compromise, and accommodation, the coordinate branches can usually satisfactorily resolve their differences over executive privilege. We cannot solve our modern dilemma by resort to the solution that was rejected by the Framers—that is, by demanding constitutional certitude.

Michael Foley makes the point that constitutional dogmatism could have the dangerous effect of exposing the unresolvable elements of the separation of powers and the inconsistencies of the constitutional system. He correctly explains that certain constitutional problems are not amenable to definitive solutions.[27] In fact, an advanced constitutional culture is one that tolerates and even cultivates the existence of what he calls "abeyances," defined as "those constitutional gaps which remain vacuous for positive and constructive purposes."[28] Foley's thesis is most germane to the analysis of how to resolve the dilemma of executive privilege.

> There is simply more to be gained by cultivating and protecting abeyances and in preventing political issues and institutional differences from inciting intransigent divisions and entrenched constitutional dogmatism. In not extending claims to their logical but provocative conclusions; in not seeking to maximize advantages irrespective of their repercussions; and in promoting "comity" by which positions are acknowledged and honoured in the cause of achieving a means of cooperation within a context brooding with adversity, political participants can transform immobilism into productive interplay. The unremitting dissonance of a separated powers system, therefore, can condition those who work within it to the need to strive continuously against a background of conflict and dispute, in order to achieve any sense of common purpose.[29]

Critics of executive privilege nonetheless make the case that such a power is potentially dangerous, thereby requiring either the elimination of that power or the imposition of severe legal constraints on its exercise. Such resolutions to the dilemma of executive privilege are antithetical to the nature of a constitutional system that tolerates and cultivates abeyances. Those resolutions demonstrate a lack of understanding of a separation of powers system in which the exercise of a power such as executive privilege is a necessity in unusual circumstances. James W. Ceaser makes the point that the exercise of prerogative powers is appropriate for unusual circumstances and that "the exception or extreme case need not define the rule."[30] Ceaser disputes the view that the legislature "performs its proper duty in a separation of powers system only when it ties the executive's hands and attempts to force the nation to run its foreign policy through the instrument of law."[31] In creating the separation of powers system, the Framers did not envision the resort to strict legalisms as the means of resolving customary interbranch disputes. Ceaser's explanation of the Framers' theory of the separation of powers is germane to this analysis.

> The executive power, although it cannot always be subject to precise limitations, can still be watched, checked, and supervised by other institutions possessing an equal or greater regard among the people. Following this theory, the founders placed the greater part of the law-making power in Congress, thereby reducing the prospect that the prerogative power would ever be carried over into normal governance. Moreover, the very presence of institutions as powerful as the Congress and the Supreme Court could serve to check the executive power. Finally, there is a sense in which the founders made the legislative power supreme not so much by giving it the law-making power as by giving it the power to impeach and convict the president. By this means the legislature can dismiss the person exercising the executive power, even though it cannot exercise that power itself.[32]

Many critics of executive privilege too readily assume that any invocation of that power is, by definition, suspect—that no one would refuse to disclose information unless he or she had something to hide. To avoid future scandals, to resolve the dilemma of executive privilege, they offer solutions that are more troublesome than the problems they wish to eliminate. The resolution to the dilemma of executive privilege is, in a sense, right before our eyes. The founders' theory of separation of powers offers the necessary mechanisms by which prerogative powers can be exercised, challenged, and constrained.

Although there is no need for any statutory definition of, or limitations on, executive privilege, it is prudent for each presidential administration to adopt a set of procedures on how it will exercise executive privilege. The failure to do so in the Ford and Carter administrations—though perhaps necessitated by the political environment of the mid to late 1970s—resulted in a great deal of confusion both within these administrations and between the political branches. There is no small irony in the fact that these two presidencies—predicated on promises of openness and dissimilarity from the Nixon administration—in failing to adopt their own executive privilege guidelines, operated officially under the guidelines established by Nixon. Reagan adopted new executive privilege guidelines in 1982, which remained in effect throughout the Reagan-Bush years, although the George H. W. Bush administration did not routinely abide by those guidelines. The Clinton administration adopted revised executive privilege guidelines in 1994, but the president clearly violated some of those new procedures during the Lewinsky scandal and other executive privilege controversies.[33] President George W. Bush's administration articulated perhaps the most uncompromising positions in defense of executive privilege under the guise of the controversial unitary executive theory. Perhaps surprising to some observers who had expected a significant shift in approach, the Barack Obama administration has adopted very similar positions as his predecessor on a number of presidential secrecy issues, including executive privilege.

To avoid confusion regarding the exercise of executive privilege, it would be eminently sensible for each new administration to promulgate a set of guidelines on the use of that power. These guidelines need not diverge substantially, or at all, from one administration to the next. But a presidential directive should be issued by each administration to make it unmistakably clear how members of the executive branch are to handle executive privilege matters. The guidelines should not be posed in the form of legalisms but should merely outline the formal procedures for handling and resolving executive privilege issues. The guidelines should identify only broad areas in which issues of executive privilege may arise; the traditional categories are national security, confidential deliberations, enforcement of criminal justice, and privacy of executive branch officials. Specific cases of executive privilege should be dealt with as they arise.

Regardless of how the guidelines are set up, ultimately, responsibility for the exercise of that prerogative resides with the president. Consequently, accountability is not compromised by the exercise of executive privilege, because the use of that power will have to be justified to the electorate at some point or to one or both of the coordinate branches of government. To accept the legitimacy of a properly constrained executive privilege in our system of separated powers is to place an important trust in our president that he will exercise this power prudently and in the public interest and to know that we can hold him accountable for the manner in which he discharges his constitutional authority.

NOTES

Introduction

1. Woodrow Wilson, *Congressional Government* (Gloucester, Mass.: Peter Smith, 1973), 198.

2. David Wise, *The Politics of Lying: Government Deception, Secrecy, and Power* (New York: Random House, 1973), 64.

3. Ibid., 140. Wise qualifies that it is acceptable for government in some cases to keep secrets, but once the information gets out, all restraints are lifted (150).

4. Ibid., 150.

5. Morton H. Halperin and Daniel N. Hoffman, *Top Secret: National Security and the Right to Know* (Washington, D.C.: New Republic Books, 1977), 31.

6. Ibid., 97.

7. Ibid., 101, 104.

8. Ibid., 104.

9. Ibid., 105.

10. James Wiggins, *Freedom or Secrecy* (New York: Oxford University Press, 1956), x.

11. Quoted in U.S. Congress, *Availability of Information to Congress,* Hearings before a Subcommittee of the Committee on Government Operations, House of Representatives, 93d Cong., 1st sess., 3, 4, 19 April 1973, 81.

12. Michael A. Ledeen, "Secrets," in *The Media and Foreign Policy,* ed. Simon Serfaty (New York: St. Martin's Press, 1991), 121.

13. Ibid., 122–23.

14. Harold Evans, "The Norman Conquest: Freedom of the Press in Britain and America," in Serfaty, *The Media and Foreign Policy,* 189.

15. Ibid., 192.

16. Stansfield Turner, *Secrecy and Democracy: The CIA in Transition* (Boston: Houghton-Mifflin, 1985), 4.

17. Daniel P. Franklin, *Extraordinary Measures: The Exercise of Prerogative Powers in the United States* (Pittsburgh: University of Pittsburgh Press, 1991), 13.

18. *Board of Education v. Pico,* 457 U.S. 853, 867 (1982); *First National Bank v. Bellotti,* 435 U.S. 765, 783 (1978); *Stanley v. Georgia,* 394 U.S. 557, 564 (1969).

19. Louis Henkin, *Constitutionalism, Democracy, and Foreign Affairs* (New York: Columbia University Press, 1990), 20.

1. The Arguments against Executive Privilege

1. Raoul Berger, *Executive Privilege: A Constitutional Myth* (Cambridge, Mass.: Harvard University Press, 1974).

2. Theodore Roosevelt, *The Autobiography of Theodore Roosevelt,* ed. Wayne Andrews (New York: Scribner's, 1958), 197–200.

3. William Howard Taft, *Our Chief Magistrate and His Powers* (New York: Columbia University Press, 1916), 138.

4. David Gray Adler, "Court, Constitution and Foreign Affairs," in *The Constitution and the Conduct of American Foreign Policy,* ed. David Gray Adler and Larry N. George (Lawrence: University Press of Kansas, 1996), 20.

5. See David Gray Adler, "The Constitution and Presidential Warmaking," in Adler and George, *Constitution and Conduct,* 215–16.

6. Harold Hongju Koh, *The National Security Constitution: Sharing Power after the Iran-Contra Affair* (New Haven, Conn.: Yale University Press, 1990), 4.

7. Louis Henkin, *Constitutionalism, Democracy, and Foreign Affairs* (New York: Columbia University Press, 1990), 36.

8. House Report No. 394, 36th Cong., 1st sess., 1860.

9. Alan Swan, "Statement before the Subcommittee on Separation of Powers of the Committee on the Judiciary," *Executive Privilege,* U.S. Senate, 92d Cong., 1st sess., 27 July 1971, 245. Raoul Berger notes that "in the Constitution the Framers provide for limited secrecy by Congress alone, thereby excluding executive secrecy from the public" ("The Incarnation of Executive Privilege," *UCLA Law Review* 22 [October 1974]: 15–16).

10. Morton H. Halperin and Daniel N. Hoffman, *Top Secret: National Security and the Right to Know* (Washington, D.C.: New Republic Books, 1977), 88.

11. Berger, "Incarnation of Executive Privilege," 17.

12. George C. Calhoun, "Confidentiality and Executive Privilege," in *The Tethered Presidency: Congressional Restraints on Executive Power,* ed. Thomas M. Franck (New York: New York University Press, 1981), 173.

13. Raoul Berger, "Executive Privilege v. Congressional Inquiry," *UCLA Law Review* 12 (1965): 1058–60.

14. Raoul Berger, "Statement before the Subcommittee on Separation of Powers of the Committee on the Judiciary," *Executive Privilege,* 278. Article I, Section 6(1), of the Constitution provides that "for any speech or debate in either House [members] shall not be questioned in any other place." Berger points out that there is no comparable guarantee in Article II against anyone else examining the executive.

15. House Report No. 271, 27th Cong., 3d sess., 1843.

16. James Richardson, comp., *A Compilation of the Messages and Papers of the Presidents* (New York: Bureau of National Literature, 1897), 4:434.

17. Berger, *Executive Privilege,* 37.

18. Ibid., 38.

19. Ibid., 3.

20. Max Farrand, *The Records of the Federal Convention of 1787* (New Haven, Conn.: Yale University Press, 1911), 1:65.

21. Adler, "The Constitution and Presidential Warmaking," 217.

22. Adler, "Court, Constitution and Foreign Affairs," 20.

23. Berger, *Executive Privilege,* 131.

24. See Adler, "Court, Constitution and Foreign Affairs," 19–56.

25. Berger, *Executive Privilege,* 127.

26. Berger, "Statement," 283.

27. J. William Fulbright, "Statement before the Subcommittee on Separation of Powers of the Committee on the Judiciary," *Executive Privilege,* 31.

28. *Inland Waterways Corp. v. Young,* 309 U.S. 518, 534 (1940).

29. *Powell v. McCormack,* 395 U.S. 486, 546 (1969). See also *United States v. Morton Salt Co.,* 338 U.S. 632, 647 (1950): once powers are "granted, they are not lost by being allowed to lie dormant, any more than nonexistent powers can be prescribed by an unchallenged exercise."

30. Sam Ervin, "Statement before the Subcommittee on Separation of Powers of the Committee on the Judiciary," *Executive Privilege,* 4; emphasis in original.

31. Stuart Symington, "Statement before the Subcommittee on Separation of Powers of the Committee on the Judiciary," *Executive Privilege,* 221.

32. *McGrain v. Daugherty,* 273 U.S. 135, 161 (1927).

33. *Exxon Corp. v. FTC,* 589 F. 2d 582, 589 (D.C. Cir. 1978), *cert. denied,* 441 U.S. 943 (1979); *FTC v. Owens-Corning Fiberglass Corp.,* 626 F. 2d 966, 970 (D.C. Cir. 1980).

34. U.S. Congress, *Executive-Legislative Consultation on Foreign Policy: Strengthening Executive Branch Procedures,* Congress and Foreign Policy Series, No. 2, U.S. House of Representatives, (Washington, D.C.: Government Printing Office, May 1981), 35–36.

35. Ibid., 30.

36. Irving Janis, *Groupthink* (Boston: Houghton-Mifflin, 1982).

37. James MacGregor Burns, *Leadership* (New York: Harper and Row, 1978), 410.

38. U.S. Congress, *Executive-Legislative Consultation on Foreign Policy,* 40.

39. Sam Ervin, "Statement," 3–4.

40. Bruce Miroff, "Secrecy and Spectacle: Reflections on the Dangers of the Presidency," in *The Presidency in American Politics,* ed. Paul Brace, Christine B. Harrington, and Gary King (New York: New York University Press, 1989), 157.

41. Ibid., 152–53.

42. Richard M. Nixon, "Statement on Establishing a New System for Classification and Declassification of Government Documents Relating to National Security," 8 March 1972, in *Public Papers of the Presidents, 1972* (Washington, D.C.: Government Printing Office), 402.

43. 5 U.S.C. §552 (1966).

44. Hanson W. Baldwin, "Managed News: Our Peacetime Censorship," *Atlantic Monthly,* April 1963, 53.

45. David Wise, *The Politics of Lying: Government Deception, Secrecy, and Power* (New York: Random House, 1973), 149–50.

46. Ibid., 149.

47. Quoted in Miles Beardsley Johnson, *The Government Secrecy Controversy* (New York: Vantage Press, 1967), 39.

48. U.S. Congress, *Freedom of Information; Executive Privilege; Secrecy in Government,* Hearings before the Subcommittee on Administrative Practice and Procedure and Separation of Powers of the Committee on the Judiciary, United States Senate and the Subcommittee on Intergovernmental Relations of the Committee on Government Operations, United States Senate, 93d Cong., 1st sess., 10, 11, 12 April; 8, 9, 10, 16 May; 7, 8, 11, 26 June 1973, 2: 209.

49. Thomas I. Emerson, "The Danger of State Secrecy," in *Watergate and the American Political Process,* ed. Ronald Pynn (New York: Praeger, 1975), 60.

50. Wise, *Politics of Lying,* 64.

51. Ibid., 343.

52. Ibid., 344. See also A. Stephen Boyan, Jr., "Presidents and National Security Powers:

A Judicial Perspective" (paper presented at the annual meeting of the American Political Science Association, Washington, D.C., 1–4 September 1988), 3: "It does not take an Iran-Contra affair or a Watergate to remind us that an appeal to national security offers a handy reason to avoid public scrutiny of unwise or mistaken policies or of abuses of constitutional rights."

53. Berger, "Incarnation of Executive Privilege," 11, 21, 26–27, 29; Norman Dorsen and John Shattuck, "Executive Privilege: The President Won't Tell," in *None of Your Business: Government Secrecy in America,* ed. Norman Dorsen and Stephen Gillers (New York: Penguin Books, 1975), 27–60; Note, "Military and State Secrets Privilege," *Yale Law Journal* (1982): 579.

54. Halperin and Hoffman, *Top Secret,* 2.

55. Stuart Symington, "Statement," 222.

56. Berger, "Incarnation of Executive Privilege," 26–27.

57. Quoted in Itzhak Galnoor, ed., *Government Secrecy in Democracies* (New York: New York University Press, 1977), vii.

2. The Arguments in Favor of Executive Privilege

1. Archibald Cox, "Executive Privilege," *University of Pennsylvania Law Review* 122 (1974): 1388.

2. Harold Laski, *The American Presidency* (New York: Harper and Row, 1940), 155.

3. Raoul Berger, "Executive Privilege v. Congressional Inquiry," *UCLA Law Review* 12 (1965): 1060.

4. On this point, see James W. Ceaser, "In Defense of Separation of Powers," in *Separation of Powers: Does It Still Work?* ed. Robert A. Goldwin and Art Kaufman (Washington, D.C.: American Enterprise Institute, 1986), 168–93.

5. Paul Peterson, "The Constitution and the Separation of Powers," in *Taking the Constitution Seriously: Essays on the Constitution and Constitutional Law,* ed. Gary McDowell (Dubuque, Iowa: Kendall/Hunt, 1981), 195.

6. Edward S. Corwin, *The President: Office and Powers, 1787–1957,* 4th revised ed. (New York: New York University Press, 1957), 10.

7. Ibid., 15–16.

8. Max Farrand, ed., *The Records of the Federal Convention of 1787* (New Haven, Conn.: Yale University Press, 1967), 3:479. Even George Mason referred to the secrecy of the Constitutional Convention as "a proper precaution" because it averted "mistakes and misrepresentations until the business shall have been completed, when the whole may have a very different complexion from that in which the several parts might in their first shape appear if submitted to the public eye" (quoted in ibid., 3:28, 32).

9. Warren Burger, "'A Republic, If You Can Keep It': A Bicentennial Commentary," *Presidential Studies Quarterly* 18 (summer 1988): 468.

10. *U.S. v. Nixon,* 418 U.S. 683, 705 (1974).

11. Michael Foley, *The Silence of Constitutions* (London: Routledge, 1989).

12. J. W. Peltason, *Corwin and Peltason's Understanding the Constitution,* 11th ed. (New York: Holt, Rinehart and Winston, 1988), 84.

13. Quoted in Robert Green McCloskey, ed., *The Works of James Wilson* (Cambridge, Mass.: Harvard University Press, 1967), 1:294, 296.

14. *Marbury v. Madison,* 1 Cranch 137, 166 (1803).

15. See Raoul Berger, "Statement before the Subcommittee on Separation of Powers of the Committee on the Judiciary," *Executive Privilege,* U.S. Senate, 92d Cong., 1st sess., 28 July 1971, 278. Madison's observation is in *Federalist 51.*

16. Peterson, "The Constitution and the Separation of Powers," 205.

17. Berger, "Executive Privilege v. Congressional Inquiry," 1060, 1117.

18. Ibid., 1117.

19. Raoul Berger, *Executive Privilege: A Constitutional Myth* (Cambridge, Mass.: Harvard University Press, 1974), 10–11.

20. Ceaser, "In Defense of Separation of Powers," 171.

21. Gary Schmitt, "Executive Privilege," in *The Presidency in the Constitutional Order,* ed. Joseph Bessette and Jeffrey Tulis (Baton Rouge: Louisiana State University Press, 1981), 157–58.

22. *Watkins v. U.S.,* 354 U.S. 178 (1957); *Wilkinson v. U.S.,* 365 U.S. 399 (1961).

23. *U.S. v. Nixon,* 418 U.S. 683 (1974).

24. Schmitt, "Executive Privilege," 159.

25. Ibid., 160.

26. Berger, "Executive Privilege v. Congressional Inquiry," 1078.

27. George Washington to James Madison, 5 May 1789, in *The Writings of George Washington,* ed. John Fitzpatrick (Washington, D.C.: Government Printing Office, 1931–1944), 30:311.

28. Glenn A. Phelps, "George Washington and the Founding of the Presidency," *Presidential Studies Quarterly* 17 (spring 1987): 350, 354.

29. 3 *Annals of Congress* 493 (1792).

30. Although this was the first request by Congress for presidential materials, it was not the first congressional investigation. During the First Congress, the House of Representatives appointed a committee to investigate the conduct of Robert Morris as superintendent of finance during the previous Continental Congress and issued its report in 1791. The significance of this incident is that although some members of Congress argued that problems within the executive branch should be investigated by the president, Congress rejected that position and declared its own right of investigation. See Louis Fisher, "Invoking Executive Privilege: Navigating Ticklish Political Waters," *William & Mary Bill of Rights Journal* 8, no. 3 (April 200): 584–85.

31. Paul Ford, ed., *The Writings of Thomas Jefferson* (New York: Putnam, 1892), 1: 189–90.

32. Adam Breckenridge, *The Executive Privilege* (Lincoln: University of Nebraska Press, 1974), 31.

33. Abraham Sofaer, "Executive Privilege: An Historical Note," *Columbia Law Review* 75 (1975): 1319.

34. Ibid.

35. Ibid.

36. Ibid., 1320.

37. Ibid.

38. Ibid., 1321; Abraham Sofaer, "Executive Power and Control over Information: The Practice under the Framers," *Duke Law Journal* 1977 (March 1977): 8.

39. James Richardson, comp., *A Compilation of the Messages and Papers of the Presidents* (New York: Bureau of National Literature, 1897), 1:186–87.

40. See 5 *Annals of Congress* 771–72 (1796).

41. Ibid., 771, 782–83.

42. Ibid., 773.

43. Henry Cabot Lodge, ed., *The Works of Alexander Hamilton,* 12 vols. (New York: Putnam, 1903), 10:107.

44. *Journal of the Executive Proceedings of the Senate of the United States of America* (Washington, D.C.: Government Printing Office, 1828), 1:185–86.

45. 5 *Annals of Congress* 771 (1796).

46. See the detailed analysis of this dispute in Fisher, "Invoking Executive Privilege," 588–92. The House ultimately voted to fund the treaty, though by a narrow margin (fifty-one to forty-eight), with James Madison voting against (5 *Annals of Congress* 1291 [1796]).

47. William Nisbet Chambers, *Political Parties in a New Nation: The American Experience, 1776–1809* (London: Oxford University Press, 1963), 134–35; Abraham Sofaer, "Executive Power and Control over Information," 13–14.

48. Sofaer, "Executive Power and Control over Information," 16–17.

49. Thomas P. Abernathy, *The Burr Conspiracy* (New York: Oxford University Press, 1954).

50. 16 *Annals of Congress* 336 (1806–1807).

51. Richardson, *Messages and Papers of the Presidents,* 1:400.

52. Letter from Thomas Jefferson to George Hay, 12 June 1807, in Ford, *Writings of Thomas Jefferson,* 9:55.

53. Letter from Thomas Jefferson to John B. Colvin, 20 September 1810, in Ford, *Writings of Thomas Jefferson,* 9:279.

54. Ford, *Writings of Thomas Jefferson,* 5:162; emphasis in original.

55. Sofaer, "Executive Power and Control over Information," 19–24.

56. Ibid., 28–45.

57. Hawkins Taylor, *Compilation of Reports of the Committee on Foreign Relations, U.S. Senate, 1789–1901,* 8 vols. (Washington, D.C.: Government Printing Office, 1901), 8:24–25.

58. *House Journal,* 18th Cong., 2d sess., 1825, 102.

59. Richardson, *Messages and Papers of the Presidents,* 2:847.

60. Ibid., 3:1172.

61. Ibid., 3:1200. Jackson later refused a House request for information on the settlement of the northeastern boundary, calling such disclosure "incompatible with the public interest" (ibid., 3:1346).

62. Ibid., 3:1255.

63. Ibid., 3:1348.

64. Ibid., 3:1351.

65. Ibid., 4:1954.

66. Ibid., 4:1958–59.

67. Ibid., 5:2011.

68. Ibid., 5:2031–32.

69. Ibid., 5:2064.

70. Ibid., 5:2075.

71. Ibid., 5:2285.

72. Ibid., 5:2415.

73. Ibid., 5:2416–17.

74. Ibid., 5:2417.

75. Ibid., 5:2454.

76. Ibid., 6:2529–37.

77. Ibid., 6:2675–76, 2687, 2695.

78. Ibid., 7:3065. See also Charles Warren, *The Making of the Constitution* (Boston: Harvard University Press, 1947), 177.

79. Richardson, *Messages and Papers of the Presidents*, 7:3234.

80. Ibid., 7:3275.

81. Ibid., 7:3350.

82. Ibid., 8:3575, 3576, 3583.

83. Ibid., 9:4315–18.

84. Ibid., 11:5123. In 1886, Cleveland supported the opinion of his attorney general that documents pertaining to the dismissal of a U.S. district attorney, George M. Duskin, should not be divulged to the Senate. See Edward S. Corwin, *The President: Office and Powers, 1787–1957*, 4th revised ed. (New York: New York University Press, 1957), 429.

85. Richardson, *Messages and Papers of the Presidents*, 12:5673–74.

86. Ibid., 13:6098.

87. Ibid., 13:6101.

88. Ibid., 14:6458.

89. Corwin, *The President: Office and Powers*, 4th ed., 429.

90. Ibid., 429–30.

91. William P. Rogers, "The Power of the President to Withhold Information from the Congress," Memorandum of the Attorney General to the Senate Subcommittee on Constitutional Rights, 85th Cong., 2d sess., 1958, 17.

In December 1906, a Senate resolution called on the president to furnish information on the dismissal of three military companies, "if not incompatible with the public interest." Senator Spooner responded that Congress could not compel disclosure of information "which, if made public, would result in very great harm to our foreign relations." Spooner noted that there are circumstances "where the president would be at liberty obviously to decline to transmit information to Congress or to either House of Congress." See debates in *Congressional Record*, 6 December 1906.

Although William Howard Taft disagreed with Roosevelt's "stewardship theory" of the presidency, Taft defended the right of the chief executive to withhold information. With regard to the constitutional provision that the president inform Congress through the state of the Union, Taft wrote that Congress did not thereby have the power "to elicit from him [the president] confidential information which he has acquired for the purposes of enabling him to discharge his constitutional duties if he does not deem the disclosure of such information prudent or in the public interest" (William Howard Taft, *Our Chief Magistrate and His Powers* [New York: Columbia University Press, 1916], 129–32).

92. 65 *Cong. Rec.* 6087 (1924).

93. "Hoover Refuses Pact Data and 2 Senators Join Foes," *New York Times*, 12 July 1930, 1; "Treaty Foes Seek Debate Limitation to Get Vote in Week," *New York Times*, 17 July 1930, 1.

94. Summarized from U.S. Congress, *Contempt of Congress*, Report of the Committee on Public Works and Transportation, House of Representatives, 97th Cong., 2d sess., 15 December 1982, 107–8.

95. Cited in William Rehnquist, "Statement before the Subcommittee on Separation of Powers of the Committee on the Judiciary," *Executive Privilege,* U.S. Senate, 92d Cong., 1st sess., July 1971, 432.

96. Francis Rourke, *Secrecy and Publicity* (Baltimore: Johns Hopkins University Press, 1961), 71.

97. *The Public Papers of the Presidents, Harry S Truman, 1948* (Washington, D.C.: Government Printing Office), 228.

98. U.S. Congress, *Investigation of the GSA Strike,* Hearings before a Special Subcommittee of the Committee on Education and Labor, House of Representatives, 80th Cong., 2d sess., 1948, pt. 2, 8.

99. Ibid., pt. 1, 12.

100. *Public Papers of the Presidents, Harry S Truman, 1950,* 240.

101. Senate Report No. 2108, 81st Cong., 2d sess., 1950, 9.

102. *Public Papers of the Presidents, Harry S Truman, 1951,* 289.

103. U.S. Congress, *Military Situation in the Far East,* Hearings before the Committee on Armed Services and the Committee on Foreign Relations, U.S. Senate, 82d Cong., 1st sess., 1951.

104. *Public Papers of the Presidents, Harry S Truman, 1952–1953,* 199.

105. Ibid.

106. Ibid., 235–36.

107. *The Public Papers of the Presidents, Dwight D. Eisenhower, 1954* (Washington, D.C.: Government Printing Office), 483–84.

108. Henry Cabot Lodge, *As It Was* (New York: Norton, 1976), 135. See also Fred I. Greenstein, *The Hidden-Hand Presidency* (New York: Basic Books, 1982), 204.

109. Greenstein, *Hidden-Hand Presidency,* 205.

110. Ibid., 205, 207.

111. Editorial, *Washington Post,* 18 May 1954, 14.

112. Speech to the National Press Club by Senator John F. Kennedy, 14 January 1960, quoted in John P. Roche and Leonard W. Levy, eds., *The Presidency* (New York: Harcourt, Brace and World, 1964), 36.

113. Text of presidential news conference, 25 January 1961, reprinted in Harold Chase and Allen Lerman, eds., *Kennedy and the Press* (New York: Thomas Y. Crowell, 1965), 8.

114. Quoted in Thomas M. Franck and Edward Weisband, eds., *Secrecy and Foreign Policy* (New York: Oxford University Press, 1974), 5.

115. U.S. Congress, *Military Cold War Education and Speech Review Policies,* Hearings before the Special Preparedness Subcommittee of the Committee on Armed Services, U.S. Senate, 87th Cong., 2d sess., 1962, 508–9.

116. Ibid., 513–14. The president subsequently wrote a letter to his secretary of state issuing the same directive given to the secretary of defense.

117. Clark R. Mollenhoff, *Washington Cover-up* (Garden City, N.J.: Doubleday, 1962), 239.

118. Richard M. Pious, *The American Presidency* (New York: Basic Books, 1979), 352.

119. *Executive Privilege,* U.S. Senate, 1971, 35.

120. Ibid., 39.

121. U.S. Congress, *Nominations of Abe Fortas and Homer Thornberry,* Hearings before the Committee on the Judiciary, U.S. Senate, 90th Cong., 2d sess., 1968, pt. 2, 1347.

122. Ibid., 1363.

123. Ibid., 1348.

124. Rehnquist, "Statement," 435.

125. Peterson, "The Constitution and the Separation of Powers," 194.

126. *First National Bank v. Banco Nacional de Cuba,* 406 U.S. 759 (1972); *Haig v. Agee,* 453 U.S. 291 (1981); *Oetjen v. Central Leather Co.,* 246 U.S. 297 (1918); *U.S. Curtiss-Wright Corp.,* 299 U.S. 304 (1936); *U.S. v. Truong Dinh Hung,* 629 F. 2d 908 (1980).

127. A. Stephen Boyan, Jr., "Presidents and National Security Powers: A Judicial Perspective" (paper presented at the annual meeting of the American Political Science Association, Washington, D.C., 1–4 September 1988), 2. See *U.S. v. Macintosh,* 283 U.S. 605 (1931), in which Justice George Sutherland wrote for the majority that constitutionally protected liberties could be suspended during wartime. Sutherland was careful to note that the exception to the rule had to be construed narrowly—only under truly extraordinary circumstances could extraordinary actions be adopted by the government.

128. 229 U.S. 304 (1936). The Court has relied on *Curtiss-Wright* in support of broad delegations of legislative authority to the chief executive. See *Ex parte Endo,* 323 U.S. 283, 298 (1944); *Zemel v. Rusk,* 381 U.S. 1, 17 (1965); *Goldwater v. Carter,* 444 U.S. 996, 1000 (1979).

129. 229 U.S. 304, 305 (1936). Writing for the majority in *Carter v. Carter Coal Co.,* 298 U.S. 238, 295 (1936), Sutherland declared that unenumerated "inherent" federal powers do not exist in domestic affairs. External affairs, he wrote, are "a wholly different matter which it is not necessary now to consider."

130. 229 U.S. 304, 307–8 (1936).

131. Ibid., 319–20.

132. *Zemel v. Rusk,* 381 U.S. 1, 17 (1965).

133. *U.S. v. Truong Dinh Hung,* 629 F. 2d 908, 913 (1980). The court held that "attempts to counter foreign threats to the national security require the utmost *stealth, speed,* and *secrecy. . . .* The executive branch not only has superior expertise in the area of foreign intelligence, it is also constitutionally designated as the preeminent authority in foreign affairs" (913, 914).

134. *INS v. Chadha,* 462 U.S. 919 (1983); *Bowsher v. Synar,* 478 U.S. 714 (1986).

135. *Chicago and Southern Airlines v. Waterman Steamship Corporation,* 333 U.S. 103, 111 (1948).

136. *U.S. v. Reynolds,* 345 U.S. 1, 10 (1953).

137. Ibid., 8.

138. See Fisher, "Invoking Executive Privilege," 612–14.

139. Michael A. Ledeen, "Secrets," in *The Media and Foreign Policy,* ed. Simon Serfaty (New York: St. Martin's Press, 1991), 123.

140. Averell Harriman, "Statement before the Subcommittee on Separation of Powers of the Committee on the Judiciary," *Executive Privilege,* U.S. Senate, 92d Cong., 1st sess., July 1971, 353.

141. William P. Bundy, "Statement before the Subcommittee on Separation of Powers of the Committee on the Judiciary," *Executive Privilege,* U.S. Senate, 92d Cong., 1st sess., July 1971, 320–21.

142. Theodore H. White, *Breach of Faith: The Fall of Richard Nixon* (New York: Atheneum, 1975), 203. Arthur S. Miller similarly writes that "executive privilege is akin to

the 'state secrets' privilege; as such, it may be invoked for the benefit of the nation, not the individual. It is not something behind which a president's peccadilloes or other derelictions can be hidden" (Arthur S. Miller, "Executive Privilege: A Political Theory Masquerading as Law," in *The Presidency and Information Policy,* ed. Harold C. Relyea [New York: Center for the Study of the Presidency, 1981], 54).

143. *U.S. v. Nixon,* 483 U.S. 683, 705–6, 708 (1974). This landmark decision shattered Berger's assertion that executive privilege is a "myth." Nonetheless, it is important to qualify that the *Nixon* case had nothing to do with congressional requests for executive branch information. For example, the courts may choose to defer to presidential assertions of secrecy for national security purposes, but Congress is not required to do so. Congress has explicit responsibilities under the Constitution for foreign affairs and national security.

144. *Federal Open Market Committee of the Federal Reserve System v. Merrill,* 413 F. Supp. 494 (D.D.C. 1979).

145. *Watkins v. U.S.,* 354 U.S. 178 (1957); *Wilkinson v. U.S.,* 365 U.S. 399 (1961).

146. *McGrain v. Daugherty,* 273 U.S. 135 (1927); *Sinclair v. United States,* 279 U.S. 263 (1929).

147. *Senate Select Committee v. Nixon,* 498 F. 2d 725, 731 (1974): "The sufficiency of the Committee's showing must depend solely on whether the subpoenaed evidence is demonstrably critical to the responsible fulfillment of the Committee's functions."

148. Robert G. Dixon, Jr., "Congress, Shared Administration, and Executive Privilege," in *Congress against the President,* ed. Harvey C. Mansfield, Sr. (New York: Praeger, 1975), 134.

149. U.S. Congress, *Contempt of Congress,* Report of the Committee on Public Works and Transportation, House of Representatives, 97th Cong., 1st sess., 15 December 1982, 83.

150. *U.S. v. Marchetti,* 466 F. 2d 1309 (1972).

151. *Weissman v. CIA,* 565 F. 2d 692 (D.C. Cir. 1977); *Phillippi v. CIA,* 655 F. 2d 1325 (1981).

152. Ledeen, "Secrets," 124–25.

153. Benjamin R. Civiletti, "Intelligence Gathering and the Law: Conflict or Compatibility," *Fordham Law Review* 48 (1980): 887–88.

154. Rehnquist, "Statement," 434.

155. *U.S. v. Pink,* 315 U.S. 203 (1942).

156. Pious, *American Presidency,* 55.

157. Ibid.

158. *New York Times v. United States,* 403 U.S. 713, 728 (1971). Stewart also wrote the following:

> I think there can be but one answer. . . . The responsibility must be where the power is. If the Constitution gives the Executive a large degree of *unshared power* in the conduct of foreign affairs and the maintenance of our national defense, then under the Constitution the Executive must have the largely *unshared duty* to determine and preserve the degree of internal security necessary to exercise that power successfully. . . . It is clear to me that it is the *constitutional duty of the executive*—as a matter of *sovereign prerogative* and not as a matter of law as the courts know law—through the promulgation and enforcement of executive regulations to *protect the confidentiality necessary* to carry out its responsibilities in the fields of international relations and national defense. (728–30)

159. *Gravel v. United States,* 408 U.S. 606 (1972).

160. David M. O'Brien, *Storm Center: The Supreme Court in American Politics,* 2d ed. (New York: W. W. Norton, 1990), 150–51.

161. *Souicie v. David,* 448 F. 2d 1067, 1080 (D.C. Cir. 1971).

162. George C. Calhoun, "Confidentiality and Executive Privilege," in *The Tethered Presidency: Congressional Restraints on Executive Power,* ed. Thomas M. Franck (New York: New York University Press, 1981), 174.

163. Raoul Berger, "The Incarnation of Executive Privilege," *UCLA Law Review* 22 (October 1974): 29.

164. Ibid.

3. Nixon and the Abuse of Executive Privilege

1. U.S. Congress, *Executive Privilege, Secrecy in Government, Freedom of Information,* Hearings before the Subcommittee on Intergovernmental Relations of the Committee on Government Operations and the Subcommittees on Separation of Powers and Administrative Practice and Procedure of the Committee on the Judiciary, U.S. Senate, 93d Cong., 1st sess., 10–12 April; 8–10, 16 May; and 7, 8, 11, 16 June 1973, 3:155.

2. Letter from Rep. John E. Moss to President Richard M. Nixon, 28 January 1969, Folder: "Executive Privilege (2)," Box 13, Edward Schmults Files, Gerald R. Ford Library, Ann Arbor, Mich.

3. Letter from President Richard M. Nixon to Rep. John E. Moss, 7 April 1969, Folder: "Executive Privilege (2)," Box 13, Edward Schmults Files, Gerald R. Ford Library.

4. Memorandum from President Richard M. Nixon to Executive Department Heads, 24 March 1969, Folder: "Executive Privilege [1973]," White House Staff Files, Ronald Ziegler Alphabetical Subject File, Nixon Presidential Materials Project, College Park, Md.

5. Ibid.

6. *The Public Papers of the Presidents, Richard M. Nixon, 1973* (Washington, D.C.: Government Printing Office), 253. In his 31 January 1973 press conference, Nixon said that he would be "as liberal as possible" about allowing White House aides to testify before Congress. He added, "We are not going to use executive privilege as a shield for conversations that might just be embarrassing to us, but that really don't deserve executive privilege" (60–61).

7. Ibid., 254.

8. Raoul Berger, *Executive Privilege: A Constitutional Myth* (Cambridge, Mass.: Harvard University Press, 1974), 254–55.

9. *Public Papers of the Presidents, Richard M. Nixon, 1973,* 253.

10. U.S. Congress, *Availability of Information to Congress,* Hearings before a Subcommittee of the Committee on Government Operations, House of Representatives, 93d Cong., 1st sess., 3, 4, 19 April 1973, 1.

11. Adam C. Breckenridge, *The Executive Privilege: Presidential Control over Information* (Lincoln: University of Nebraska Press, 1974), 119–20.

12. Louis Fisher, "Congress and the Removal Power," *Congress and the Presidency* 10 (spring 1983): 75.

13. Letter from Sen. Sam Ervin, Jr., to Rep. L. H. Fountain, 2 April 1974; U.S. Con-

gress, *Survey on Executive Privilege,* Subcommittee on Separation of Powers of the Committee on the Judiciary, U.S. Senate, 93d Cong., 1st sess., 5 March 1973.

14. Breckenridge, *Executive Privilege,* 7–8.

15. Ibid., 93–94; Berger, *Executive Privilege,* 259.

16. *Environmental Protection Agency v. Mink,* 410 U.S. 73 (1973).

17. See Breckenridge, *Executive Privilege,* 19–20, 94–96.

18. See *The White House Transcripts* (New York: *New York Times*/Bantam, 1974), 163–64.

19. Memorandum from President Richard M. Nixon to Leonard Garment, 2 May 1973, White House Staff Files, H. R. Haldeman, Folder: "Action Completed—Outbox Material," Box 281, Larry Higby Files, Nixon Presidential Materials Project.

20. *U.S. v. Nixon,* 418 U.S. 683 (1974).

21. Stephen E. Ambrose, *Nixon: Ruin and Recovery, 1973–1990* (New York: Simon and Schuster, 1991), 384.

22. 418 U.S. 683, 712 (1974).

23. Ibid., 708.

24. Ibid., 712.

25. *Nixon v. Administrator of General Services,* 433 U.S. 425 (1977).

26. Brief of Richard M. Nixon in Opposition to Plaintiffs' Motion for Summary Judgment, *Senate Select Committee on Presidential Campaign Activities v. Nixon,* 366 F. Supp. 51 (D.D.C. 1973).

27. Brief of Richard M. Nixon in Opposition, *In re Grand Jury Subpoena Duces Tecum to Nixon,* 360 F. Supp. 1 (D.D.C 1973), 12–13; hereafter Brief II.

28. "Nixon: A President May Violate the Law," *U.S. News and World Report,* 30 May 1977, 65.

29. Ibid.

30. U.S. Congress, *Availability of Information to Congress,* 308.

31. Brief II, 4.

32. Letter from President Richard M. Nixon to Judge John Sirica, 25 July 1973, White House Central Files, FE4-1 (1 May 1973 to 30 September 1973), Nixon Presidential Materials Project.

33. Quoted in the U.S. Congress, *Executive Privilege—Secrecy in Government,* Hearings before the Subcommittee on Intergovernmental Relations of the Committee on Government Operations, U.S. Senate, 94th Cong., 1st sess., 29 September and 23 October 1975, 598.

34. U.S. Congress, *Freedom of Information; Executive Privilege; Secrecy in Government,* Hearings before the Subcommittee on Administrative Practice and Procedure and Separation of Powers of the Committee on the Judiciary, U.S. Senate, and the Subcommittee on Intergovernmental Relations of the Committee on Government Operations, U.S. Senate, 93d Cong., 1st sess., 10–12 April; 8–10, 16 May; 7, 8, 11, 26 June 1973, 1:35.

35. Ibid., 39.

36. "Nixon: A President May Violate the Law," 65.

37. Quoted in U.S. Congress, *Availability of Information to Congress,* 308.

38. U.S. Congress, *Executive Privilege, Secrecy in Government, Freedom of Information,* 158–59.

39. Quoted in U.S. Congress, *Freedom of Information, Executive Privilege; Secrecy in Government,* 39.

40. Quoted in Ambrose, *Nixon,* 76.

41. Ibid.

42. Quoted in Congressional Quarterly, *Watergate: Chronology of a Crisis* (Washington, D.C.: Congressional Quarterly Press, 1974), 2:6.

43. Brief II, 23.

44. Ibid., 2–3.

45. Letter from President Richard M. Nixon to Sen. Sam J. Ervin, 6 July 1973, White House Central Files, FE4-1 (1 May 1973 to 30 September 1973), Nixon Presidential Materials Project.

46. Letter from President Richard M. Nixon to Sen. Sam J. Ervin, 4 January 1974, White House Central Files, FE4-1 (1 May 1973 to 30 September 1973), Nixon Presidential Materials Project.

47. *Public Papers of the Presidents, Richard M. Nixon, 1973,* 253.

48. Brief II, 18.

49. Quoted in William S. Moorhead, "Operation and Reform of the Classification System in the United States," in *Secrecy and Foreign Policy,* ed. Thomas M. Franck and Edward Weisband (New York: Oxford University Press, 1974), 99–100.

50. *White House Transcripts,* 163–64.

51. "Nixon: A President May Violate the Law," 65.

52. Ambrose, *Nixon,* 114. In a memorandum to John Ehrlichman, the president advocated that to counter press criticism of the administration's claims of executive privilege and its use of the FBI for domestic surveillance, they assert that the previous Democratic administrations had engaged in similar activities. See letter from President Richard M. Nixon to John Ehrlichman, 4 March 1973, President's Personal File: "Memoranda: 1969–1974," Nixon Presidential Materials Project.

4. The "Open" Presidencies of Ford and Carter

1. Letter from John E. Moss to President Gerald R. Ford, 15 August 1974, Folder: "Executive Privilege (2)," Box 13, Philip W. Buchen Files, Gerald R. Ford Library, Ann Arbor, Mich.; hereafter, GRFL.

2. Letter from Max L. Friedersdorf to John E. Moss, 16 August 1974, Folder: "Executive Privilege (2)," Box 13, Philip W. Buchen Files, GRFL.

3. Letter from Reps. John N. Erlenborn and William S. Moorhead to President Gerald R. Ford, 13 August 1974; Letter from Sens. Sam Ervin, Edmund S. Muskie, and William V. Roth to President Gerald R. Ford, 22 August 1974; Letter from Max Friedersdorf to Rep. John N. Erlenborn, 16 August 1974; Letters from William E. Timmons to Sens. Sam Ervin, Edmund S. Muskie, and William V. Roth, 28 August 1974, Folder: "Executive Privilege—General (2)," Box 13, Edward Schmults Files, GRFL.

4. Memorandum from Stanley Ebner to Philip W. Buchen, 19 September 1974, Folder: "Executive Privilege (2)," Box 13, Philip W. Buchen Files, GRFL.

5. Memorandum from William E. Timmons to Philip W. Buchen, 23 September 1974, Folder: "Executive Privilege (2)," Box 13, Philip W. Buchen Files, GRFL.

6. White House Schedule Proposal, 23 September 1974, Folder: "Executive Privilege (2)," Box 13, Philip W. Buchen Files, GRFL.

7. Agenda: Meeting with Moorhead and Erlenborn, 9 October 1974, Folder: "Executive Privilege (2)," Box 13, Philip W. Buchen Files, GRFL.

8. Memorandum from Doug Metz to Philip W. Buchen, 24 September 1974, Folder: "Executive Privilege—General (2)," Box 13, Edward Schmults Files, GRFL.

9. Memorandum from Dudley Chapman to Philip W. Buchen, 25 September 1974, Folder: "Executive Privilege—General (2)," Box 13, Edward Schmults Files, GRFL.

10. Memorandum from Dudley Chapman to Philip W. Buchen, et al., 5 November 1974, Folder: "Executive Privilege—General (1)," Box 13, Edward Schmults Files, GRFL.

11. Participants in the discussion included Solicitor General Robert Bork; the assistant attorney general for the Office of Legal Counsel, Antonin Scalia; former adviser to presidents Kennedy and Johnson, Martin Richman; Department of Justice officer Robert L. Keuch; and two members of Ford's White House staff, Rod Hills and James Wilderotter. Note from Robert L. Keuch to Rod Hills, 7 April 1975, Folder: "Executive Privilege (4)," Box 13, Philip W. Buchen Files, GRFL.

12. Memorandum from Philip W. Buchen to Members of the Cabinet and Senior White House Staff, 21 November 1975, Folder: "Executive Privilege (5)," Box 13, Philip W. Buchen Files, GRFL.

13. Memorandum from the Office of the Attorney General—Privilege of the Executive Branch to Withhold Information from Congressional Committees, November 1975, Folder: "Executive Privilege (3)," Box 13, Philip W. Buchen Files, GRFL.

14. Gerald R. Ford, A Time to Heal (Norwalk, Conn.: Easton Press, 1987), 134.

15. Clifton Daniel, "Ford's Speech: Same Priorities," New York Times, 13 August 1974, 21.

16. Author interview with John W. Hushen, Washington, D.C., 14 May 1990.

17. Stanley I. Kutler, The Wars of Watergate: The Last Crisis of Richard Nixon (New York: Alfred A. Knopf, 1990), 570.

18. Quoted in Memorandum from Philip W. Buchen to Members of the Cabinet and Senior White House Staff, 21 November 1975, Folder: "Executive Privilege (5)," Box 13, Philip W. Buchen Files, GRFL.

19. Dom Bonafede, Daniel Rapoport, and Joel Havemann, "The President versus Congress: The Score since Watergate," National Journal, 29 May 1976, 738; Robert G. Dixon, "Congress, Shared Administration, and Executive Privilege," in Congress against the President, ed. Harvey C. Mansfield, Sr. (New York: Praeger, 1975), 129.

20. See Memorandum from Dudley Chapman to Philip W. Buchen, et al., 5 November 1974, Folder: "Executive Privilege (1)," Box 13, Edward Schmults Files, GRFL. See also Memorandum from Philip W. Buchen to Members of the Cabinet and Senior White House Staff, 21 November 1975.

21. Memorandum from Philip W. Buchen to Members of the Cabinet and Senior White House Staff, 21 November 1975.

22. This section is summarized from the following sources: Memorandum from Philip W. Buchen to Members of the Cabinet and Senior White House Staff, 21 November 1975; Richard Ehlke, "Congressional Access to Information from the Executive: A Legal Analysis," in CRS Report to Congress (Washington, D.C.: Congressional Research Service, 10 March 1986), 41–43; Peter M. Shane, "Negotiating for Knowledge: Administrative Responses to Congressional Demands for Information," Administrative Law Review 44 (spring 1992): 202–3.

23. 50 U.S.C. Appl. 2406(c) (1969).

24. U.S. Congress, *Contempt Proceedings against Secretary of Commerce, Rogers C. B. Morton,* Hearings before the Subcommittee on Oversight and Investigations of the Committee on Interstate and Foreign Commerce, House of Representatives, 94th Cong., 1st sess., 1975, 11.

25. This section is summarized from the following sources: Richard Ehlke, "Congressional Access to Information: Selected Problems and Issues," in *CRS Report to Congress* (Washington, D.C.: Congressional Research Service, 16 October 1979), 19–21; Ehlke, "Congressional Access to Information from the Executive," 20n; Memorandum from Philip W. Buchen to Members of the Cabinet and Senior White House Staff, 21 November 1975.

26. House Report No. 94-693, 94th Cong., 1st sess., 1975, quoted in Ehlke, "Congressional Access to Information: Selected Problems and Issues," 19–20.

27. Letter from President Ford to Rep. Otis Pike, 19 November 1975, in *The Public Papers of the Presidents, Gerald R. Ford* (Washington, D.C.: Government Printing Office, 1975), 1889.

28. Memorandum from Philip W. Buchen to Members of the Cabinet and Senior White House Staff, 21 November 1975.

29. This section is summarized from A. Stephen Boyan, ed., *Constitutional Aspects of Watergate,* vol. 5 (Dobbs Ferry, N.Y.: Oceana, 1979), 183–88; Ehlke, "Congressional Access to Information from the Executive," 9–14.

30. Boyan, *Constitutional Aspects of Watergate,* 184.

31. *United States v. AT&T,* 419 F. Supp. 454 (D.D.C. 1976).

32. *United States v. AT&T,* 551 F. 2d 384 (D.C. Cir. 1976).

33. *United States v. AT&T,* 567 F. 2d 121 (D.C. Cir. 1977).

34. Ibid., 131–33.

35. Letter from Reps. Richardson Preyer and Paul N. McCloskey, Jr., to President Jimmy Carter, 13 June 1977, File: "Executive Privilege, 3–6/77," Box 130, Margaret McKenna Files, Jimmy Carter Library, Atlanta, Ga.; hereafter JCL.

36. Letter from Rep. Richardson Preyer to Robert J. Lipshutz, 1 June 1978, File: "Executive Privilege, 1/78–7/79," Box 130, Margaret McKenna Files, JCL.

37. Letter from Reps. Richardson Preyer and Paul N. McCloskey, Jr., to President Jimmy Carter, 27 September 1978, File: "Executive Privilege, 1/78–7/79," Box 130, Margaret McKenna Files, JCL.

38. Letters from Frank Moore to Reps. Richardson Preyer and Paul N. McCloskey, Jr., 10 October 1978, Box FE 2-1, White House Central File (WHCF)—Subject File, JCL.

39. In July 1979, Rep. John Erlenborn (R-Ill.) also requested that the White House respond to the Preyer-McCloskey letters. At this late date in Carter's term, the general counsel to the Office of Management and Budget wrote a memorandum to Lipshutz asking if there had been any response to various executive privilege inquiries and how to reply to members of Congress seeking information about the administration's policy. Memorandum from Robert P. Bedell to Robert J. Lipshutz, 12 July 1978, File: "Executive Privilege, 1/78–7/79," Box 130, Margaret McKenna Files, JCL.

40. There are numerous memoranda on these White House discussions in File: "Executive Privilege, 7–12/77," Box 130, Margaret McKenna Files, JCL. In particular, see, Memorandum from Edward C. Newton to Margaret McKenna, 12 May 1977; Memorandum from Patricia M. Wald to Heads of Offices, Bureaus, and Divisions, 29 June 1977; Memorandum from Bob Lipshutz to Margaret McKenna, 6 July 1977; Memorandum from James W. Moorman to Patricia M. Wald, 8 July 1977; Memorandum from Thomas J. Madden to Patricia M.

Wald, 11 July 1977; Memorandum from Myron C. Baum to Patricia M. Wald, 13 July 1977; Memorandum from Kevin D. Rooney to Patricia M. Wald, 14 July 1977; Memorandum from John M. Harmon to Patricia M. Wald, 19 July 1977; Memorandum from Patricia M. Wald to Heads of Offices, Boards, and Divisions, 20 July 1977; Memorandum from Gilbert G. Pompa to Patricia M. Wald, 20 July 1977.

41. See the following memoranda in File: "Executive Privilege, 7–12/77," Box 130, Margaret McKenna Files, JCL: Memorandum from Margaret McKenna to Patricia M. Wald and John Harmon, 18 July 1977; Memorandum from Eric L. Richard to Margaret McKenna, 25 July 1977; Memorandum from Margaret McKenna to Doug Huron, 10 August 1977; Memorandum from Doug Huron to William Nichols, 15 August 1977; Route Slip from Ron Kienlen to Doug Huron, 14 October 1977 (this correspondence contains copies of all departmental responses to the proposed executive order); Memorandum from Eric L. Richard to Working Group on Disclosure of Information to Congress, 25 October 1977; Memorandum from Eric L. Richard Working Group on Disclosure of Information, 3 November 1977.

42. See "Congressional Requests for Information from the Executive Branch" and other memoranda on executive privilege in Box FE-1, WHCF—Subject File, JCL.

43. Memorandum, "Congressional Requests for Information from the Executive Branch," 1977 [no specific date provided], Box FE-1, WHCF—Subject File, JCL.

44. Letter from Rep. John E. Moss to President Jimmy Carter, 11 October 1977, Box FE 2-1, WHCF—Subject File, JCL. Frank Moore wrote to Moss acknowledging that Carter had received the letter and would take the congressman's "comments under consideration." Letter from Frank Moore to Rep. John E. Moss, 20 October 1977, Box FE 2-1, WHCF—Subject File, JCL.

45. Memorandum from Robert Lipshutz to White House Staff, 8 February 1979, Box FE-2, WHCF—Subject File, JCL.

46. Memorandum from Doug Huron and Barbara Bergman to Lloyd Cutler, 6 March 1980, File: "Executive Privilege, 6/77–11/80," Box 74, Lloyd Cutler Files, JCL.

47. Memorandum from Lloyd Cutler to Reubin O'D. Askew, 22 October 1980, File: "Executive Privilege, 6/77–11/80," Box 74, Lloyd Cutler Files, JCL.

48. Memorandum from Lloyd N. Cutler to Heads of All Units within the Executive Office of the President and the Senior White House Staff, 31 October 1980, File: "Executive Privilege, 6/77–11/80," Box 74, Lloyd Cutler Files, JCL.

49. Memorandum from Lloyd N. Cutler to the Attorney General, 31 October 1980, File: "Executive Privilege, 6/77–11/80," Box 74, Lloyd Cutler Files, JCL.

50. Memorandum from Zoe E. Baird to Lloyd N. Cutler, 10 November 1980, File: "Executive Privilege, 6/77–11/80," Box 74, Lloyd Cutler Files, JCL.

51. Memorandum from Robert Lipshutz and Margaret McKenna to President Jimmy Carter, 30 April 1977, Box FE-1, WHCF—Subject File, JCL.

52. Memorandum from Margaret McKenna and Robert Lipshutz to President Jimmy Carter, 11 May 1977, File: "Executive Privilege, 1977," Box 15, Robert Lipshutz Files, JCL.

53. Memorandum from Juanita M. Kreps to President Jimmy Carter, 21 November 1977, File: "Executive Privilege, 1977," Box 15, Robert Lipshutz Files, JCL.

54. Letter from Juanita M. Kreps to Rep. Benjamin S. Rosenthal, 21 November 1977, File: "Executive Privilege, 1977," Box 15, Robert Lipshutz Files, JCL.

55. Memorandum from Robert Lipshutz to President Jimmy Carter, 29 November 1977, File: "Executive Privilege, 1977," Box 15, Robert Lipshutz Files, JCL.

56. Memorandum from Robert Lipshutz to Stuart Eizenstat, 23 November 1977, File: "Executive Privilege, 1977," Box 15, Robert Lipshutz Files, JCL.

57. Memorandum from Robert Lipshutz to President Jimmy Carter, 30 November 1977, File: "Executive Privilege, 1977," Box 15, Robert Lipshutz Files, JCL.

58. Letter from Rep. Benjamin S. Rosenthal to James Griffin, 12 July 1978, File: "Executive Privilege, 1978," Box 15, Robert Lipshutz Files, JCL.

59. Memorandum of Conversation, 25 July 1978, File: "Executive Privilege, 1978," Box 15, Robert Lipshutz Files, JCL.

60. Letter from C. Fred Bersten to Rep. Benjamin S. Rosenthal, 25 July 1978, File: "Executive Privilege, 1978," Box 15, Robert Lipshutz Files, JCL.

61. Memorandum from Robert H. Mundheim to Robert Lipshutz, 13 September 1978, File: "Executive Privilege, 1978," Box 15, Robert Lipshutz Files, JCL. Lipshutz agreed with Mundheim's recommendation. See Memorandum from Robert J. Lipshutz to Robert H. Mundheim, 18 September 1978, File: "Executive Privilege, 1978," Box 15, Robert Lipshutz Files, JCL.

62. U.S. Congress, *Contempt Proceedings against Secretary of Health, Education and Welfare, Joseph A. Califano, Jr.,* Hearings before the Subcommittee on Oversight and Investigations of the Committee on Interstate and Foreign Commerce, House of Representatives, 95th Cong., 2d sess., 16 August 1978.

63. Letter from Sarah Weddington to Sen. Harrison A. Williams, 31 January 1979, File: "Executive Privilege, 1979," Box 15, Robert Lipshutz Files, JCL.

64. Transcript of 31 January 1979 news conference, File: "Executive Privilege, 1979," Box 15, Robert Lipshutz Files, JCL.

65. Memorandum from Robert Lipshutz to Margaret McKenna and Doug Huron, 2 February 1979, File: "Executive Privilege, 1979," Box 15, Robert Lipshutz Files, JCL.

66. Memorandum from Robert Lipshutz to White House Staff, 8 February 1979, File: "Executive Privilege, 1979," Box 15, Robert Lipshutz Files, JCL.

67. Memorandum from Robert Lipshutz and Margaret McKenna to President Jimmy Carter, 23 May 1977, File: "Executive Privilege, 1977," Box 15, Robert Lipshutz Files, JCL.

68. Letter from Lloyd Cutler to Rep. Samuel S. Stratton, 30 September 1980, File: "Executive Privilege, 6/77–11/80," Box 74, Lloyd Cutler Files, JCL. Cutler noted that the president had previously taken the exceptional position of waiving the privilege with regard to testimony by White House aides when the president's brother had been implicated in a scheme to represent Libyan interests in the United States for a substantial fee.

69. Proclamation No. 4744, 45 *Fed. Reg.* 22, 864 (3 April 1980).

70. U.S. Congress, *The Petroleum Import Fee: Department of Energy Oversight,* Hearings before a Subcommittee of the Committee on Government Operations, House of Representatives, 96th Cong., 2d sess., 8, 24, 29 April 1980, 1–8.

71. Ibid., 35.

72. Ibid., 96–101.

73. Ibid., 116–17.

74. Ibid., 146.

75. Ibid., 134–39.

76. Ibid., 142. *Independent Gasoline Marketers Council v. Duncan,* 492 F. Supp. 614 (D.D.C. 1980).

5. Reagan, Bush, and the Era of Divided Government

1. Memorandum from President Reagan to Heads of Executive Departments and Agencies, "Procedures Governing Responses to Congressional Requests for Information," 4 November 1982.

2. Diana M. T. K. Austin, "The Reagan Administration and the Freedom of Information Act," in *Freedom at Risk: Secrecy, Censorship, and Repression in the 1980s,* ed. Richard O. Curry (Philadelphia: Temple University Press, 1988), 71–72; David Sadofsky, *Political and Legal Control of Information* (New York: Praeger, 1990), 84.

3. Austin, "Reagan Administration," 72.

4. Ibid.

5. Quoted in David S. Broder, *Behind the Front Page: A Candid Look at How the News Is Made* (New York: Simon and Schuster, 1987), 187.

6. Austin, "Reagan Administration," 72.

7. Ibid., 73–74; Donna A. Demac, *Keeping America Uninformed: Government Secrecy in the 1980s* (New York: Pilgrim Press, 1984), 96.

8. Demac, *Keeping America Uninformed,* 92.

9. John D. Lees, "Environmental Deregulation and Intelligence Gathering under Reagan—Contrasting Experiences of Policy Change," in *Reagan's First Four Years: A New Beginning?* ed. John D. Lees and Michael Turner (New York: Manchester University Press, 1988), 221.

10. Ibid., 219–20; Austin, "Reagan Administration," 73.

11. "Protection of Classified National Security Council and Intelligence Information," *Weekly Compilation of Presidential Documents* 18 (January 1982): 24–25.

12. Stephen Hess, *The Government/Press Connection: Press Officers and Their Offices* (Washington, D.C.: Brookings Institution, 1984), 90.

13. Ibid., 91–92.

14. Lees, "Environmental Deregulation," 219.

15. Demac, *Keeping America Uninformed,* 96.

16. Ibid., 97.

17. *Time,* 7 November 1983, 66.

18. Quoted in Broder, *Behind the Front Page,* 186.

19. Quoted in Mark Hertsgaard, *On Bended Knee: The Press and the Reagan Presidency* (New York: Farrar Straus Giroux, 1988), 222.

20. The following events are summarized from two congressional reports: U.S. Congress, *Executive Privilege: Legal Opinions Regarding Claim of President Ronald Reagan in Response to a Subpoena Issued to James G. Watt, Secretary of the Interior,* Subcommittee on Oversight and Investigations, Committee of Energy and Commerce, House of Representatives, 97th Cong., 1st sess. (Washington, D.C.: Government Printing Office, 1981); U.S. Congress, *Contempt of Congress,* Committee on Energy and Commerce, House of Representatives, 97th Cong., 2d sess. (Washington, D.C.: Government Printing Office, 1982).

21. William French Smith, "Assertion of Executive Privilege in Response to a Congressional Subpoena," Opinion of the Office of Legal Counsel (1981); hereafter Smith Opinion.

22. Ibid.

23. Ibid.

24. U.S. Congress, *Contempt of Congress,* Committee on Energy and Commerce, 42–45.

25. U.S. Congress, *Investigation of the Role of the Department of Justice in the Withholding of Environmental Protection Agency Documents from Congress in 1982–1983,* House of Representatives, Committee on the Judiciary, 99th Cong., 1st sess. (Washington, D.C.: Government Printing Office, 1985), 28.

26. The following events are summarized from ibid., U.S. Congress, *Contempt of Congress,* Committee on Public Works and Transportation, House of Representatives, 97th Cong., 2d sess. (Washington, D.C.: Government Printing Office, 1982); Jonathan Lash, Katherine Gillman, and David Sheridan, *A Season of Spoils: The Reagan Administration's Attack on the Environment* (New York: Pantheon Books, 1984).

27. In the midst of this controversy, Gorsuch married Robert Burford and changed her surname. For purposes of clarity, I refer to her throughout this chapter as Gorsuch.

28. U.S. Congress, *Contempt of Congress,* Committee on Public Works and Transportation, 42–43.

29. Ibid., 36.

30. Ibid., 37.

31. *United States of America v. The House of Representatives,* 556 F. Supp. 150 (D.D.C. 1983). Some members of Congress objected to the administration being referred to in the suit as the "United States of America." They had a point, given the fact that the case involved a conflict between coequal branches of the U.S. government. See Lash, Gillman, and Sheridan, *Season of Spoils,* 76.

32. Lash, Gillman, and Sheridan, *Season of Spoils,* 76–77.

33. 556 F. Supp. 150, 153 (D.D.C. 1983).

34. Ibid., 152.

35. U.S. Congress, *Investigation of the Role of the Department of Justice,* 11.

36. Ibid., 17.

37. The events surrounding the Rehnquist memos are derived from reports in *Congressional Quarterly Weekly Reports* and the *Washington Post.* See Nadine Cohodas, "Rehnquist Rebuts Criticism, Confirmation Seems Likely," *Congressional Quarterly Weekly Reports,* 2 August 1986, 1764–65; Nadine Cohodas, "Rehnquist, Scalia Headed for Confirmation," *Congressional Quarterly Weekly Reports,* 9 August 1986, 1844–46; Al Kamen and Howard Kurtz, "Rehnquist Told in 1974 of Restriction in Deed," *Washington Post,* 6 August 1986, A1, 6; David Broder, "Those Memos Will Tell," *Washington Post,* 6 August 1986, A15; Howard Kurtz and Al Kamen, "Rehnquist Not in Danger over Papers," *Washington Post,* 7 August 1986, A1, 14; Howard Kurtz, "Rehnquist Memos Described," *Washington Post,* 7 August 1986, A15.

38. The events surrounding the controversy over Reagan's diaries are summarized from several *Washington Post* news reports: Bob Woodward and David Hoffman, "President's Memoir File Includes Iran Notes," *Washington Post,* 1 February 1987, A1, 16; Al Kamen, "'Executive Privilege' Hailed," *Washington Post,* 1 February 1987, A16; W. Dale Nelson, "Reagan Iran Notes Report Confirmed," *Washington Post,* 2 February 1987, A16; David Hoffman, "President Offers to Share Iran Sales Notes with Hill," *Washington Post,* 3 February 1987, A1, 8.

39. Louis Fisher, "Congress as Macromanager of the Executive Branch," in *The Managerial Presidency,* ed. James P. Pfiffner (Pacific Grove, Calif.: Brooks/Cole, 1991), 232.

40. Woodward and Hoffman, "President's Memoir File," A16.

41. Nelson, "Reagan Iran Notes," A16.

42. Ibid.

43. Kamen, "'Executive Privilege' Hailed," A16.

44. Hoffman, "President Offers to Share," A1.

45. Ibid., A8.

46. Author interview with Jim Lewin, by telephone, 19 November 1992.

47. Letter from Reps. Bob Wise and Al McCandless to President George Bush, 26 July 1989, Case No. 058917, FE002-01, White House Office of Records Management (WHORM): Subject File, "Presidential Powers," Bush Presidential Library, College Station, Tex.; hereafter Bush Library.

48. Letters from Frederick D. McClure to Reps. Bob Wise and Al McCandless, 3 August 1989, Case No. 058917, FE002-01, WHORM: Subject File, "Presidential Powers," Bush Library. A White House correspondence tracking sheet shows that the Wise-McCandless letter and a draft of the McClure response were circulated among a number of officials, including the attorney general, White House counsel, and national security adviser. The sheet included the comments "no further response required" and "close out." See Case No. 059817, FE002-01, WHORM: Subject File, "Presidential Powers," Bush Library.

49. William P. Barr, "Congressional Requests for Confidential Executive Branch Information," Memorandum Opinion for the General Counsel's Consultative Group, 19 June 1989 (on file with author).

50. Smith Opinion.

51. Memorandum from Douglas M. Kmiec to Oliver B. Revell, "Congressional Requests for Information from Inspectors General Concerning Open Criminal Investigations," 24 March 1989, 1; reprinted in U.S. Congress, *Department of Justice Authorization for Appropriations for Fiscal Year 1990*, House of Representatives, Committee on the Judiciary, 101st Cong., 1st sess. (Washington, D.C.: Government Printing Office, 1989); hereafter Kmiec memo.

52. Memorandum from Steven R. Ross and Charles Tiefer, "Justice Department Memorandum Directing the Withholding from Congress of Inspector General Information," 2 May 1989, 2; reprinted in ibid., 78.

53. Kmiec memo, 7–8; reprinted in ibid., 71–72.

54. Ross and Tiefer, "Justice Department Memorandum," 12; reprinted in ibid., 88.

55. Author interview with Charles Tiefer, by telephone, 23 November 1992.

56. This section is summarized from various news reports in the *New York Times, Washington Post,* and *Wall Street Journal.*

57. David Johnston, "Reagan Is Ordered to Provide Diaries in Poindexter Case," *New York Times,* 31 January 1990, A20.

58. Tracy Thompson, "Justice Department Asks Delay on Reagan Diary Ruling," *Washington Post,* 3 February 1990, A3.

59. David Johnston, "Reagan Rejects Poindexter Plea to Yield Diaries," *New York Times,* 6 February 1990, A1.

60. Ibid.

61. Paul M. Barrett and Amy Dockser Marcus, "Reagan's Videotaped Testimony Ordered," *Wall Street Journal,* 6 February 1990, B10. Reagan's attorney, Theodore B. Olson, had met the 5 February 1990 deadline for formally refusing to release the diary entries but never used the phrase *executive privilege* in so refusing. That led to some confusion over whether Reagan had met Judge Greene's condition of having to assert executive privilege by that date as the basis for the refusal. Olson made it clear on 7 February 1990 that Reagan had indeed

relied on executive privilege as the basis for withholding the diaries: "No court has declared that the protection afforded the privilege for confidential presidential communications may be invoked only by reciting the phrase executive privilege. However, if this court intended . . . that the privilege may only be invoked in that fashion, the former president reaffirms that was, indeed [his] intention" (Joe Pichirallo, "Reagan Attorneys Assert Executive Privilege," *Washington Post,* 8 February 1990, A4).

62. David Johnston, "Reagan to Give Tape Testimony on Iran-Contra," *New York Times,* 10 February 1990, 28.

63. David Johnston, "Poindexter Loses Fight for Reagan Notes," *New York Times,* 22 March 1990, A20. The issue of executive privilege also arose in connection to the Iran-contra trial of Lt. Col. Oliver North. In this case, North sought to subpoena Reagan's diaries and the testimonies of then President Reagan and President-elect Bush, but the three subpoenas were quashed. Because earlier conspiracy charges against North had been dropped, Judge Gerhard A. Gesell determined that the defendant's needs in this case did not overcome the "presumptive privilege" accorded to the president and the president-elect. See Comment, "Legitimacy: The Sacrificial Lamb at the Altar of Executive Privilege," *Kentucky Law Journal* 78 (1990): 822–25; Joe Pichirallo and Ruth Marcus, "Reagan, Bush Subpoenaed by North; White House to Fight Testimony Demand," *Washington Post,* 31 December 1988, A1, 12; Ruth Marcus, "Subpoenaing the President," *Washington Post,* 11 January 1989, A7; Michael Wines, "Key North Counts Dismissed by Court," *New York Times,* 14 January 1989, 1, 7; George Lardner, Jr., "North Asks Court to Overturn Convictions," *Washington Post,* 7 February 1990, A3.

64. Peter Schmeiser, "Shooting Pool," *New Republic,* 18 March 1991, 21; Sydney H. Schanberg, "A Muzzle for the Press," in *The Gulf War Reader: History, Documents, Opinions,* ed. Micah L. Sifry and Christopher Cerf (New York: Random House, 1991), 370.

65. H. Res. 19, 102d Cong., 1st sess., 3 January 1991.

66. Letter from C. Boyden Gray to Rep. Dante B. Fascell, 23 January 1991.

67. Letter from Reps. Dante B. Fascell and Les Aspin to President George Bush, 7 February 1991.

68. Letter from Brent Scowcroft to Rep. Dante B. Fascell, 20 February 1991.

69. The following events are summarized from Letter from Rep. Ted Weiss to Rep. John Conyers, Jr., 21 May 1991; Memorandum from Steven R. Ross and Charles Tiefer to Rep. Ted Weiss, 20 June 1991; Kenneth J. Cooper, "Executive Privilege at Education Department," *Washington Post,* 17 May 1991, A23.

70. Letter from Edward Stringer to Rep. Ted Weiss, 7 May 1991.

71. Letter from Edward Stringer to Rep. Ted Weiss, 13 May 1991.

72. Memorandum from Steven R. Ross and Charles Tiefer to Rep. Ted Weiss, 20 June 1991.

73. This section is based on Patricia A. Gilmartin, "Congress Increases C-17 Scrutiny in Wake of Reported Cost Overruns," *Aviation Week & Space Technology,* 2 September 1991, 25–26; personal interviews with Charles Tiefer, deputy general counsel to the clerk of the House of Representatives, 23 November 1992; Eric Thorson, staff member, House Committee on Government Operations, 20 November 1992; and Morton Rosenberg, specialist in American public law, American Law Division, Congressional Research Service, 21 November 1992; U.S. Congress, *Oversight Hearing on the A-12 Navy Aircraft,* Hearings before the Legislation and National Security Subcommittee of the Committee on Government Operations,

House of Representatives, 102d Cong., 1st sess., 11 April and 24 July 1991; U.S. Congress, *A-12 Navy Aircraft: System Review and Recommendations,* Twenty-first Report by the Committee on Government Operations, House of Representatives, 102d Cong., 2d sess., 27 August 1992.

74. Memorandum from President George Bush to Secretary of Defense Richard Cheney, "Congressional Subpoena for an Executive Branch Document," 8 August 1991.

75. This section is based on U.S. Congress, *The Quayle Council's Plans for Changing FDA's Drug Approval Process: A Prescription for Harm,* Twenty-sixth Report by the Committee on Government Operations, House of Representatives, 102d Cong., 2d sess., 9 October 1992; Dana Priest, "Competitiveness Council under Scrutiny," *Washington Post,* 26 November 1991, A19.

76. Letter from Kay Holcombe, Acting Associate Commissioner for Legislative Affairs, FDA, to Rep. Ted Weiss, 16 October 1991; quoted in U.S. Congress, *The Quayle Council's Plans,* 6.

77. Letter from Rep. Ted Weiss to Commissioner David A. Kessler, 21 November 1991.

78. This section is based on author interviews with Charles Tiefer, Morton Rosenberg, and Monica Wrobelewski and various congressional documents provided by Ms. Wrobelewski, including Statements of Rep. Howard Wolpe before the Subcommittee on Investigations and Oversight of the House Committee on Science, Space and Technology, 23 September, 2 and 5 October 1992.

79. Letter from Rep. Howard Wolpe to President Bush, 24 September 1992.

80. Letter from C. Boyden Gray to Rep. Howard Wolpe, 1 October 1992.

81. Letter from Rep. Howard Wolpe to Attorney General William P. Barr III, 5 October 1992.

82. Letter from Assistant Attorney General W. Lee Rawls to Rep. Howard Wolpe, 5 October 1992.

83. This section is based on Joan Biskupic, "Panel Challenges Thornburgh over Right to Documents," *Congressional Quarterly Weekly Reports,* 27 July 1991, 2080; David Johnston, "Administration to Fight House Panel's Subpoena," *New York Times,* 30 July 1991, A12; U.S. Congress, *Department of Justice Authorization for Appropriations, Fiscal Year 1992,* Hearings before the Committee on the Judiciary, House of Representatives, 102d Cong., 1st sess., 11 and 18 July 1991; interviews with Morton Rosenberg, 21 November 1992, and Charles Tiefer, 23 November 1992.

84. This section is based on Biskupic, "Panel Challenges Thornburgh," 2080; U.S. Congress, *The Attorney General's Refusal to Provide Congressional Access to "Privileged" INSLAW Documents,* Hearings before the Subcommittee on Economic and Commercial Law of the Committee on the Judiciary, House of Representatives, 101st Cong., 2d sess., 5 December 1990; U.S. Congress, *Department of Justice Authorization for Appropriations, Fiscal Year 1992;* "The INSLAW Investigation," *Washington Post,* 29 May 1993, A30.

85. David Johnston, "Administration to Fight House Panel's Subpoena," *New York Times,* 30 July 1991, A12.

6. Clinton and Executive Privilege

1. Kenneth T. Walsh, "Seeking a Support Group: Clinton, under Fire, Finds Solace in the Trials of His Predecessors," *U.S. News & World Report,* 29 August–5 September 1994, 29.

2. Memorandum from Lloyd Cutler to All Executive Department and Agency General Counsels, 28 September 1994 (copy on file with author).

3. See Letter from Janet Reno, United States Attorney General, to President Bill Clinton, 30 September 1996 (copy on file with author); Letter from Janet Reno, United States Attorney General, to President Bill Clinton, 20 September 1996 (copy on file with author).

4. U.S. Congress, House of Representatives, *Proceedings against John M. Quinn, David Watkins, and Matthew Moore,* Report of the Committee on Government Reform and Oversight, 29 May 1996, 6; hereafter Clinger Report.

5. Letter from John M. Quinn to Rep. William F. Clinger, Jr., 9 May 1996 (on file with author).

6. Letters on file with author.

7. Letter from John M. Quinn to Rep. William F. Clinger, Jr., 2 May 1996 (on file with author).

8. Clinger Report, 3.

9. Ibid., 9 n. 13.

10. Letter from Attorney General Janet Reno to President Bill Clinton, 23 May 1996 (on file with author). Reno had written earlier that the president could properly claim executive privilege over "the entire set of White House Counsel's Office documents currently being withheld from the committee, pending a final Presidential decision on the matter" (Letter from Attorney General Janet Reno to President Bill Clinton, 8 May 1996 [on file with author]).

11. Committee staff notes and copies of documents (on file with author).

12. Memorandum from Special Counsel to the President, Jane C. Sherburne, to Sens. Alfonse M. D'Amato and Paul S. Sarbanes, 12 December 1995 (on file with author).

13. Letter from Counsel to the President John M. Quinn to Rep. Newt Gingrich, 18 December 1995 (on file with author).

14. Letter from Rep. Newt Gingrich to Counsel to the President John M. Quinn, 21 December 1995 (on file with author).

15. Letter from Rep. James Leach to Rep. Newt Gingrich, 21 December 1995 (on file with author); Memorandum from Morton Rosenberg, American Law Division of the Congressional Research Service, to Rep. James Leach, 21 December 1995.

16. *In re Sealed Case,* 121 F. 3d 729 (D.C. Cir. 1997).

17. Ibid., 754.

18. Ibid., 752.

19. Ibid., 746.

20. Ibid., 737–38.

21. Ruth Larson, "White House Yields Papers on Utah Wilderness Decision," *Washington Times,* 23 October 1997, A3.

22. A detailed presentation of the various facets and details of this controversy are in the congressional hearing report. See U.S. Congress, House Committee on Government Reform and Oversight, *Investigation of Political Fundraising Improprieties and Possible Violations of the Law,* 105th Cong., 2d sess., 5 November 1998, 3:3111–54.

23. Note from President Bill Clinton to Chief of Staff Leon Panetta, undated, in ibid.: 3826.

24. Letter from White House Counsel Charles Ruff to Richard D. Bennett, chief counsel to the Committee on Government Reform and Oversight, 21 October 1997 (on file with author).

25. White House Privilege Log, 21 October 1997 (on file with author).

26. Letter from Rep. Dan Burton to White House Counsel Charles F. C. Ruff, 4 November 1997 (on file with author).

27. Letter from Rep. Dan Burton to White House Counsel Charles F. C. Ruff, 18 November 1997 (on file with author).

28. Letter from Richard D. Bennett to Special Counsel to the President Lanny Breuer, 26 November 1997 (on file with author).

29. Letter from Richard D. Bennett to Special Counsel to the President Lanny Breuer, 6 December 1997 (on file with author).

30. Morton Rosenberg, "Substantiality of White House Claims of Executive, Attorney-Client and Work Product Privileges for Documents Relating to the Hudson Dog Track Matter," Congressional Research Service, 3 December 1997. This document is a wonderfully detailed legal analysis of the various aspects of the executive privilege controversy in the Hudson casino application controversy.

31. Letter from Lanny A. Breuer to Richard D. Bennett, 9 December 1997 (on file with author).

32. Letter from Richard D. Bennett to Special Counsel to the President Lanny Breuer, 16 December 1997 (on file with author).

33. Letter from John M. Quinn to Rep. William H. Zeliff, Jr., 1 October 1996 (on file with author).

34. Letter from Rep. Benjamin A. Gilman to Jack Quinn, 9 September 1996 (on file with author).

35. Letter from Rep. Benjamin A. Gilman to Jack Quinn, 19 September 1996 (on file with author).

36. Letter from Attorney General Janet Reno to President Bill Clinton, 20 September 1996 (on file with author).

37. Letter from Jack Quinn to Rep. Benjamin A. Gilman, 23 September 1996 (on file with author).

38. Letter from White House Counsel Charles Ruff to Rep. Dan Burton, 30 April 1997 (on file with author).

39. Letter from Rep. Dan Burton to White House Counsel Charles Ruff, 2 May 1997 (on file with author).

40. Letter from Rep. Dan Burton to White House Counsel Charles Ruff, 9 May 1997 (on file with author).

41. Letter from Special Counsel to the President Lanny A. Breuer to House Government Reform and Oversight Chief Counsel John P. Rowley, III, 14 May 1997 (on file with author).

42. U.S. Congress, *Investigation of Political Fundraising Improprieties,* 57.

43. Letter from White House Counsel Charles Ruff to Rep. Dan Burton, 17 June 1997, containing nonwaiver agreement (on file with author).

44. Letter from Rep. Dan Burton to White House Counsel Charles Ruff, 27 June 1997 (on file with author).

45. U.S. Congress, *Investigation of Political Fundraising Improprieties,* 58.

46. Ibid.

47. Letter from Rep. Dan Burton to White House Counsel Charles Ruff, 25 February 1998 (on file with author).

48. Letter from White House Counsel Charles Ruff to Rep. Dan Burton, 25 February 1998 (on file with author).

49. U.S. Congress, *Investigation of Political Fundraising Improprieties*, 59.

50. See House Report No. 105-830. The original language of Article IV of the House impeachment report included the statement that Clinton had "frivolously asserted executive privilege" (84). Republican members were convinced that Clinton had abused executive privilege, but not all were confident that this behavior constituted an impeachable offense.

51. See "Ruff's Argument for Executive Privilege," unsealed 27 May 1998, at *www.wash ingtonpost.com/wp-srv/politics/special/clinton/stories/ruff05289.htm*. See also "White House Motion Seeking Privilege," filed 17 March 1998, at *www.washingtonpost.com/wp-srv/politics/ special/clinton/stories/whitehouse05289.htm*.

52. "Judge Johnson's Order on Executive Privilege," issued 26 May 1998, at *www.wash ingtonpost.com/wp-srv/politics/special/clinton/stories/order05298.htm*.

53. "Ruff's Argument."

54. "White House Motion Seeking Privilege."

55. "Judge Johnson's Order."

56. "Starr Report," 1998, Referral to the U.S. House of Representatives Pursuant to Title 28, U.S. Code, 595C, Submitted by the Office of Independent Counsel, 9 September 1998.

57. Letter from Cheryl Mills to Rep. Dan Burton, 16 September 1999 (on file with author).

58. From statement of White House Counsel Office spokesman Jim Kennedy, quoted in Andrew Cain, "Clinton Invokes Executive Privilege on FALN Decision," *Washington Times*, 17 September 1999.

7. George W. Bush, Barack Obama, and the Growing Discord over Executive Privilege

1. See, for example, Steven G. Calabresi and Christopher S. Yoo, *The Unitary Executive: Presidential Power from Washington to Bush* (New Haven, Conn.: Yale University Press, 2008); William Crotty, "Presidential Policymaking in Crisis Situations: 9/11 and Its Aftermath," *Policy Studies Journal* 31 (August 2003): 451–464; Ron Suskind, *The One Percent Doctrine: Deep inside America's Pursuit of Its Enemies Since 9/11* (New York: Simon & Schuster, 2006); John Yoo, *The Powers of War and Peace* (Chicago: University of Chicago Press, 2005).

2. "The Vice President Appears on ABC's This Week," 27 January 2002, http:// georgewbush-whitehouse.archives.gov/vicepresident/news-speeches/speeches/vp20020127 .html [accessed 5 July 2009].

3. Letter from Rep. Dan Burton to Attorney General John Ashcroft, 29 August 2001 (on file with author).

4. "Memorandum on the Congressional Subpoena for Executive Branch Documents," *Weekly Compilation of Presidential Documents* 37 (12 December 2001), 1783.

5. Quoted in Ellen Nakashima, "Bush Invokes Executive Privilege on Hill," *Washington Post*, 14 December 2001, A43.

6. Statement of Michael E. Horowitz, Chief Of Staff, Criminal Division, Department of Justice, before the Committee on Government Reform of the U.S. House of Representatives, 13 December 2001 (on file with author). This prepared statement is a truly unimpressive brief on behalf of the administration's claim of privilege. It contains a string of unconnected quotations taken out of context to try to prove the obvious point that administrations have secrecy needs. The statement never gets beyond broad generalities to make a

case why secrecy was needed in this particular dispute. Some of the evidence presented is simply wrong (e.g., the claim that George Washington withheld all information from Congress in the St. Clair incident), leaves out important facts (e.g., that four days after a former Bush administration stand on executive privilege the president relented and gave everything to Congress), and claims as authoritative a widely discredited assertion by former attorney general Benjamin Civiletti that allowing members of Congress to investigate the process of federal prosecutions would destroy the civil liberties of persons under investigation (Benjamin R. Civiletti, "Justice Unbalanced: Congress and Prosecutorial Discretion," speech at the Heritage Foundation, Washington, D.C., 19 August 1993).

7. Letter from Daniel J. Bryant to Rep. Dan Burton, 19 December 2001 (on file with author).

8. Letter from Rep. Dan Burton to Attorney General John Ashcroft, 3 January 2001 (on file with author).

9. Letter from Judge Alberto R. Gonzales to Rep. Dan Burton, 10 January 2001 (on file with author); Letter from Rep. Dan Burton to Judge Alberto R. Gonzales, 11 January 2001 (on file with author).

10. Letter from Hon. Rep. Dan Burton to Attorney General John Ashcroft, 4 February 2002 (on file with author).

11. U.S. Congress, House Committee on Government Reform and Oversight, *The History of Congressional Access to Deliberative Justice Department Documents*, 107th Cong., 2nd sess., February 6, 2002 (author, Mark J. Rozell, testified as expert witness).

12. See testimony of Mark J. Rozell in ibid.

13. Letter from Counsel to the President, Alberto R. Gonzales to Rep. Stephen Horn (R-Calif.), 2 November 2001 (on file with author).

14. U.S. Congress, Subcommittee on Government Efficiency, Financial Management and Intergovernmental Relations of the House Committee on Government Reform, *Hearings on the Presidential Records Act*, 107th Cong., 1st sess., November 6, 2001 (hearing attended by author, Mark J. Rozell, as expert witness).

15. *American Historical Association v. National Archives and Records Administration, et al.,* 516 F. Supp. 2d. 90 (D.D.C. 2007).

16. Executive Order 12267, issued January 18, 1989.

17. 50 U.S.C. §403(d)(3).

18. Mark J. Rozell, testimony before the Subcommittee on Government Efficiency, Financial Management and Intergovernmental Relations of the House Committee on Government Reform, *Hearings on the Presidential Records Act*, 107th Cong., 1st sess., 6 November 2001.

19. "The Vice President Appears on ABC's This Week," 27 January 2002, http://georgewbush-whitehouse.archives.gov/vicepresident/news-speeches/speeches/vp20020127.html [accessed 5 July 2009].

20. "Remarks Prior to a Meeting with the Energy Policy Development Group and an Exchange with Reporters," *Weekly Compilation of Presidential Documents* 37 (29 January 2001), 236–37.

21. U.S. General Accounting Office, "Energy Task Force: Process Used to Develop the National Energy Policy [hereinafter GAO report]," GAO-03-894, August 2003 (citing Presidential Memorandum, 29 January 2001), http://www.gao.gov/new.items/d03894.pdf [accessed 5 July 2009].

22. The following were also NEPDG members: the Secretaries of State, Treasury, Interior, Agriculture, Commerce, Transportation, and Energy; the Administrator of the Environmental Protection Agency; the Director of the Federal Emergency Management Agency; the Director of the Office of Management and Budget; the Assistant to the President and Deputy Chief of Staff for Policy; the Assistant to the President for Economic Policy; and the Deputy Assistant to the President for Intergovernmental Affairs. Ibid., 8.

23. Ibid., 9.

24. David S. Addington to W. J. "Billy" Tauzin, Dan Burton, John Dingell, and Henry Waxman, 4 May 2001, http://oversight.house.gov/Documents/20040831095650-29059.pdf [accessed 5 July 2009].

25. GAO report, 5.

26. U.S. President, Report of the National Energy Policy Development Group, "National Energy Policy," May 2001, http://georgewbush-whitehouse.archives.gov/energy/2001/National-Energy-Policy.pdf [accessed 5 July 2009].

27. U.S. Department of Energy, "National Energy Policy Status Report on Implementation of NEP Recommendations," January 2005, http://www.energy.gov/media/NEP_Implementation_Report.pdf [accessed 5 July 2009].

28. John Dingell and Henry Waxman to Andrew Lundquist, 19 April 2001, http://oversight.house.gov/Documents/20040831095838-21952.pdf [accessed 5 July 2009].

29. Federal Advisory Committee Act, 5 U.S.C.A. App. 2 (2006).

30. Now called the Government Accountability Office. See "GAO's Name Change and Other Provisions of the GAO Human Capital Reform Act of 2004," http://www.gao.gov/about/namechange.html [accessed 5 July 2009].

31. David S. Addington to W. J. "Billy" Tauzin, Dan Burton, John Dingell, and Henry Waxman, 4 May 2001, http://oversight.house.gov/Documents/20040831095650-29059.pdf [accessed 5 July 2009].

32. John Dingell and Henry Waxman to Andrew Lundquist, 15 May 2001, http://oversight.house.gov/Documents/20040831095447-76303.pdf [accessed 5 July 2009].

33. David S. Addington to Anthony Gamboa, 16 May 2001, http://oversight.house.gov/Documents/20040831095214-51332.pdf [accessed 5 July 2009].

34. John Dingell and Henry Waxman to David S. Addington, 22 May 2001, http://oversight.house.gov/Documents/20040831094829-47374.pdf [accessed 5 July 2009].

35. David S. Addington to Reid Stuntz and Phil Barnett, 25 May 2001 (emphasis added), http://oversight.house.gov/Documents/20040831095041-19071.pdf [accessed 5 July 2009].

36. Anthony Gamboa to David S. Addington, 1 June 2001, http://oversight.house.gov/Documents/20040831095041-19071.pdf [accessed 5 July 2009].

37. David S. Addington to Anthony Gamboa, 7 June 2001, http://oversight.house.gov/Documents/20040831010840-55687.pdf [accessed 5 July 2009].

38. Ibid.

39. Anthony Gamboa to David S. Addington, 22 June 2001, http://oversight.house.gov/Documents/20040831010638-49718.pdf [accessed 5 July 2009]; David Walker to Richard Cheney, 18 June 2001, http://oversight.house.gov/Documents/20040831004316-29355.pdf [accessed 5 July 2009].

40. Richard Cheney to the House of Representatives, 2 August 2001, http://oversight.house.gov/Documents/20040830233716-42929.pdf [accessed 5 July 2009].

41. GAO Statement, 6 August 2001, http://oversight.house.gov/Documents/20040830 233320-50377.pdf [accessed 5 July 2009].

42. John Dingell and Henry Waxman to Richard Cheney, 29 August 2001, http://over sight.house.gov/Documents/20040831103738-88498.pdf [accessed 5 July 2009].

43. GAO Statement on the National Energy Policy Development Group, 7 September 2001, http://oversight.house.gov/Documents/20040831103615-65132.pdf [accessed 5 July 2009].

44. Statement of Comptroller General David Walker on the National Energy Policy Development Group, 28 September 2001, http://oversight.house.gov/Documents/200408311 03404-31650.pdf [accessed 5 July 2009].

45. Henry Waxman to Richard Cheney, 4 December 2001, http://oversight.house.gov/ Documents/20040831103250-77482.pdf [accessed 5 July 2009].

46. David S. Addington to Henry Waxman, 3 January 2002, http://oversight.house.gov/ Documents/20040830155258-34566.pdf [accessed 5 July 2009].

47. Henry Waxman to Richard Cheney, 8 January 2002, http://oversight.house.gov/ Documents/20040830155227-58704.pdf [accessed 5 July 2009].

48. Henry Waxman to Richard Cheney, 16 January 2002, http://oversight.house.gov/ Documents/20040830154908-42327.pdf [accessed 5 July 2009]; Henry Waxman to Richard Cheney, 25 January 2002, http://oversight.house.gov/Documents/200408301 54529-45198.pdf [accessed 5 July 2009].

49. Statement of Comptroller General David Walker on the National Energy Policy Development Group, 9 January 2002, http://oversight.house.gov/Documents/2004083015512 6-21933.pdf [accessed 5 July 2009].

50. Joseph Lieberman, Ernest Hollings, Carl Levin, and Byron Dorgan to David Walker, 22 January 2002, http://oversight.house.gov/Documents/20040830154810-75641.pdf [accessed 5 July 2009].

51. John Dingell and Henry Waxman to David Walker, 24 January 2002, http://over sight.house.gov/Documents/20040830154700-91281.pdf [accessed 5 July 2009].

52. "The Vice President Appears on ABC's This Week," 27 January 2002, http://www .whitehouse.gov/vicepresident/news-speeches/speeches/vp20020127.html [accessed 5 July 2009].

53. General Statement of Decision of the Comptroller General Concerning NEPDG litigation, 30 January 2002, http://oversight.house.gov/Documents/20040830154126-19726 .pdf [accessed 5 July 2009].

54. *Walker v. Cheney*, 230 F. Supp. 2d 51 (D.D.C. 2002).

55. GAO Statement Concerning Litigation, 22 February 2002, http://oversight.house .gov/Documents/20040830153549-62303.pdf [accessed 5 July 2009].

56. *Walker v. Cheney*, 230 F. Supp. 2d 51, 75.

57. GAO Press Statement on *Walker v. Cheney*, 7 February 2003, http://oversight.house .gov/Documents/20040625103334-22539.pdf [accessed 5 July 2009].

58. GAO report, 3.

59. *Judicial Watch, Inc. v. Nat'l Energy Pol'y Dev. Group*, 219 F. Supp. 2d 20, 25–27 (D.D.C. 2002). The National Resources Defense Council also initiated a suit.

60. Federal Advisory Committee Act, §1, 5 U.S.C.A. App. 2 (2006).

61. *Judicial Watch, Inc. v. Nat'l Energy Pol'y Dev. Group*, 219 F. Supp. 2d 20, 56–57.

62. Ibid., 30.

63. Ibid., 44.

64. *Judicial Watch, Inc. v. Nat'l Energy Pol'y Dev. Group,* 230 F. Supp. 2d 12, 15 (D.D.C. 2002).

65. Ibid., 16.

66. Ibid.

67. *Judicial Watch, Inc. v. Nat'l Energy Pol'y Dev. Group,* 233 F. Supp. 2d 16, 23 (D.D.C. 2002).

68. *In re Cheney,* 334 F. 3d 1096, 1101 (D.C. Cir. 2003).

69. Ibid., 1105.

70. Ibid., 1107.

71. *Cheney v. U.S. Dist. Court for Dist. of Columbia,* 540 U.S. 1088 (2003).

72. Opinion Clause: the president "may require the Opinion, in writing, of the principal Officer in each of the executive Departments, upon any Subject relating to the Duties of their respective Offices." Article II, section 2 of the U.S. Constitution. Recommendations Clause: the president "shall from time to time give to the Congress Information of the State of the Union, and recommend to their Consideration such Measures as he shall judge necessary and expedient." Article II, section 3 of the U.S. Constitution.

73. Brief for the Petitioners, *Cheney v. United States District Court for the District of Columbia* (2004) (No. 03-475), 11. "Those Clauses allow the President a zone of autonomy in obtaining advice, including with respect to formulating proposals for legislation." Ibid., 12.

74. Brief for the Petitioners, *Cheney v. United States District Court for the District of Columbia* (2004) (No. 03-475), 11.

75. Ibid., 12.

76. Ibid., 32.

77. Ibid., 34.

78. Ibid., 42.

79. *Cheney v. U.S. Dist. Court for Dist. of Columbia,* oral argument transcript, 27 April 2004, 18, http://www.supremecourtus.gov/oral_arguments/argument_transcripts/03-475 .pdf [accessed 5 July 2009].

80. Ibid., 21.

81. Ibid.

82. *Cheney v. U.S. Dist. Court for Dist. of Columbia,* 542 U.S. 367, 378 (2004).

83. Ibid., 382.

84. Ibid., 384.

85. Ibid., 384 (citing *United States v. Nixon,* 418 U.S. 683, 707 [1974]).

86. Ibid., 384–85.

87. Ibid., 385.

88. Ibid., 388 (citing *In re Cheney,* 334 F. 3d 1096, 1096 [D.C. Cir. 2003]).

89. Ibid., 389. (citing *United States v. Reynolds,* 345 U.S. 1, 7 [1953]).

90. Ibid., 389.

91. Ibid., 391.

92. Michael J. Mongan, "Fixing FACA: The Case for Exempting Presidential Advisory Committees from Judicial Review under the Federal Advisory Committee Act," *Stanford Law Review* 58 (December 2005), 917.

93. *In re Cheney,* 406 F.3d 723, 731 (D.C. Cir. 2005).

94. Ibid., 728.

95. Ibid.

96. Ibid.

97. Mongan, "Fixing FACA," 918.

98. Louis Brandeis, *Other People's Money and How the Bankers Use It* (New York: F. A. Stokes, 1914; reprint, New York: St. Martin's Press, 1995), 89.

99. John Yoo, "How the Presidency Regained Its Balance," *New York Times,* 17 September 2006, http://www.nytimes.com/2006/09/17/opinion/17yoo.html?ei=5090&en=2db 683b71a2b4606&ex=1316145600&partner=rssuserland&emc=rss&pagewanted=print [accessed 5 July 2009].

100. John Yoo, "Former Deputy Assistant Attorney General John Yoo Talks about Terrorism, the Justice Department and the Supreme Court," http://www.cfif.org/htdocs/freedom line/current/in_our_opinion/general_john_yoo.htm [accessed 5 July 2009].

101. Louis Fisher, *The Politics of Executive Privilege* (Durham, N.C.: Carolina Academic Press, 2004), 198.

102. *Judicial Watch v. Department of Justice*. 365 F.3d 1108 (D.C. Cir. 2004), 1010.

103. Elisabeth Bumiller, "White House Withholding Documents on Pardons," *New York Times*, 28 August 2002, A17.

104. *Judicial Watch v. Department of Justice,* 259 F. Supp. 2d 86 (D.D.C. 2003), 87.

105. *Judicial Watch v. Department of Justice* 2004, 1112.

106. Ibid., 1114.

107. Ibid., 1114–15.

108. Ibid., 1116–17.

109. Ibid., 1118.

110. 28 U.S.C. §547 (2000).

111. 28 U.S.C. §541(a) (2000).

112. 28 U.S.C. §546 (2000).

113. P.L. 109-177 §502, 120 Stat. 246 (2006).

114. P.L. 110-34, 121 Stat. 224 (2007).

115. Amy Goldstein, "Report Suggests Laws Broken in Attorney Firings," *Washington Post,* 25 July 2007, A3.

116. Eric Lipton, "Colleagues Cite Partisan Focus by Justice Official," *New York Times,* 11 May 2007, A1.

117. David Johnston and Eric Lipton, "'Loyalty' to Bush and Gonzales Was Factor in Prosecutors' Firings, E-Mail Shows," *New York Times*, 13 March 2007, A18.

118. Dan Eggen and John Solomon, "Firings Had Genesis in White House; Ex-Counsel Miers First Suggested Dismissing Prosecutors 2 Years Ago, Documents Show," *Washington Post,* 13 March 2007, A1.

119. David Johnston and Eric Lipton, "E-Mail Identified G.O.P. Candidates for Justice Jobs," *New York Times,* 13 April 2007, A1.

120. Eggen and Solomon, "Firings Had Genesis in White House," A1.

121. David Johnston and Eric Lipton, "Gonzales Met with Advisers on Dismissals," *New York Times*, 24 March 2007, A1.

122. David Johnston and Eric Lipton, "'Loyalty' to Bush and Gonzales Was Factor in Prosecutors' Firings," *New York Times,* 14 March 2007, A18.

123. Associated Press, "List of 8 Dismissed U.S. Prosecutors" *Boston.com*, 6 March 2007, http://www.boston.com/news/nation/washington/articles/2007/03/06/list_of_8_dismissed _us_prosecutors/ [accessed 5 July 2009].

124. Dianne Feinstein, Letter from Patrick Leahy and Dianne Feinstein to Alberto Gonzales [attached to a January 11 press release], 9 January 2007, http://feinstein.senate.gov/public/index.cfm?FuseAction=NewsRoom.PressReleases&ContentRecord_id=18a696d7-7e9c-9af9-7a2b-397a786a69fc&Region_id=&Issue_id= [accessed 5 July 2009].

125. Mark Pryor, Press Release: Senators Feinstein, Leahy, Pryor to Fight Administration's Effort to Circumvent Senate Confirmation Process for U.S. Attorneys, 11 January 2007, http://pryor.senate.gov/newsroom/details.cfm?id=267495 [accessed 5 July 2009].

126. U.S. Senate, Committee on the Judiciary, *Department of Justice Oversight,* 110th Cong., 1st sess., 18 January 2007, 24.

127. U.S. Senate, Committee on the Judiciary, *Preserving Prosecutorial Independence: Is The Department of Justice Politicizing the Hiring and Firing of U.S. Attorneys?* 110th Cong., 1st sess., 6 February 2007, 2.

128. Ibid.

129. Ibid., 14.

130. Ibid., 17.

131. Alberto Gonzales, "They Lost My Confidence," *USA Today,* 7 March 2007, 10A.

132. Rebecca Carr and Ken Herman, "Gonzales, Rove Had Early Role in Firings; E-mails Show High White House Interest," *Atlanta Journal-Constitution,* 16 March 2007, 1C.

133. Dan Eggen and Carol D. Leonning, "Officials Describe Interference by Former Gonzales Aide," *Washington Post,* 23 May 2007, A4.

134. George W. Bush, "Remarks on the Department of Justice and an Exchange with Reporters," *Weekly Compilation of Presidential Documents,* 43, 26 March 2007, 359.

135. Ibid., 359–60.

136. Ibid., 360.

137. Ibid., 361.

138. Carl Hulse, "Panel Approves Rove Subpoena on Prosecutors," *New York Times,* 22 March 2007, A1.

139. Paul Kane, "Senate Panel Approves Subpoenas for 3 Top Bush Aides," *Washington Post,* 23 March 2007, A4.

140. Alberto Gonzales, "Transcript of Media Availability with Attorney General Alberto R. Gonzales," 13 March 2007, http://www.usdoj.gov/archive/ag/speeches/2007/ag_speech_070313.html [accessed 5 July 2009].

141. Dan Eggen and Paul Kane, "Ex-Aide Contradicts Gonzales on Firings," *Washington Post,* 30 March 2007, A1.

142. Dan Eggen, "House Panel Issues First Subpoena over Firings," *Washington Post,* 11 April 2007, A1.

143. Patrick Leahy, "Chairman Leahy Issues Subpoena For 'Lost' Karl Rove E-Mails," 2 May 2007, http://leahy.senate.gov/press/200705/050207.html#Letter [accessed 5 July 2009].

144. U.S. Department of Justice, Office of the Solicitor General, "Letter from Paul D. Clement to George W. Bush," 27 June 2007, http://georgewbush-whitehouse.archives.gov/news/releases/2007/06/LetterfromSolicitorGeneral06272007.pdf [accessed 5 July 2009].

145. The White House, Letter from Fred F. Fielding to John Conyers and Patrick Leahy, 28 June 2007, http://georgewbush-whitehouse.archives.gov/news/releases/2007/06/LetterfromCounseltothePresident06282007.pdf [accessed 5 July 2009].

146. The White House, Letter from Fred F. Fielding to John Conyers and Patrick Leahy, 9 July 2007, http://georgewbush-whitehouse.archives.gov/news/releases/2007/07/Memo_070907.pdf [accessed 5 July 2009].

147. Neil A. Lewis, "Panel Votes to Hold Two in Contempt of Congress," *New York Times*, 25 July 2007, A13.

148. Ibid.

149. Ibid.

150. Jon Ward, "Democrats Seek Gonzales Probe, Subpoena Rove," *Washington Times*, 27 July 2007, A3.

151. Ibid.

152. The White House, "Letter from Fred F. Fielding to Patrick Leahy and Arlen Specter," 1 August 2007, http://leahy.senate.gov/press/200708/07-08-01%20white%20house%20rove.pdf [accessed 5 July 2009].

153. Patrick Leahy, "Comment of Sen. Patrick Leahy . . . on White House Letter Regarding Testimony of Karl Rove and J. Scott Jennings," 1 August 2007, http://leahy.senate.gov/press/200708/080107c.html [accessed 5 July 2009].

154. U.S. Senate, Committee on the Judiciary, Letter from Patrick Leahy to George W. Bush, 14 August 2007, http://leahy.senate.gov/press/200708/081407LetterToPresident.pdf [accessed 5 July 2009].

155. U.S. Senate, Committee on the Judiciary, Letter from Patrick Leahy to Glenn A. Fine, 16 August 2007, http://leahy.senate.gov/press/200708/8-16-07%20PJL%20ltr%20to%20Glenn%20Fine-AG.pdf [accessed 5 July 2009].

156. U.S. Department of Justice, Office of the Inspector General, Letter from Glenn A. Fine to Patrick Leahy, 30 August 2007, http://leahy.senate.gov/press/200708/8-30-07%20fine%20to%20pjl.pdf [accessed 5 July 2009].

157. Paul Kane, "Rove, Bolten Found in Contempt of Congress; Senate Committee Cites Top Bush Advisers in Probe of U.S. Attorney Firings," *Washington Post*, 14 December 2007, A8.

158. Ibid.

159. Ibid.

160. Paul Kane, "West Wing Aides Cited for Contempt," *Washington Post*, 15 February 2008.

161. *Committee on the Judiciary v. Miers et al.* 2008a, Civil No. 1:08-cv-00409 (D.D.C.).

162. Stephen G. Bradbury, "Immunity of Former Counsel to the President from Compelled Congressional Testimony," Office of Legal Counsel memorandum, 10 July 2007, http://www.usdoj.gov/olc/2007/miers-immunity-Opinion071007.pdf [accessed 4 September 2009].

163. Plaintiff's Motion 2008, 32 (emphasis in original).

164. *In re Sealed Case* 1997, 737–38.

165. *Committee on the Judiciary v. Harriet Miers, et al.* 2008a, 3.

166. Ibid., 78.

167. Ibid., 78–81.

168. Ibid., 81–82.

169. Ibid., 83.

170. Ibid., 84.

171. Ibid.

172. Ibid., 84–85.

173. Ibid., 85.

174. Ibid., 86.

175. Ibid., 3–4.

176. Editorial, "The Contempt Citation," *Washington Post,* 22 September 1998, A16.

177. *U.S. v. House of Representatives,* 556 F. Supp. 150, 153 (D.D.C. 1983).

178. 8 O.L. C. 101 (1984).

179. Richard E. Levy, *The Power to Legislate: A Reference Guide to the United States Constitution* (Westport, Conn.: Greenwood Press, 2006), 33.

180. 19 U.S. 204.

181. 19 U.S. 204, 228 (1821).

182. Josh Gerstein, "Rove Testimony Hangs in the Balance," *Politico,* 19 February 2009, http://www.politico.com/politico44/perm/0209/deadline_for_privilege_c630914e-62ba-4056-a8ef-b883d9c7eb2e.html [accessed 2 July 2009].

183. Ibid.

184. Christopher P. Bliley, Letter to Henry A. Waxman, 20 June 2008, http://oversight.house.gov/documents/20080620114653.pdf [accessed 5 July 2009].

185. Ibid.

186. Henry Waxman, *Opening Statement of Rep. Henry A. Waxman,* 20 June 2008, http://oversight.house.gov/documents/20080620121418.pdf [accessed 5 July 2009].

187. Michael B. Mukasey, Letter to George W. Bush, 19 June 2008, www.oversight.house.gov/documents/20080620114653.pdf [accessed 4 September 2009].

188. *In re Sealed Case* 1997, 752.

189. 42 USC 7543(b)(1) [2006].

190. Michael B. Mukasey, Letter to George W. Bush, 19 June 2008 (emphasis added).

191. Ibid.

192. Ibid.

193. 42 USC 7543(b)(1) [2006].

194. *Kendall v. U.S.* 1838, 612–13.

195. Ibid., 613.

196. David A. Fahrenthold, "EPA to Let California Set Own Emissions Standards," *Washington Post,* 1 July 2009, A2.

197. Keith B. Nelson, Letter to Henry A. Waxman, 16 July 2008, http://oversight.house.gov/documents/20080716104053.pdf [accessed 5 July 2009].

198. Michael B. Mukasey, Letter to George W. Bush, 19 June 2008, http://oversight.house.gov/documents/20080620114653.pdf [accessed 5 July 2009].

199. Ibid.

200. Ibid.

201. *In re Sealed Case,* 1997, 745.

202. Keith B. Nelson, Letter to Henry A. Waxman, 16 July 2008, http://oversight.house.gov/documents/20080716104053.pdf [accessed 5 July 2009].

203. Patrick J. Fitzgerald, Letter to Henry A. Waxman, 3 July 2008, http://oversight.house.gov/documents/20080708103231.pdf [accessed 5 July 2009].

204. Jason Leopold, "Obama Backs Bush in Refusing to release Cheney CIA Leak Transcript," 19 June 2009, http://www.pubrecord.org/law/955-obama-backs-bush-in-refusing-to-release-cheneys-cia-leak-transcript.html [accessed 5 July 2009].

205. Barack Obama, Memorandum for the Heads of Executive Departments and Agencies, "Transparency and Open Government", 21 January 2009, at http://www.whitehouse.gov/the_press_office/Transparency_and_Open_Government/ [accessed 5 July 2009].

206. Mark J. Rozell and Mitchel A. Sollenberger, "Obama Opens the Books," *Politico,* 2 February 2009, at http://www.politico.com/news/stories/0209/18266.html [accessed 3 July 2009].

207. See Mark J. Rozell and Mitchel A. Sollenberger, "Taking Executive Privilege to Absurd Levels," *Roll Call,* 6 February 2009, at http://www.rollcall.com/news/32134-1.html [accessed 5 July 2009]; Mark J. Rozell and Mitchel A. Sollenberger, "End the Nonsense, Make Rove Testify," *Politico,* 6 March 2009, at http://www.politico.com/news/stories/0309/19662.html [accessed 5 July 2009].

208. Rozell and Sollenberger, "End the Nonsense."

209. Michael Shear, "Obama Criticized for Withholding Visitor Logs," *Washington Post,* 17 June 2009, p. A4.

210. R. Jeffry Smith, "Judge Questions Justice Department Effort to Keep Cheney Remarks Secret," *Washington Post,* 19 June 2009, p. A17.

211. R. Jeffrey Smith, "New Evidence Cheney Swayed Reaction to Leak; Discussions of CIA Agent Listed in Filing," *Washington Post,* 3 July 2009, p. A4.

212. Barack Obama, "Statement of President Barack Obama on Release of OLC Memos," White House, Office of the Press Secretary, 16 April 2009, http://www.whitehouse.gov/the_press_office/Statement-of-President-Barack-Obama-on-Release-of-OLC-Memos/ [accessed 5 July 2009].

213. Barack Obama, "Statement by the President on the Situation in Sri Lanka and Detainee Photographs," White House, Office of the Press Secretary, http://www.whitehouse.gov/the_press_office/Statement-by-the-President-on-the-Situation-in-Sri-Lanka-and-Detainee-Photographs/ [accessed 5 July 2009].

214. *Mohamed, et al., v. Jeppesen Dataplan, et al.,* Petition for Rehearing or Rehearing En Banc (Circuit docket No. 08-15693).

215. *Mohamed, et al., v. Jeppesen Dataplan, et al.,* 5:07-CV-02798-JW Opinion (28 April 2009).

216. Carrie Johnson, "U.S. Urges New Look at State-Secrets Case," *Washington Post,* 13 June 2009, p. A2.

217. Ibid.

218. Barack Obama, "Remarks by the President on National Security," White House, Office of the Press Secretary, http://www.whitehouse.gov/the_press_office/Remarks-by-the-President-On-National-Security-5-21-09/ [accessed 5 July 2009].

219. Ibid.

Conclusion

1. Raoul Berger, "The Incarnation of Executive Privilege," *UCLA Law Review* 22 (October 1974): 29.

2. Ibid.

3. See the commentary of Sen. J. William Fulbright in U.S. Congress, *Executive Privilege,* Hearings before the Subcommittee on Separation of Powers of the Committee on the Judiciary, U.S. Senate, 92d Cong., 1st sess., 4 August 1971, 18–47.

4. James W. Ceaser, "In Defense of Separation of Powers," in *Separation of Powers—Does It Still Work?* ed. Robert A. Goldwin and Art Kaufman (Washington, D.C.: American Enterprise Institute, 1986), 190.

5. Brief of Richard M. Nixon in Opposition to Plaintiffs' Motion for Summary Judgment, *Senate Select Committee on Presidential Campaign Activities v. Nixon,* 366 F. Supp. 51 (D.D.C. 1973), 16.

6. *U.S. v. Sirica,* 487 F. 2d 700, 742 (D.C. Cir. 1973).

7. Louis W. Koenig, *The Chief Executive* (New York: Harcourt, Brace, Jovanovich, 1986), 11.

8. John Locke, *The Second Treatise of Government,* ch. 14, sec. 160.

9. L. Peter Schultz, "The Separation of Powers and Foreign Affairs," in Goldwin and Kaufman, *Separation of Powers,* 119.

10. See, for example, James Hamilton and John C. Grabow, "A Legislative Proposal for Resolving Executive Privilege Disputes Precipitated by Congressional Subpoenas," *Harvard Journal of Legislation* 22 (winter 1984): 145–72.

11. Letter from Edward Levi to Vice President Nelson Rockefeller, 13 June 1975.

12. Sotirios A. Barber, "The Supreme Court and Congress's Responsibilities in Foreign Affairs," in *Taking the Constitution Seriously: Essays on the Constitution and Constitutional Law,* ed. Gary L. McDowell (Dubuque, Iowa: Kendall/Hunt, 1981), 231.

13. J. William Fulbright, *The Arrogance of Power* (New York: Vintage Books, 1966), 46.

14. Koenig, *The Chief Executive,* 11–12.

15. Letter from William French Smith to Rep. John D. Dingell, 30 November 1982, cited in U.S Congress, *Contempt of Congress,* Report of the Committee on Public Works and Transportation, House of Representatives, 97th Cong., 2d sess., 15 December 1982, 79.

16. President George W. Bush actually initiated such a policy, only to quickly back down in the face of widespread congressional and public opposition. On 5 October 2001, the president sent a memorandum to the heads of various departments directing that, when providing briefings to Congress about the antiterrorism campaign, they speak only to certain designated members: Speaker of the House, House minority leader, Senate majority and minority leaders, and chairs and ranking members of the House and Senate Intelligence Committees. Memorandum from President George W. Bush to the Secretary of State, Secretary of the Treasury, Secretary of Defense, the Attorney General, the Director of Central Intelligence, and the Director of the Federal Bureau of Investigation, 5 October 2001 (on file with author).

17. William Rehnquist, "Statement before the Subcommittee on Separation of Powers of the Committee on the Judiciary," *Executive Privilege,* U.S. Senate, 92d Cong., 1st sess., July 1971, 434.

18. *Atlee v. Laird,* 347 F. Supp. 689 (E.D. Pa. 1972), affirmed without opinion, 935 S. Ct. 1545 (1973); *Chicago & Southern Airlines v. Waterman Steamship Co.,* 333 U.S. 111 (1948); *Coleman v. Miller,* 307 U.S. 433 (1939); *Crockett v. Reagan,* 558 F. Supp. 893 (1982); *Holtzman v. Schlesinger,* 484 F. 2d 1307 (2d Cir. 1973), cert. denied 94 S. Ct. 1935 (1974); *New York Times Co. v. United States,* 403 U.S. 713 (1971; Justice Stewart concurring); *Oetjen v. Central Leather Corp.,* 246 U.S. 297 (1918); *U.S. v. Belmont,* 57 S. Ct. 758 (1937); *U.S. v. Cutiss-Wright Corp.,* 299 U.S. 304 (1936); *U.S. Presbyterian Church in U.S.A. v. Reagan,* 557 F. Supp. 61 (1982).

19. Louis Fisher, "War Powers: The Need for Collective Judgment," in *Divided Democracy: Cooperation and Conflict Between the President and Congress,* ed. James A. Thurber (Washington, D.C.: Congressional Quarterly Press, 1991), 215.

20. *U.S. v. Nixon,* 418 U.S. 683, 706 (1974).

21. Ibid., 706, 710.

22. Ibid., 713.

23. See *Senate Select Committee on Presidential Campaign Activities v. Nixon,* 498 F. 2d 725 (D.C. Cir. 1974); *United States v. AT&T,* 521 F. 2d 384 (D.C. Cir. 1976) and 567 F. 2d 121 (D.C. Cir. 1977).

24. *Farnsworth Cannon v. Grimes,* 635 F. 2d 268 (4th Cir. 1980); *Nixon v. Sirica,* 487 F. 2d 700 (D.C. Cir. 1973); *U.S. v. Boyce,* 594 F. 2d 1246 (9th Cir.), cert. denied, 100 S. Ct. 112 (1979); *U.S. v. Jolliff,* 548 F. Supp. 229 (1981); *U.S. v. Lyon,* 567 F. 2d 777 (8th Cir., 1977), cert. denied, 98 S. Ct. 1476 (1978).

25. *Committee for Nuclear Responsibility, Inc. v. Seaborg,* 463 F. 2d 788 (D.C. Cir. 1971); *Kaiser Aluminum & Chemical Corp. v. U.S.,* 157 F. Supp. 939 (1958).

26. *U.S. v. Burr,* 25 Fed. Cas. 187, 190, 191–92 (No. 14, 694) (1807).

27. Michael Foley, *The Silence of Constitutions* (London: Routledge, 1989), 77.

28. Ibid., xi.

29. Ibid., 76.

30. Ceaser, "In Defense of Separation of Powers," 176.

31. Ibid., 190.

32. Ibid., 176.

33. See Mark J. Rozell, "Executive Privilege and the Modern Presidents: In Nixon's Shadow," *Minnesota Law Review,* May 1999, 1069–126.

INDEX